D⁴

# Women Writers of the English Renaissance

## Twayne's English Authors Series

Arthur F. Kinney, Editor

*University of Massachusetts, Amherst*

TEAS 521

ESTHER INGLIS, SELF-PORTRAIT INSERTED IN HER 1624 MANUSCRIPT
BOOK OF GEORGETTE DE MONTENAY'S EMBLEMES CHRESTIENS.

*Reproduced by permission of the British Library, London, from Royal Ms. 17 D XVI, folio 7.*

# Women Writers of the English Renaissance

## Kim Walker

*Victoria University of Wellington*

**Twayne Publishers**
An Imprint of Simon & Schuster Macmillan
New York

**Prentice Hall International**
London • Mexico City • New Delhi • Singapore • Sydney • Toronto

Twayne's English Authors Series No. 521

*Women Writers of the English Renaissance*
Kim Walker

Twayne Publishers
An Imprint of Simon & Schuster Macmillan
1633 Broadway
New York, New York 10019

**Library of Congress Cataloging-in-Publication Data**

Walker, Kim.
     Women Writers of the English Renaissance / Kim Walker.
         p. cm. — (Twayne's English authors series ; TEAS 521)
     Includes bibliographical references and index.
     ISBN 0-8057-7017-8 (cloth)
         1. English literature—Women authors—History and criticism. 2. English
literature—Early modern, 1500–1700—History and criticism. 3. Pembroke, Mary
Sidney Herbert, Countess of, 1561–1621—Criticism and interpretation. 4. Cary,
Elizabeth, Lady, 1585 or 6–1639—Criticism and interpretation. 5. Wroth, Mary,
Lady, ca. 1586–ca. 1640—Criticism and interpretation. 6. Women and
literature—England—History—16th century. 7. Women and literature—
England—History—17th century. 8. Renaissance—England. I. Title.
II. Series.
     PR113.W35    1996
     820.9'9287'09031—dc20                                              96-12874
                                                                                                   CIP

10 9 8 7 6 5 4 3 2

Printed in the United States of America

# Contents

# Editor's Note

"Did women have a Renaissance?" Joan Kelly-Gadol raised that question as recently as 1977; since that time, a large part of the most active and significant scholarship in Renaissance studies has attempted to answer it. Kim Walker's book will take a commanding lead among the responses. In a careful but current and wide-ranging survey of Renaissance women writers, she examines the conditions under which women wrote, their attempts to move from the margins to the center of literary production, and their establishment of careers as professional writers. Both major and minor writers—poets, diarists, letter writers, novelists, playwrights, and biographers—are discussed here in revealing, reliable, and provocative ways. Major writers, such as Mary Sidney and Elizabeth Cary, are seen in new and important perspective. This volume is a signal accomplishment for the Twayne English Authors Series in the Renaissance that should be read by every scholar and student who sees the culture and literature of Tudor and Stuart England as an important area of study.

Arthur F. Kinney

# Preface

*Women Writers of the English Renaissance* is an unusual book in Twayne's English Authors Series in that it takes as its subject not the works of one writer but those of a group of writers. It attests to the growing impact of recent feminist scholarship on early modern women, and I have no doubt that in the not too distant future we will see the publication of Twayne texts on individual women writers of the period. Writers such as Mary Sidney, Countess of Pembroke, and her niece, Lady Mary Wroth, are now attracting substantial critical attention, and while it is not the aim of this book to "canonize" such women, their works are already acquiring institutional status in an academic world politicized by feminism.

*Women Writers* has, primarily for reasons of space, taken shape around the literary writings of English women working in the 80-year period 1560–1640. I treat "English" here as both a geographical and a linguistic term: I exclude Scottish women writers such as Elizabeth Melville, Lady Culross; English women living and publishing on the Continent like Jane Weston; and the works of women writing in languages other than English (Jane Weston again, and the tombstone elegies of the Cooke sisters, in Latin and Greek). Women were, of course, writing prior to 1560, but much of their work in the early years of the Reformation consisted of religious tracts and translations. After 1640, women writers flourished in the pamphleteering of the Civil War as well as in more central literary genres; their prolific output and the unusual conditions of the commonwealth period deserve another book.

I have focused in this book on genres that largely conform to traditional notions of literary writing. In excluding polemical tracts, religious treatises, controversy literature, and mother's advice books, I do not wish to reaffirm the very canon that labels such women's texts as marginal or minor. As a gesture toward a less restrictive notion of genre, I include a chapter that explores letters, diaries, and autobiographical writing, kinds of writing which need a great deal more critical and editorial attention. I also consider both published and unpublished material, though much of the manuscript material and, for that matter, many of the early printed texts are still not readily available or accessible. Editorial work currently being carried out both by individual scholars and by such groups as the Brown University Women Writers Project is likely to make many more of these texts accessible in the next few years. To focus on print alone, as Margaret Ezell has pointed out, would certainly be anachronistic for a period still in transition between two modes of literary production. Manuscript circulation continued to be a significant form of exchange, even as the technology of print transformed literary relations.

In the exploration of the works of individual writers such as Mary Sidney, Elizabeth Cary, and Mary Wroth, and in the chapters that look more generally at the writing of groups of women, I have always attempted to consider both the pressures (social, ideological, and material) against writing that confronted Renaissance Englishwomen and the negotiations in which women writers engaged to produce the works that have come down to us today in manuscript, printed text and tombstone engraving. My hope is that, in some small way, *Women Writers* will help to negotiate a space for the voices of those women in our own time.

Whatever contribution this book makes to the status of early modern women writers would not have been possible without the institutional support of the Turnbull Library and Victoria University of Wellington and the individual support of friends, colleagues, and family. My first debt is to Arthur Kinney, whose kind suggestion prompted me to begin work on this book several years ago. To Victoria University, I owe grants for research materials and assistance, and for academic leave and travel. Without the early modern collection of the Turnbull Library in Wellington, my research would have foundered hopelessly in geographical isolation; I am grateful to the Turnbull librarians for their help and interest in my work. I owe a further debt to the reference librarians of the Victoria University Library for their assistance; my thanks to Justin Cargill in particular for his indefatigable good humor and bad jokes in the face of an endless stream of interlibrary loan requests. Throughout my work on *Women Writers*, I have been helped and hindered by my dear friend and colleague Linda Hardy; her vast memory has been a tremendous resource, and her admirable intellect a constant if sometimes uncomfortable spur. To Ruth Turnbull and Kristen Jensen, who have helped me with the typing of the manuscript, and to Sue McDowall, who has been a precise and able research assistant in the final stages of my work, I owe more than they were ever paid. Last, but far from least, my heartfelt thanks to Jock Phillips; his willing ear, warm support, and good cooking have kept me from becoming one more silent woman.

## Note on Quotations

I have retained the original spelling and punctuation of all quotations cited from early modern texts, with certain exceptions. Contractions have been silently expanded, and the typographical peculiarities of the early modern printing press are generally modernized. I have silently substituted "s" for the old long "ſ ", and have modernized usage of "i"/"j" and "u"/"v" throughout.

Kim Walker
*Victoria University of Wellington*

# Chronology

1528    Elizabeth (Cooke) Russell born.

1533    Elizabeth Tudor born.

1535    Anne (Vaughan) Locke Prowse born.

1552    Grace (Sharington) Mildmay born.

1556    Anne (Cecil) de Vere born.

1558    Elizabeth I ascends the throne. Anne (Dacre) Howard born.

1560    Anne Locke Prowse's *Sermons of John Calvin* published. ?Margaret (Russell) Clifford born.

1561    Mary Sidney born.

1567    Isabella Whitney's *The Copie of a letter* published.

1569    Aemilia Lanyer born.

1571    Margaret (Dakins) Hoby born. Esther (Inglis) Kello born.

1573    Isabella Whitney's *A sweet Nosgay* published.

1574    Anne of Denmark (later Queen Anne) born. Anne (Harris) Southwell born.

1576    Frances Aburgavenny dies.

1578    Margaret Tyler's *The Mirrour of Princely deedes and Knighthood* published.

1581    Jane (Meautys) Cornwallis born. Lucy (Harington) Russell born.

1582    Verses of Frances Aburgavenny and Elizabeth Tyrwhit published in Thomas Bentley's *Monument of Matrones*.

1584    Anne de Vere's sonnets published in John Soowthern's *Pandora.*

1585    Elizabeth (Tanfield) Cary born.

1587    ?Mary (Sidney) Wroth born.

1588    Anne de Vere dies.

1589    Anne Clifford born. Anne Dowriche's *The French Historie* published. Elizabeth I's poem, "The doubt of future foes," published in George Puttenham's *Arte of English Poesie.*

1590    Anne Locke Prowse's translation of John Taffin's *Of the markes of the children of God* published. Anne (Clifford) Sackville born.

1592    Mary Sidney's translations of *A Discourse of Life and Death* and *Antonius, a Tragedie* published.

1593    Philip Sidney's *The Countesse of Pembrokes Arcadia* (authorized edition) published.

1595    Mary Sidney's translation of *Antonius* republished as *The Tragedie of Antonie.* Mary Sidney's "The Doleful Lay of Clorinda" published in Edmund Spenser's *Colin Clouts Come home againe.*

1596    Elizabeth Stuart born.

1597    ?Rachel Speght born.

1599    Presentation copy of the Sidney Psalms prepared for Queen Elizabeth.

1600    Brilliana (Conway) Harley born.

1601    Margaret Clifford's epitaph to Richard Candish inscribed on a wall at Hornsey Church, Middlesex.

1602    Mary Sidney's "Dialogue . . . in praise of Astrea" published in Francis Davison's *A Poeticall Rhapsody.*

1603    Queen Elizabeth I dies. James VI of Scotland ascends the throne as James I.

1609    Elizabeth Russell dies.

1611    Aemilia Lanyer's *Salve Deus Rex Judaeorum* published.

1612    Prince Henry dies.

1613    Elizabeth Cary's *The Tragedie of Mariam* published. Princess Elizabeth marries Frederick, Elector Palatine.

1616    Margaret Clifford dies.

1617    Grace Mildmay's manuscript journal written. Rachel Speght's *A Mouzell for Melastomus* published.

1619    Queen Anne dies.

1620    Grace Mildmay dies.

1621   Rachel Speght's *Mortalities Memorandum* published.
       Mary Wroth's *Urania* published. Mary Sidney dies.

1624   Esther Inglis dies.

1625   King James I dies. Charles I ascends to the throne and
       marries Henrietta Maria.

1626   Anne Southwell dates the title page of her manuscript
       journal.

1627   Mary Cornwallis dies. Lucy Russell dies.

1628   Elizabeth Cary's *Edward II* written.

1630   Anne Howard dies. Diana Primrose's *A Chaine of Pearl*
       published.

1633   Margaret Hoby dies.

1634   Alice Sutcliffe's *Meditations of Man's Mortalitie* published.

1636   Anne Southwell dies.

1637   Mary Fage's *Fames Roule* published. Elizabeth Middle-
       ton's manuscript poem, "The Death and Passion of our
       Lord Jesus Christ," written.

1639   Suzanne Du Verger's *Admirable Events* published.
       Elizabeth Cary dies.

1640   Judith Man's *An Epitome of the History of Faire Argenis
       and Polyarchus* published.

1641   Diana Primrose dies.

1643   Brilliana Harley dies.

1645   Aemilia Lanyer dies.

1652   ?Mary Wroth dies.

1655   ?Life of Elizabeth Cary written by her daughter.

1659   Jane Cornwallis dies.

1662   Elizabeth Stuart, Queen of Bohemia, dies.

1676   Anne Clifford dies.

1680   Elizabeth Cary's *Edward II* published in two separate
       editions.

# Chapter One

# Wise Virgins: Authority and Authorship[1]

*Then shall the kingdom of heaven be likened unto ten virgins, which took their lamps, and went forth to meet the bridegroom. And five of them were wise, and five were foolish. They that were foolish took their lamps, and took no oil with them: But the wise took oil in their vessels with their lamps.*

Matthew 25:1–4

The title of this chapter implicitly sets biblical wise virgins and Renaissance women writers in grammatical apposition, a relationship that implies semantic affinity. Indeed, such affinity is often claimed by women writers in the Renaissance, either for themselves or for the women readers they address.[2] Aemilia Lanyer, in the dedicatory verses prefaced to *Salve Deus Rex Judaeorum* (1611) addressed "To all vertuous Ladies in generall," links the wisdom of the biblical virgins with the wisdom of Greek goddess Pallas Athene, and claims that both are supported by the Muses.[3] Learning and the arts, she asserts, are fit companions for "faire mindes." Lanyer's association of the wise virgins with the Muses is unconventional; the company of the Muses was frequently proscribed or carefully constrained for women in the Renaissance, and associated not with virtue and godly labors but with idleness, pride, and sexual license.[4] The wise virgin, then, is a double-edged figure for the Renaissance woman writer, a figure marked by the problematic relationship between wisdom, sex, and sexuality. This chapter sketches conditions of literary production in Renaissance England, and outlines some of the social, educational, economic, and ideological contexts of female authorship.

## Renaissance and Reformation

The Renaissance is a heterogeneous era, chronologically, geographically, and politically. Even within the boundaries set by this book, Renaissance England from 1560 to 1640 provides a disparate context for women writers. At the outer margins of that period, conditions for literary production differ markedly; the Civil War environment is quite distinct from that of the Reformation a century earlier. The notion of "rebirth" that is bound up with the word Renaissance (a rebirth envisaged by early humanists in the revival of the learning of ancient Greece and Rome) is now often displaced by the term "early modern" in order to stress continuity between social, economic, and political relations that emerged in the period and those that exist in the present.[5] Feminist historians have displaced the notion in another way: following the lead of Joan Kelly-Gadol, they have pointed to the gender bias in the traditional conceptualization of the Renaissance. "There was no renaissance for women," Kelly asserts, "at least, not during the Renaissance."[6] Since her seminal essay, the relative position of women in the period has been much debated, and new knowledge of gender-specific conditions is in turn feeding the exploration of an associated question: was there a renaissance for women writers?[7]

The developments taking place in the social, economic, political, and religious life of Renaissance England, as recent studies have increasingly emphasized, did not affect men and women equally.[8] As capitalism developed and the household lost its centrality as the place of production, the growing segregation of public and private spheres, work and home, led to a division of labor that took men outside the household into the "public" world to earn an individual wage, while women (in theory at least) were relegated to the "private" domestic sphere of "huswifery," a wageless activity that became invisible as productive work. Women were encouraged to be good housewives to prevent "idleness," a vice that was increasingly perceived to affect women in the expanding middle classes as well as aristocratic women.[9]

The rise of professionalism—in disciplines such as medicine, law, and education as well as in government service—was encouraged by the secular ideals promulgated by humanism.[10] With a new belief in the freedom and dignity of Man, humanists emphasized the potential for self-determination and self-fulfillment in worldly affairs.[11] Secular education promised secular rewards, new knowledge promised control of society and the world, and rhetoric and eloquence were privileged as valuable tools of public life.[12]

Humanism, despite its belief in the freedom and dignity of Man, was phallocentric: Man was free, but women were subject to men. Indeed, the humanist promotion of engagement in the secular world was dependent on gender differentiation. Ruth Kelso and Ann Rosalind Jones have pointed to the displacement onto women of Christian virtues such as piety, humility, charity, and withdrawal from the world, as the notion of the ideal humanist gentleman came to embody secular, pagan virtues such as justice.[13] Humanism, moreover, was able to support the development of capitalism through its discourses of sexual difference: Lorna Hutson has argued that acquisitive activities outside the household were supported by humanist texts that represented husband and wife as a new kind of economic unit.[14] The prudent wife in the home maintained and preserved the gains of the husband in the secular world beyond the home, while the "household" was redefined to include all activities from which a man could profit. In *De Republica Anglorum* (a text that went through 11 editions between 1583 and 1640), Sir Thomas Smith's description of the commonwealth can thus locate its origin in this "natural" division of labor in the family: husband and wife form the "naturalest and first conjunction . . . after a diverse sorte ech having care of the familie: the man to get, to travaile abroad, to defende: the wife, to save that which is gotten, to tarrie at home to distribute that which commeth of the husbandes labor for the nurtriture of the children and family of them both, and to keepe all at home neat and cleane."[15]

Protestant theology and moral philosophy interacted with humanism and capitalism to relegate women to the private domestic sphere of home and family.[16] While Protestantism asserted the common spirituality of women and men, and granted access to religious texts to both sexes, emphasis on the Pauline epistles only reasserted the traditional theological assumption of the inferiority of women.[17] In Protestant writings, women were above all represented as wives, with responsibility for the care of the household and family under the guidance and direction of their husbands.[18] As a wife, a woman must acknowledge her husband's authority.[19] The analogy between the positions of God, monarch, and husband/father (an analogy encouraged by Church and state alike in support of the Reformation and the centralization of the monarchy) helped to confirm the outlines of the patriarchal Protestant family. As the male head of the family displaced the priest, so the family became a "little Church."[20] With celibacy no longer the privileged state, marriage acquired new value in relation to companionate partnership as well as reproduction, and the duties of women as wives and mothers were extolled. Under the guidance of her husband, the good wife was expected to raise her children as good subjects who had internalized their moral and political duties; in return, she would be loved, protected, and supported (as the "weaker vessel") by her husband. The Protestant ideology of the family, then, was dependent on and contributed to discourses of sexual difference.

The development of the printing press has often been linked to the rise of Protestantism in England as well as in Europe, since the Reformers themselves acknowledged and exploited the potential of print as a means of mass communication.[21] The new medium paradoxically intensified both religiosity and secularism at once; printing and publishing helped to undermine the Church's control of knowledge even as it allowed the Church to disseminate doctrine and propaganda to a mass audience. Elizabeth Eisenstein has argued that print effected a genuine transformation in cultural history and in the conditions of intellectual life, and is therefore a decisive factor helping to mark and produce the new epoch of the Renaissance (1983, 110–21).[22] Print and print culture helped to transform English society for both sexes, but women's access to print (as readers and as writers) was limited by gender and influenced by class.

Women did not stand "on a footing of perfect equality with men" in Renaissance England[23]; social, political, and economic developments affected women differently, both in terms of the actual conditions of their existence and in relation to the gender differentiations of contemporary ideology. Discourses of sexual difference inscribed in fields of knowledge such as theology, law, medicine, education, moral philosophy, and politics reiterated women's "proper" and "natural" subordination to men.[24] Even women who were highly educated were subject to cultural attitudes that insisted on their inferiority to men and on their exclusion from public affairs and public language. Inevitably, such conditions had an impact on women's writing: the few women in the Renaissance who were able to write were confronted not only by social prohibitions against writing (and, more intensively, against publication) but also by a literary tradition that was almost totally male. Nevertheless, though their numbers are far fewer than men writers, some women did negotiate their way into existence as writers.

## Education and the Ideal Woman

Educational practice and ideology provided both stepladder and obstacle to women writers. The vast majority of women in Renaissance England were largely if not wholly illiterate. David Cressy has estimated that 90 percent of women were still unable to sign their names in the middle of the 17th century.[25] Both class and gender factors contributed to low literacy rates. Education was on the whole the privilege of the upper and growing middle classes, and educators, whether liberal or severe, delineated separate programs of learning for men and women. Vives, whose *Instruction for a Christen Woman* ran to seven English editions between its first translation (by Richard Hyrde) in 1529 and 1592, asserted that "it is mete that the man have knowlege of many and dyvers thynges, that may both profite hymselfe and the common welthe, bothe with the use and increasynge of lernynge. But I wolde the woman shulde be altogether in that parte of philosophy, that taketh upon hit to enfourme, and teche and amende the conditions" (sigs. E2–E2v).[26]

Likewise, the schoolmaster Richard Mulcaster introduces the education of young girls into his treatise, but marks the distinction between the sexes: "young maidens must give me leave to speake of boyes first: bycause naturally the male is more worthy, and politikely he is more employed, and therfore that side claimeth this learned education. . . . [T]he bringing up of young maidens in any kynd of learning, is but an accessory by the waye."[27] Humanists and Reformers alike produced treatises in the Renaissance advocating the education of women, but such encouragement was clearly a mixed blessing in terms of its paternalism. The education of daughters was seen primarily as an education in virtue and in good "huswifery," best conducted by their mothers or by matrons of good repute. Richard Brathwait's list of exemplary mothers in his 17th-century conduct book indicates the priority accorded to feminine virtue: "Cornelia instructed hers in all piety; Portia hers in exemplary grounds of chastity; Sulpitia hers in precepts of conjugall unity; Edesia hers in learning and morality; Paulina hers in memorials of shamefaste modesty."[28] Henry Bullinger, whose *Christen State of Matrimonye* is one of the early texts idealizing the "honest faithfull houswyfe" confined to the home, insists that "Mothers must also teach their daughters to worke, to love theyr housbandes and chyldren. And let them laye their handes to spynne, sewe, weave" (sig. K4v).[29]

Humanist education principles brought a brief spell in which aristocratic women were encouraged to study classical literature and languages (including Greek, French, Latin, and Italian) as well as more decorative and practical skills. Writers like Vives posited that if women were of weaker intellect, then there was all the more reason to educate them. Sir Thomas More, for example, wrote to the tutor of his daughters: "if the female soil be in its nature stubborn, and more productive of weeds than fruits, it ought, in my opinion, to be more diligently cultivated."[30] Geographical and historical comparisons provided other contexts for the encouragement of women's education. Antonio de Guevara used classical models to chastise contemporary women: "the tyme whyche the auncient women spente, in vertues and studyes: these of this presente, consume in pleasurs and vyces."[31] Mulcaster boasted of some English women who could be compared with "the best Romaines or Greekish paragonnes" (168); nationalism provides the context for his celebration, but even here these women are defined as paragons, "rarely qualified," and accepted as honorary men.

The standard argument for women's education was not that it would provide a basis for female involvement in statecraft and politics, but rather that cultivation and learning was an "accessory" suited to the gentlewoman's existence in a civilized society, making her a fit wife and companion for men of her class. Vives sets out a familial context for a woman's learning: "A wise woman shulde have in mynde myry tales, and histories (howe be it yet honest) wherwith she may refreshe her husbande, and make hym mery, whan he is wery. And also she shal lerne preceptes of wisedome, to exhorte hym unto vertue, or drawe him from vice with al, and some sage sentences agaynst the assautes and rages of both fortunes. . . . Neyther a vertuous mother ought to refuse lernynge on the boke, but nowe and than studye and rede holy and wyse mennes bokes: and though she do it nat for her owne sake, at the least wyse for her children, that she may teache them and make them good" (sigs. e2, l3v).[32] Vives specifies that public matters are not a woman's concern: "you women that wyll medle with comen matters of realmes and cites, and wene to governe people and nacions with the braydes of your stomackes, you go about to hurle downe rownes afore you and you lyght upon an hard rocke . . . your owne house is a cite great inough for you" (sig. h2v). A woman's learning, then, was to be carefully contained within the bounds of the family and the home.

The early humanist encouragement of a relatively broad education in the liberal arts for women has been dated as lasting for a period of about 40 years, from 1520 to 1560.[33] After this, writers either promoted an elegant aristocratic model like that of the gentlewomen in Baldassare Castiglione's *The Book of the Courtier* (1528), which placed less emphasis on letters than on social graces (such as music, painting, dancing, and needlework), or, more often, outlined a bourgeois model that emphasized modest piety, "huswifery," and family-centered usefulness.[34] In 1605, Pierre Erondelle could wonder at the lack of books teaching French to women, and in his series of dialogues "my chiefe ayme hath beene to furnish English Ladyes and Gentle-women with such conference and familiar talk as is incident unto them specially."[35] His lessons include vocabulary for women's clothing and "necessaries for a sucking

Childe" (dialogue 5), and discussions of child education; in the third dialogue, a mother talks to her daughters about their "cut-work" and tapestry, and their lessons in dancing, singing, and music. There is nothing to suggest a more extensive program of studies for these fictional pupils. Brathwait's concern for the "improved education" of his English gentlewoman is little concerned with her learning, and the few recommendations he provides for her studies appear significantly in a chapter on gentility.

Thomas Salter's Elizabethan treatise is overtly suspicious; a woman's vocation makes a liberal education unnecessary and even dangerous:[36]

> It is not mete nor convenient for a Maiden to be taught or trayned up in learnyng of humaine artes . . . for in learnyng and studiyng of the artes there are twoo thynges finallie proposed unto us, that is recreation and profitte[;] touchyng profitte, that is not to bee looked for, at the handes of her that is geven us for a companion in our labours, but rather every woman ought wholelie to be active and diligent about the governement of her housholde and familie, and touchyng recreation by learnyng that cannot bee graunted her, without greate daunger and offence to the beautie and brightnesse of her mynde; seying then that the governement of estates and publike weales are not committed into the handes of women. (sigs. C1–C1v)

A woman's mind, Salter suggests, can shine only within the confines of the household; its brightness will be stained by learning that has any association with the masculine public sphere. The "light" of learning becomes "vaine glorie" in a woman, a sign of vanity and pride rather than wisdom and cultivation. The humanist emphasis on the private and familial context of women's education provides the grounds for Salter's more restrictive program of education in good "huswifery."

Learned women, particularly after the mid-16th century, were likely to be mocked or viewed as a threat. Margaret King and Lisa Jardine have pointed to the link that was perceived between learning in women and their aggression or deviancy (often specifically sexual deviancy).[37] The association between learning and deviancy can be seen at work in such texts as Thomas Heywood's *Nine Bookes of Various History Concerning Women* (1624), which links women poets and witches in its eighth book, "Intreating of Women everie way Learned."[38] Writers who discussed women's learning could not dissociate the topic from their chastity and virtue. Edward Hake, for example, in citing examples of learned women of the past, describes Hortensia as "not more famous for hir learning

then loved for hir vertue, and honoured for hir chastity."[39] Learned
women were urged to be "wise virgins," or attacked for their lack of
chastity. This association, however, like the identification of women with
the home, provided a paradigm that was both enabling and constraining
for female learning. On the one hand, Hyrde can state that "I never
herde tell, nor reed of any woman well lerned, that ever was (as plentu-
ous as yvell tonges be) spotted or infamed as vicious. But on the other-
side, many by their lernyng taken suche encrease of goodnesse, that
many may beare them wytnesse of their vertue" (in Roper, sig. a4v).[40]
On the other hand, Salter argues against women's learning because, he
says, such famous women "never got so muche fame by their learnyng,
as thei did defame, for their unhonest and losse livyng . . . where these
obstinate defendoures of learning to be meete and necessarie in women,
can bryng in one example, I will alledge a nomber to the contrarie" (sigs.
B8v–C1). The chastity of a learned woman was put in question by male
writers regardless of their educational stance; women could not escape a
gendered and sexualized analysis of the "brightnesse" of their minds. At
the same time, however, contradictory positions within the paradigm
allowed a certain amount of room for maneuver.

Models of education for women, because of their concern with female
virtue, were closely related to models delineating the "ideal woman." A
flood of publications in a variety of genres (publications often associated with the literature of controversy surrounding the *querelle des femmes*,
or debate about women) occupied itself with providing such models in
the Renaissance—from conduct and courtesy book to satire and sermon.[41] Often, as Ann Rosalind Jones has argued, these texts are cen-
trally concerned not with women but rather with redefining
masculinity; their representations of the ideal woman provide specular
endorsement which helps to construct the ideal man.[42] While this did
not necessarily lessen the ideological impact of such rhetorical fictions
on women, more than one model existed; different and competing
frameworks for "proper" feminine behavior were available. As with educational writing, contradictions between these models allowed for productive manipulation.

Perhaps the most dominant prescription for the ideal woman in the
Renaissance was the triad of chastity, silence, and obedience, an inter-
linked set of virtues that posed specific problems for the woman writer.
Protestant emphasis on the Pauline epistles encouraged an insistent
recourse to the injunctions in Ephesians (5:22–24, on the submission of
wives to their husbands) and 1 Corinthians (14:34–35, on women's

silence in church), as well as 1 Timothy (2:11–14): "Let the woman learn in silence with all subjection. But I suffer not a woman to teach, nor to usurp authority over the man, but to be in silence. For Adam was first formed, then Eve. And Adam was not deceived, but the woman being deceived was in the transgression." On the basis of such scriptural texts, silence was regularly propounded as a virtue in a woman, while excessive speech became a sign of transgression, the usurpation of masculine authority. Brathwait, for example, repeats a proverbial saying: "what is spoken of Maids, may be properly applyed by an usefull consequence to all women: They should be seene, and not heard" (41). Drawing on the concept of the self-contained and well-governed household, Peter de la Primaudaye asserts that "a woman must have a speciall care to be silent, and to speake as seldome as she may, unlesse it be to hir husband, or at his bidding: reserving household wantes and affaires secret to hirselfe, and not publish them abroad."[43] Women's speech was popularly linked with disobedience and disruption in the home, while the Corinthian prohibition of women's speech in church was also generalized to any public place (beyond the home).[44] Henry Bullinger, counseling parents on the religious instruction of their daughters, reminds them that this instruction should be kept within the house: "yet shall they not be to busye in teachinge and reasoninge openly, but ere to use sylence and to lerne at home, openly to heare, and at home let them reasone and teche eche other" (1541, sig. K4).

Chastity, seen as the very foundation of a woman's value and worth, was problematically interconnected with the virtues of silence and obedience.[45] Vives reminded women that chastity was their fundamental virtue: "For as for a man nedeth many thynges, as wysedome, eloquence, knowlege of thynges . . . in a woman no man wyll loke for eloquence, great witte, or prudence, or crafte to lyve by, or ordrynge of the commen weale, or justice, or liberalite. . . . [G]yve her chastite, and thou hast gyven her al thynges" (sigs. G4–G4v). Yet a woman's chastity could be tainted by her speech, which was associated with temptation and seduction through the story of Eve. Richard Tofte, for example, cites a verse that links verbal and bodily expression: "A slow soft Tongue betokens Modestie, / But, quicke and loud signe's of Inconstancy: / Words, more then swords the inward Heart doe wound, / And glib'd tongue'd Women seldome chaste are found."[46] Similarly, Brathwait warns that "[women's] tongues are held their defensive armour; but in no particular detract they more from their honour, than by giving too free scope to that glibbery member" (88).

Humanist writers who encouraged and celebrated male eloquence (spoken or written) became profoundly ambivalent on the subject where women were concerned. Vives repeatedly hesitates over eloquence in women: "As for eloquence I have no great care, nor a woman nedeth it nat: but she nedeth goodnes and wysedom. Nor it is no shame for a woman to holde her peace. . . . Nor I wyl nat here condempne eloquence" (sigs. E1v–E2). "For as for eloquence, or lernyng in the lawe, or feattes of warre are no matters for women to wynne worship by" (sig. Y4v). "I wolde nat have a woman to speke, excepte it be a thynge that shulde do hurte to be kepte in" (sig. h1v). Antonio de Guevara, in the middle of a discussion of pregnant wives and nursing mothers in Book 2 of *The Diall of Princes*, inserts a chapter on the importance of eloquence. He concludes by giving a reason for his digression: it is of eloquence in gentlemen he speaks, to persuade Princes and lords that their (male) children should be taught not only how to live but also how to speak (ff. 122–123v). Richard Brathwait, in his chapter on decency, can conclude that "Silence in a Woman is a moving Rhetoricke, winning most, when in words it wooeth least" (90).[47]

Salter's ambivalence is more pervasive, appearing even in his advice on reciting scriptures in company: "when it behoves her through request to recite any Psalme, or other Spirituall song, or godlie sentence, she shall set her self forthe to doe it with a milde refusall, yet altogether voide of undecent affectyng" (sig. D4v). The good woman should simultaneously ready herself to comply and refuse; yet this duplicity should be paradoxically truthful, "voide of undecent affectyng." Salter's text shows the difficulty encountered when the injunction to silence comes into conflict with that of obedience; the conflict, for him, is best marked on the woman's body itself: "where it behoveth her to shewe her vertue, she shall bee readie but not to bolde, and by a sodaine blushyng, whiche immediatly will overspread her lillie cheekes with roseat read, she shall shewe that she beareth in her breaste a reverente harte, farre separated from infamous and reprochfull shame" (sig. D4v). In showing her virtue, in displaying herself verbally in public, only the woman who blushes evades suspicion of duplicity, boldness, and pride.

Silence was a heavy injunction for the potential woman writer, particularly since it was intertwined so closely with chastity. Where eloquence in a woman is praised, it is often in terms that make her a sexually ambiguous figure. Thomas Heywood, for example, cites the example of a Roman woman who pleaded her own cause "with such a manly yet modest constancie, that from that time forward shee was called

Androgine" (373); a more cautionary example follows, moreover, of a woman "whose common rayling and loquacitie before the Bench, grew to that scandall that it almost stretcht to the injurie of the whole Sex" (374). Like learning in general, eloquence in a woman is often associated with aggression or sexual deviancy. A woman's tongue was popularly represented as her phallic weapon.[48] Not only was silence enjoined on women, then, but speech itself, given the association between silence and chastity, was eroticized.

Other virtues supported the foundational triad of chastity, obedience, and silence in the model woman. A woman's modesty, for example, would prevent her from inciting male lust; her humility and obedience would evade male anger and violence; her temperance in relation to food and drink would help to preserve her chastity and ward off the temptations of contact with men.[49] A woman's reputation, in this heavily male-oriented context, was represented as fragile and easily spotted, and male writers warned of the dangers of public display, of going outside the home. Brathwait remarks that "no place can be more mortally danger-ous. . . . What an excellent impregnable fortresse were Woman, did not her Windowes betray her to her enemy? But principally, when shee leaves her Chamber to walke on the publike Theatre" (41–43). Vives becomes particularly expansive on this topic: "A woman shulde be kepte close, nor be knowen of many, for hit is a token of no great chastite or good name, to be knowen of many, or be songen about in the cite in songes, or to be markedde or named by any notable marke, as whyte, lame, gogle eied, lyttell, great, fat, maymed, or stuttynge, these ought nat to be knowen abrode in a good woman" (sig. N3).[50] Inscribed in his statement is an elision of physical marking ("notable markes" on the woman's body) and verbal or visual marking (by men who visually mark or verbally name these "markes"). By means of this elision, bodily defect slides into defect in virtue, outer mark into inner taint, "a token of no great chastite." "The greatest vertue of a woman (said Euboides) is not to be known but of hir husband: and hir praise (said Argeus) in a strange mouth is nothing else but a secret blame" (de la Primaudaye, 516). The model woman was not only a silent woman but also the woman least talked about.

Rhetorical fictions of the ideal woman encouraged women to make themselves less visible, even as they confirmed women as the objects of men's gaze, and treatises on wifely duties repeatedly emphasized the importance of staying at home.[51] Scriptural texts were called on to warn of the dangers of public display for a woman's reputation. Cleaver, for example, cites St. Paul and Solomon in his commentary on the term "huswife": "Lastly, wee call the wife Huswife, that is, house-wife, not a street-wife, one that gaddeth up and downe, . . . to shew that a good wife, keepes her house, and therefore Paul biddeth Titus, to exhort women that they bee chaste, and keeping at home: presently after chaste, hee saith, keeping at home: as though home were chastities keeper. And therefore Salomon depainting, and describing the quallities of a whore, setteth her at the doore, now sitting upon her staull, now walking in the streetes, now looking out of the window. . . . But chastitie careth to please but one, and therefore shee keepes her closet, as if shee were still at prayer" (218–19). Cleaver's ideal woman becomes doubly confined not just to the house but to the privacy of her closet within the house.

Humanists and Reformers alike promoted the figure of the housewife. As Lorna Hutson has argued, the housewife and her domestic prudence complemented and helped to justify the acquisitive dealings of men in the "outside" world (1994, 22). "The office of the husbande is to bring in necessaries, of the wife, well to keepe them. The office of the husbande is, to go abroad in matters of profite, of the wife, to tarrye at home, and see all be well there. The office of the husbande is, to provide money, of the wife, not wastfully to spende it. The office of the husbande is, to deale, and bargaine with all men, of the wife, to make or meddle with no man" (Tilney, sig. C5v). Robert Cleaver adds a paradoxical duty for women: "The dutie of the man is, to bee skilfull in talke: and of the wife, to boast of silence" (169). In this fiction, the well-trained and well-governed woman in the home was essential to the representation of the ideal man as good governor in family and state, a man morally and spatially freed for the negotiations and exchanges of the market and the public world.

The prudent, chaste, and silent woman, then, was a signifier of male sovereignty in a secular world; it is as if, in "possessing" her, a man could lay claim to Christian virtues at the heart of his own secular activities. Relegated to the private sphere of the home, with her mouth, her body, her doors closed to all but the proper owner, she provided a justification of humanist endeavor.[52]

Despite the pervasiveness of this model, however, alternative versions of the ideal woman emphasized class distinctions between women—distinctions that provided potential loopholes for the woman writer.[53] The eloquence of some women was valued. Courtesy literature and its promotion of courtly conversation is particularly significant in this respect. Ann Rosalind Jones has pointed to the necessarily ambivalent position of courtesy writers on the subject of women's conversation at court ( Jones

1990, 15–20). Given the eroticization of women's speech, such conversation is fraught with danger: the potential seduction of their words must be "bridled" by the "chastity" of their ideas. Yet, like the ideal housewife, women at court are necessary figures who help to define the ideal courtier; consequently, their conversation is important in its capacity to elicit and admire male eloquence and male accomplishments. The sweetness of women's speech in such literature, then, offers a restrained alternative to silence. Brathwait's *English Gentlewoman* too, despite its strictures on the danger of public report for women's reputations, offers more liberal advice in accordance with rank: "Now for publike Employments, I know all are not borne to be Deborahs, to beare virile spirits in feminine bodies. Yet, in chusing the better part, you may fit and accommodate your persons to publike affaires, well sorting and suting with your ranke and quality. . . . [A] modest and well Behaved Woman may by her frequent or resort to publike places, conferre no lesse benefit to such as observe her behaviour, than occasion of profit to her private family, where shee is Overseer. . . . Words spoken in season, are like apples of gold with pictures of silver" (51–52).

The model of the prudent housewife also offered loopholes when it paid attention to class distinctions between women. Such attention could take the form of attacks on the idleness of aristocratic women in contrast to the industrious bourgeois housewife.[54] Class distinctions provided opportunity for women writers of both the upper and the middle classes. On the one hand, "idleness" in aristocratic women became the very vice which could be avoided in reading and writing. The title page of *The Needles Excellency*, a 17th-century needlework manual that assumes a middle-class female audience, illustrates this possibility in its emblematic representation of Wisdom, Industry, and Folly (see figure one).[55] Both Wisdom and Folly are marked off from Industry as aristocratic women by their jewelry and elaborate clothing, but they are also differentiated from each other. Folly appears to be wearing the fashionable attire of the 1620s, with a high, short-waisted bodice rather than a long stomacher, and soft flowing skirts. She wears pearls lavishly at her neckline and throat, and her hair is tied in an elaborate knot. Wisdom, on the other hand, is less fashionable; she wears a farthingale (out of favor by the 1620s) and has a more restrained neckline.[56] The illustration of Folly accords with the reiterated strictures in conduct books and sermons against women's extravagance in clothing. Edward Hake, for example, exclaims: "Of a trueth, the substaunce whiche is consumed in two Yeares space upon the apparaill of one meane Gentlemans Daughter, or upon

The Needles Excellency

A New Booke wherin are diuers Admirable Workes wrought with the Needle. Newly inuented and cut in Copper for the pleasure and profit of the Industrious.

WISDOME

INDVSTRIE

FOLLIE

TITLE PAGE OF JOHN TAYLOR, *The Needles Excellency* (1631).

*Reproduced by permission of the Master and Fellows, Magdalene College, Cambridge, England.*

the Daughter or Wife of one Citizen, woulde bee sufficient to finde a poore Student in the Universitye, by the space of fowre or five yeeres at the least" (sigs. D2–D2v). Folly, moreover, stands with her arms openly gesturing and appears to be talking, whereas Wisdom stands in composed meditation as she reads the book she is holding. Her reading is set off visually as the wise alternative to foolish and unguarded talk. Industry, however, is the focal point of the illustration. She sits between Wisdom and Folly, busily working at her needle. She is dressed in the plain but respectable clothes of a woman of the lesser gentry, with an unpatterned gown and sleeves neither split nor stuffed, a high bodice, and her hair covered with a hat. The signs of her modesty and industry are linked in the representation: she displays neither the fashionable excesses of Folly nor the leisured learning of Wisdom. The illustration suggests that learning is an appropriate endeavor for the leisured upper-class woman, but an inappropriate one for women of lesser rank. Yet, despite conventional warnings, the "industry" of the prudent housewife had the potential to be expanded to include such activities as writing.[57]

## Reading and Writing

Reading and writing by women, even according to the more liberal early humanist writers on education, were subjects that provoked anxiety. Both activities (taught separately in Renaissance England) were represented as potentially dangerous activities for women, activities that without careful surveillance could lead to transgressive behavior. While humanists celebrated the transformative power of reading for men, its capacity to provide men with a store of resources that could be called on at need in their daily exchanges in public life, this same transformative power provoked anxiety and prohibitions wherever women readers were identified.[58] If reading could transform men, then surely it could also transform women; it could provide women with their own store of knowledge and with an alternative source of authority unmediated by their husbands and fathers. Vives, in his *Instruction*, seems to be aware of the danger when he warns women to consult "wyse and sad men" about their reading: "the woman ought nat to folowe her owne jugement, lest whan she hath but a lyght entryng in lernyng, she shuld take false for true: hurtful in stede of holsome, folyshe and pevyshe for sad and wyse" (sig. F2). Protestant writers also acknowledged this dangerous possibility as the Reformation displaced the authority of the priest with that of the Bible; it was, in some circumstances, seen as appropriate for a woman to resist the commands of her husband if such commands were contradictory to the word of God.[59]

Gender ideology was inscribed in defenses of as well as attacks on reading. Reading was not, for women, promoted as an activity that could equip them as able servants of the commonwealth; rather, it was represented as an activity preventing idleness and loose talk, gossip, and even loose thoughts: "womens myndes shulde be occupied," said Vives, "either with worke, or els holy study and communication, leest they fall in to vyce by idelnesse" (*Instruction*, sig. H4v). In the same way, de la Primaudaye warns a woman to avoid plays, dancing, and hunting, and instead encourages her to "bestow as much time as she can steale from domesticall affaires, in the studie of notable sayings, and of the morall sentences of auncient Sages and good men" (518). Any time spent in reading is "stolen" from her primary duties as housewife, and only acceptable insofar as she is obedient to her husband's will; the fruits of her reading are wholly domestic.

The title page of Foxe's Book of Martyrs, a Reformation text recommended to women even by the severe Salter, provides a visual illustration of the paternalism of Protestant support of women's reading (see figure two).[60] The two bottom panels contrast Protestant and Catholic communities as they gather around a preacher in their midst. The representations of women in the two panels are significant. In each case, there are two token women among the crowd of men who fill the majority of the spiritual space. In the Catholic panel, the hand gesture of one of the women suggests that she is talking to the man opposite her, while the second woman sits turned away from the preacher with beads on her lap and her head in her hand. The preacher himself is turned away from the women and toward a group of men. In the Protestant panel, on the other hand, the two women sit together (as "sisters"), with a child kneeling behind them. The women face two men opposite, and each pair has an open book before them. The group, which can be interpreted as a "family" composed of sisters and brothers (including a couple with child), is visually confirmed by a compositional triangle with the preacher (who looks down on the two women and the child) at its apex. The women sit on a more equal level with the men than the women in the Catholic panel, yet their gaze appears to be focused on the men opposite, one of whom is actively consulting the text as the other listens to the preacher. While the women have access to the word, their access is still implicitly mediated by men. The illustration indicates the centrality of representations of the family in the rise of Protestantism and suggests how the good woman and wife could be used to define the good (Protestant) husband. Godly reading may have been supported to encourage the virtue of the good woman, but such reading was to be conducted under the watchful supervision of men.

This watchful supervision is not only apparent in a wide range of texts; it is also incorporated into arguments in favor of women's reading. Reading, as several writers describe it, is an activity that allows increased surveillance of women's minds. Mary Ellen Lamb has drawn attention to Richard Hyrde's concentration on the control of women's imagination and desire: "Also, redyng and studyeng of bokes so occupieth the mynde, that it can have no leyser to muse or delyte in other fantasies, whan in all handy werkes, that men saye be more mete for a woman, the body may be busy in one place, and the mynde walkyng in another: and while they syt sowing and spinnyng with their fyngers, maye caste and compasse many pevysshe fantasyes in their myndes" (in Roper, sig. a4).[61] Vives, too, emphasizes the useful control of women's thoughts in his *Instruction:* "Womans thought is swyfte, and for the most part unstable, walkyng and wandrynge out from home, and sone wyl slyde, by the reason of it owne sypernes, I wote nat howe far. Therfore redyng were the best, and ther unto I gyve them counsaile specially" (sigs. C3v–C4). Even Du Bosque's liberal treatise, which argues that reading is "necessary for all women, what kinde of spirit soever they be of," agrees that reading provides a mechanism to control women's thoughts when they are alone: women "who have some knowledge or reading, afford great pleasure in Conversation, and receive no lesse in solitude when they are alone. Their Idea hath somewhat to content them, while the ignorant are subject much to evill thoughts" (1639, 24). Du Bosque's support of reading assumes that well-read women will improve their virtue and also provide better entertainment for men.

Educational treatises that support reading for women repeatedly prohibit certain kinds of material. Vives outlines a relatively liberal program, encouraging reading in the Bible, classical authors such as Plato, Cicero, and Seneca; and the Church Fathers. However, he excludes chivalric romances and Ovid ("a schole maister of baudry," sig. B2v) and rejects material to do with war, armor, or love. Bullinger likewise specifies the exclusion of popular romance and books of love, which could only incite lust in women readers: "let them not reade bokes of fables of fonde and lyght love. . . . Bokes of Robyn hode, Beves of Hampton, Troilus, and such lyke fables do but kyndle in lyers lyke lyes and wanton love" (sig. K4v). The danger of books of love for women readers is

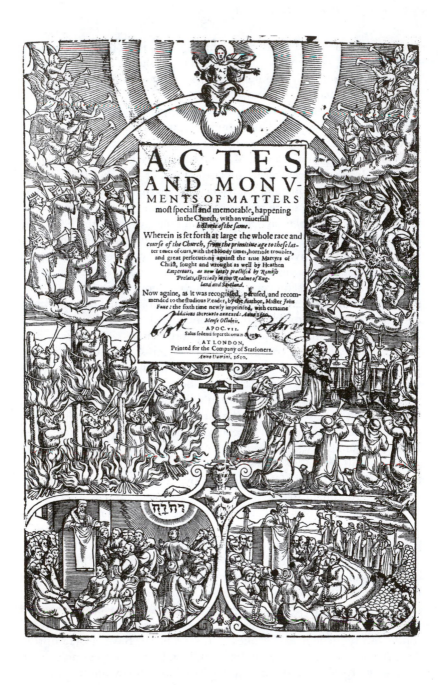

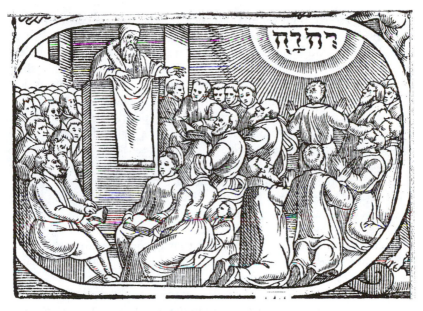

COMPLETE TITLE PAGE, LEFT, AND DETAILS, THIS PAGE, OF JOHN FOXE, *Actes and Monuments* (1563), FROM THE 5TH EDITION OF 1610.

*Reproduced by permission of the Alexander Turnbull Library, Wellington, New Zealand.*

repeatedly asserted. Hake, in 1574, bewails the state of contemporary education for women: "Eyther shee is altogither kept from exercises of good learning, and knowledge of good letters, or else she is so nouseled in amorous bookes, vaine stories and fonde trifeling fancies, that shee smelleth of naughtinesse even all hir lyfe after. . . . [S]uch parents as doe bring up their daughters in learning, do it to none other ende, but to make them companions of carpet knightes, and giglots, for amorous lovers" (sigs. C4–C6). Du Bosque's unusual acceptance of the reading of Ovid is qualified by the translator, N. N., in a preface addressing potential critics. The author, he says, has recognized that women cannot be weaned from the *Metamorphoses*, so "he hath taken away from them an idle tale, and given them a Morall: A divine Metamorphosie. . . . [T]heir poyson is become their Antidote" (1639, sigs. F3–F3v).

Other treatises were less supportive of women's reading as a result of such concerns. Thomas Salter argued that once a woman was able to read, control over her would be lost: "Some perhaps will alledge that a Maiden beyng well learned, and able to searche and reade sonderie authors, maie become chaste and godlie, by readyng the godlie and chaste lives of diverse: but I aunswere who can deny, that, seyng of her self she is able to reade and understande the Christian Poetes . . . that shee will not also reade the Lascivious bookes" (sig. B7v). While Salter truculently allows reading of "the holie scripture, or other good bookes" (sig. C3v), such as those that deal with the lives of virtuous women, or Foxe's "worthie booke of Martyres" (sig. C4), he repeatedly condemns books of love, "sonnettes, and Ditties of daliance" (sig. B2v), as well as "lascivious Songes, filthie Ballades, and undecent bookes" (sig. C3). Discourses of sexual difference that saw women as inferior in body and intellect contributed to the fear that women's reading might become carnal misreading.[62] Mary Ellen Lamb has shown that Sidney's *Arcadia* was treated as a serious political, philosophical, and moral work where male readers were envisaged, but became dangerously sexual when its readers were women (1990, 72–114). Published texts, moreover, rarely addressed women readers. Suzanne Hull, in her survey of books for women published between 1475 and 1640, has identified only 163 texts that were "specifically directed to or printed for women readers," the majority of which appeared after 1570.[63] While the book trade was beginning to recognize a female market, writers generally assumed a male audience, denying women subjectivity as readers.

If reading was an activity fraught with anxiety, writing was perhaps worse. The idealization of silence in the model woman could be applied to all language, the distinction between speech and writing effaced. In *The French Academie*, de la Primaudaye could say that "the same rules and precepts that belong to speaking, agree also to writing. Besides, writing is called of many, a dumb speech, which ought to be short and full of instruction" (132). Speech was popularly conceived as the original and primary form of expression; writing, whether privileged or not, was a materialization of speech, so a woman's public writing was potentially as transgressive as her public speech.[64]

The skill of handwriting itself was sometimes discouraged for women. Martin Billingsley prefaces his writing manual with an argument against "that ungrounded opinion of many, who affirme Writing to bee altogether unnecessary for women. If by it many foule businesses are contracted, and thereby much hurt effected: Is this to be laid upon the Art it selfe?"[65] He acknowledges that women are "phantasticall and humorsome," lack patience, have poor memories, and must "bee taught that which they may instantly learne" (sig. C2v). Yet he promotes writing for women on the grounds of these very failings: "if any Art be commendable in a woman, (I speake not of their ordinary workes wrought with the needle, wherein they excell) it is this of Writing; wherby they, commonly having not the best memories (especially concerning matters of moment) may commit many worthy and excellent things to Writing, which may, occasionally, minister unto them matter of much solace" (sig. B4v).

If writing as a skill was not always encouraged for women, literary writing was even more problematic, particularly if publication was involved. Writing might have been called a "dumb speech," but it was also differentiated from speech in debates about the relative value of the two. While speech was able to be adapted to its immediate context and audience, written words were more permanent and inflexible: "we ought to be much more staied and advised in writing any thing, than in bare speaking: bicause a rash and inconsiderate worde may be corrected presently, but that which is once set down in writing can no more be denied, or amended but with infamy" (de la Primaudaye, 132).

Writing also posed a problem specific to women: what was a legitimate audience? Who was a woman writer to address, given the scriptural injunction against teaching and preaching? More worrisome still, print was perceived as a public medium, as Thomas Bentley's preface to his collection of pious writing by women suggests; by publishing this collection, he says, what was once "private to my selfe, and a few of my freends, [is] now publike and common also to you good christian readers."[66] Such a characteristic could be celebrated by Reformers intent on spreading the Word, but it was condemned by aristocrats and others who disliked the democratization of a mass audience (Eisenstein 1983, 145–48).[67] Publication was problematic for male writers; for women, the "stigma of print" was intensified. Even relatively enlightened figures like Sir Thomas More, whose daughter was one of the most educated women of her time, is careful to praise her for employing her learning in a private context only: "You never hunt after vulgar praises," he says in a letter to her, "you esteem me and your husband a sufficient and ample theatre for you to content you with."[68] The audience for her display of intelligence, he implies, is properly those male members of her family who can appreciate and guide her; it is not appropriate for her to aim for a public reputation, which could only entail "vulgar praises." A variety of criticisms were leveled at women writers, from assertions of plagiarism and theft (from men) to mockery of empty repetition rather than true imitation. To complicate matters further, in exceeding the conventional boundaries of feminine accomplishment, women writers could be accused of sexual transgression and abnormality; women's language, whether speech or writing, was eroticized or made sexual. Twentieth-century women writers have pointed to the way that their books are "treated as though they themselves were women"; as Christiane Rochefort puts it, "we are read below the belt."[69] In the Renaissance, a similar equation was made between women's language and their bodies. Salter's strictures against learning for women extended specifically to writing, an activity associated with sexual transgression:

> [I]n suche studies, as yeldeth recreation and pleasure, there is no lesse daunger, that they will as well learne to be subtile and shamelesse Lovers, as connyng and skilfull writers, of Ditties, Sonnetes, Epigrames, and Ballades. . . . For suche as compare the small profit of learnyng with the greate hurt and domage that commeth to them by the same shall sone perceive (although that they remaine obstinate therein) how far more convenient the Distaffe, and Spindle, Nedle and Thimble were for them with a good and honest reputation, then the skill of well using a penne or wrightyng a loftie vearce with diffame and dishonour, if in the same there be more erudition then vertue. (sigs.C1v–C2)

With a male audience assumed, a woman's public speech and writing could be metaphorically equated with licentious behavior, behavior that somehow put the body as well as the words of the woman on display for men. Ann Rosalind Jones cites a particularly vivid example of this equation from an Italian conduct book that asserts that the "speech of a noblewoman can be no less dangerous than the nakedness of her limbs."[70] The eroticization of female authorship posed a gender-specific difficulty for women writers in the Renaissance. The virginity or chastity of a woman is repeatedly represented by male writers as a virtue put at risk by book learning; consequently, emphatic declarations of bodily integrity recur in women's writing, both in their own statements and in the statements of men who write prefatory material for their printed texts.

Such anxiety is hardly surprising, given the metaphorical association of literary creativity with masculine potency. Sandra Gilbert and Susan Gubar have argued that in Western civilization, "the text's author is a father. . . . More, his pen's power, like his penis's power, is not just the ability to generate life but the power to create a posterity to which he lays claim."[71] Where male writers in the Renaissance figured their texts as the "natural" issue of a heterosexual communion between author and female Muse, the relation between a woman writer and her Muse could be cast as unnatural, her issue monstrous and abortive. Ben Jonson, for example, in "An Epigram on The Court Pucell," castigates a woman for her writing activities by identifying textual with sexual transgression:

> What though with Tribade lust she force a Muse,
> And in an Epicoene fury can write newes
> Equall with that, which for the best newes goes,
> As aërie light, and as like wit as those?[72]

Her relationship to her Muse is defined as lesbian rape, her writing the product of a fury that blurs gender boundaries and makes her both more and less than a woman.[73] Women writers, in the context of such a sexualized poetics, become suspiciously transgressive, assuming a phallic position of masculine authority. Their writing raises the specter of an autonomous female subject able to threaten the stability of the sovereign male self.

Constraints on secular reading, on learning, and on the public display of that learning generated particular problems for women writers in the Renaissance; in such a context, writing was an emphatically gendered activity, and writing practices reflected this. Prohibitions related to reading material operated to constrain certain kinds of writing. The majority of writing by women, for example, was devoted to religion (whether doctrine or practice, whether translation or original composition). Out of bounds were privileged and public genres such as epic; tragedy; and political, philosophical, and religious theory. Since preaching was forbidden to women, sermon writing was not condoned. Nor were books of love, with their dangerously sexual concerns.

Yet women, as several critics have pointed out, were not doomed to victimization. As the following chapters will show, ideological contradictions existed in and between discourses of sexual difference, enabling women to circulate their writing in manuscript and even to make their way into print. Certain kinds of writing were more readily accessible to women than others. Translation of male-authored texts, particularly texts with religious and moral subjects, was a popular form of writing which fitted with notions of female obedience and subjection to men.[74] Original devotional works such as prayers, meditations, and confessions could be represented as both pious and private, in accordance with the Christian virtues of the ideal woman. Bentley, in his *Monument of Matrones*, commends those women "who to shew themselves woorthie paternes of all pietie, godlinesse, and religion to their sex, and for the common benefit of their countrie, have not ceased . . . to spend their time, their wits, their substance, and also their bodies, in the studies of noble and approved sciences, and in compiling and translating of sundrie most christian and godlie bookes" (sig. B1). His praise guarantees the virtue of such work by suggesting that these godly studies "spend" rather than display the woman's body. Elegies for children and husbands likewise could be promoted as pious and chaste expressions of familial affection. Even the literature of love, so often condemned by male writers, could be represented not as sexual transgression but as a private concern set off from the masculine public world. Outside the conventional boundaries of "literature," practical texts on cooking and works dealing with child rearing were less problematic for women writers also, since they conformed to the domesticity and family-centered usefulness of the model housewife. Times of turmoil, moreover, brought opportunities for publication even in restricted genres. Beyond the boundaries of this book, during the Civil War, for example, censorship of the book trade was relaxed. Radical religious sects proliferated, and political tracts and religious prophesies were published by men and women alike.

Manuscript circulation among friends and family provided an audience that could be contrasted with the public and uncontrollable readership of print. Even print had its productive contradictions. Market relations operating in the book trade could be usefully exploited and denied simultaneously; texts by women writers provided novelty value at the very least, as prefaces by printers and editors often imply. While print was a problematic medium which seemed to transgress injunctions to silence and put the body as well as the language of the woman writer on public display, it could also be differentiated from public speech. Writing, after all, was a solitary activity. Repeatedly, women writers (and their editors) insist on the privacy of their writing, often figured in terms of the spatial isolation of their closet. Such a metaphorical enclosure effaces the audience and the signs of dialogue, and in their place substitutes a silent woman alone with her thoughts.

Material and ideological conditions provide an important context for any study of Renaissance women writers. Despite the gendered conditions of literary production; despite the social, economic, and ideological constraints on female authorship; despite the difficulties inscribed in the notion of the "wise virgin," English women writers produced a wide range of literary texts in the Renaissance. Often, as recent critics have argued, what is not said, what is only half-said, what cannot be said, is as interesting as what *is* said in these texts.[75] The following chapters show a range of responses to the constraints faced by women writers— responses that include conformity and compromise but also, more radically, appropriation and confrontation.

## Chapter Two

# "Busie in my Clositt": Letters, Diaries, and Autobiographical Writing[1]

The spatial isolation of the closet is frequently called on by women writing in even the most marginal and ostensibly private genres. Her writing figuratively bounded by the confines of this retired chamber, the woman herself may become an enclosure, implicitly bounded and sealed, for knowledge: "where learning and wisdome meet in a vertuous disposed woman, she is the fittest closet for all goodnesse."[2] In this chapter I wish to address modes of writing that are peripheral to accepted "literary" forms—letters, diaries, and autobiographical writing—so as to explore some of the ways in which literate Renaissance women articulate their identity and stretch the boundary between private and public writing. These modes of writing have often been read for the apparently privileged access they offer to a mind or to experience, as "spontaneous thinking" or as "discontinuous forms . . . important to women because they are analogous to the fragmented, interrupted, and formless nature of their lives."[3] Yet, however "spontaneous" and "discontinuous" these forms of writing are, we cannot assume that they are transparent accounts of the self or of experience. Like autobiography, letters and diaries involve selection and interpretation of experience. In the wake of Sigmund Freud, Juliet Mitchell can remind us that "at every moment of a person's existence he [sic] is living and telling in word, deed or symptom the story of his life."[4] Such stories are bound up with historically and culturally specific ways of thinking. Letters, diaries, and autobiographies provide a space for constructing a personal voice, constituting the self, shaping a self-image, and articulating an identity within and against available structures of meaning. How experience is represented, how a life is told, depends also on conventions of writing.

## Letters

The letter occupies a position that is poised between private and public realms, often written in the closet but sent out into the world. The social practice of correspondence showed a marked growth in the 16th century.[5] Practical manuals for letter writing, which included model letters, were published, and fictional letters found their way into genres such as the romance. At the same time, the theory of letter writing flourished, and after 1560 collections of familiar letters were increasingly popular. The letter is extremely flexible, able to incorporate humble as well as elevated subject matter, to include details of daily life and a profusion of things, to speak in a variety of voices more or less familiar. As a functional mode of writing outside the literary marketplace, it belongs to the private domain, but its literary possibilities were increasingly exploited during the Renaissance. Whether a letter is functional or fictional, the author is engaged in shaping not only a version of the self, but also a particular moment of an interpersonal relation and the audience he or she addresses.

While the letter was promoted as a genre, manuals largely addressed a male audience and no collections of letters by women were published until 1638, when Du Bosque's collection was translated from the French as *The Secretary for Ladies*. The prefatory material to this collection repeatedly draws attention to the book's astonishing novelty, and, while it serves to open up a new literary field to women, it is marked by its attempt to preserve boundaries between masculine and feminine writing. Letter writing by English women was a social practice if not a literary practice well before 1638, of course. A large number of letters survive by women from a variety of backgrounds, though few are accessible in printed collections. As Maureen Bell argues, a "rereading of the huge and scattered mass of letters, in manuscript and in print, despite all its difficulties, would open up a rich area for the study of women's handling of language."[6] Inevitably, the letters that have been printed (primarily in editions published since the 18th century), often in collections of family papers or to illustrate the lives of politically significant men, are largely written by women of the upper classes. Even among such published collections, a remarkable range of writing is evident. Gender roles, religion, and social and geographical position complicate a class structure which in itself is jealous of the fine gradations between members of nobility and gentry. I make a foray here into this "rich area" of writing by exploring the letters of several women from a range of backgrounds

who span the period 1560–1640. While all these women—Queen
Elizabeth I; Lady Jane Cornwallis; her correspondents Lucy Russell,
Countess of Bedford, and Mary, Countess of Bath; and Lady Brilliana
Harley—write from positions of class privilege, their letters show strik-
ing differences of voice as they constitute their identities within various
structures available to them.[7]

The letters of Elizabeth I make particularly visible the potential for
maneuver within these structures.[8] The distinction between public and
private spheres becomes blurred, if not meaningless, in her case. The
most reliable indication of a personal letter is her use of the first-person
singular pronoun rather than the royal "we"; but the shift of pronoun
does not guarantee the woman rather than the queen. Even in her most
private and personal letters, she constitutes herself above all as England's
sovereign. In a brief message to her young godson, John Harington, for
example, whom she addresses familiarly as "Boy Jack," Elizabeth sends a
copy of her Parliamentary speech and tells him to "play with them till
they enter thine understanding; so shalt thou hereafter, perchance, find
some good fruits hereof when thy Godmother is out of remembrance;
and I do this because thy father was ready to serve and love us in trouble
and thrall" (Harrison 1935, 123). The simple gift of a godmother, what
she calls her "poor words," is simultaneously the gift of a learned sovereign; her final sentence pointedly shifts from singular to plural pronoun
as she links this personal gift to the public service required of the good
subject. Political understanding appears to displace moral or spiritual
advice; or rather, godliness is implicitly associated with the words of a
Christian prince.

Elizabeth's letters adapt themselves, as epistolary theory recommended, to the occasion and the audience they address. They can be read as
more or less polished rhetorical performances, and they range stylistical-
ly from plain statement to witty and sententious flourish, from clarity to
enigmatic abstraction, according to the demands of the situation.
Repeatedly, they show Elizabeth at work manipulating her self-representation by playing with the conflicting attributes of femininity and sovereignty. At times, she sets gender and rank at odds and overtly excludes
the feminine from her identity as sovereign. Thus she writes in indigna-
tion to the French King, Henry IV: "Can you imagine that the softness
of my sex deprives me of the courage to resent a public affront? The
royal blood I boast could not brook, from the mightiest Prince in
Christendom, such treatment" (Harrison 1935, 218). She attributes to
Henry a gross misreading of her nature by setting body against blood;

genealogy is made to displace gender as the primary source of identity. Yet her sex is nevertheless available to define Henry's treatment of her as shamefully uncivil and unmanly; she allows her troops to remain on the Continent, "blushing, meantime, that I am made to the world the spectacle of a despised princess" (219). Elsewhere, she calls on gender to construct an androgynous identity that composes a complementary whole. In a letter of condolence written to Lady Elizabeth Drury, for example, she proffers a doubled assistance: "you can enjoy with comfort, a King for his power, and a Queen for her love, who leaves not now to protect you when your case requires care" (200).

Marriage negotiations involve her in some particularly striking maneuvers in this respect. In her correspondence during the years 1579–84 with the Duke of Anjou, a suitor 23 years her junior, her letters draw on conventional notions of the ideal woman to represent her as mistress and potential good wife. Passivity, modesty, beauty, simplicity, spotless faith, constancy, obedience, and even inferior understanding and lack of wit are attributes to which she lays claim in these letters. The Duke of Anjou appears as the active lover. It is his desires that ostensibly drive the negotiations, while she, in contrast, is passive, pious, and obedient: "I feel myself so bound by the charm which you lay on me that I cannot persuade myself other than that the Holy Spirit this Pentecost has inspired me to obey your desires" (Harrison 1935, 146). Advice is accompanied by mention of the "foolishness of my understanding" (139) and protestations that she recognizes her "lack of wit to instruct you" (129); warnings are playfully undercut with gendered conceits: "But at this moment I muse as old women are wont in their dreams, not having slept well" (138). Age difference is made a very different signifier in letters to the young James VI of Scotland: "You deal not with one whose experience can take dross for good payments. . . . No, no, I mind to set to school your craftiest Councillor" (159). Here, it is the wise experience of age that is emphasized, and in the process an ungendered metaphor can displace the "old woman": "we old foxes can find shifts to save ourselves by others' malice, and come by knowledge of greatest secret" (163).

Gender and royal blood often sit in uneasy relationship in these negotiations. While patently debating the terms of the proposal, Elizabeth calls on the mythology of marriage as a spiritual union rather than a material contract, ostensibly indignant that the duke should be seeking her fortune rather than her person; her letter goes on to outline the gifts of body and mind she brings to her suitor, while simultaneously concerned to assert her appropriately feminine modesty. This, she declares, is no negotiation with "a Princess that had either some def[ect] of body or some other notable defect of nature, or l[acking gif]ts of the mind fit for one of our place and quality"; rather, since "it hath pleased God to bestow His gifts upon us in good measure, which we do ascribe to the Giver, and not glory in them as proceeding from ourselves (being no fit trumpet to set out our own praises), we may in true course of modesty think ourself worthy of as great a Prince as Monsieur is" (133–34). God is called on to validate both the virtues and the modesty of a female sovereign who is engaged in arranging her own marriage. It is noteworthy that Elizabeth is identified as a "princess" in this instance, a label that attempts to signify the propriety of a potential union with a suitor who is no king by leveling the disparity of rank between herself and her male suitor.

The term "princess" is used for rather different purposes in Elizabeth's letters to Mary, Queen of Scots. In a letter following the murder of Mary's second husband, Lord Darnley, Mary is advised to "show the world what a noble Princess and loyal woman you are" by taking revenge on Darnley's murderers (Harrison 1935, 49). The choice of terms suggest the need to avoid a scandal to Mary's reputation as both sovereign and woman; to squash rumours of her implication in the murder, she is to preserve her honor by displaying her loyalty as a wife as well as the proper response of a just ruler. Mary's later involvement in plots against Elizabeth is represented as the action of a monstrous woman as her trial begins in England: "Let your wicked murderess know how, with hearty sorrow, her vile deserts compel these orders"; her fault is "far passing woman's thought, much less a Princess" (180). Often, Mary's letters are mirrored back to her as emotional outbursts that lack judgment and order: "But now finding by your last letter . . . an increase of your impatience, tending also to uncomely, passionate, ireful and vindictive speeches, I thought to change my former opinion, and by patient and advised words to move you to stay or qualify your passions" (103). Elizabeth's voice, by contrast, is identified as the voice of calm reason. Such letters appear to position Elizabeth as the masculine to Mary's weak and wayward feminine, marking out her superiority in gendered terms.

The conflicting structures of sovereignty and gender allow for a flexibility of voice in Elizabeth's letters that women of lesser rank could not emulate. Yet similar strategies are visible in their self-representation as they draw on various sources of authority that qualify or even counter the injunction to be chaste, silent, and obedient. Lady Jane Cornwallis, for example, widowed at 30 by the death of her first husband and left in control of a sizable estate and fortune, makes use of the ideology of the marriage manuals to negotiate the terms of her second marriage with Nathaniel Bacon in much the same way as Elizabeth did.[9] Thirty years after the queen's negotiations with Anjou, she represents herself as a passive recipient of her suitor's advances: "this gentleman being so desierous to see me, as you said he was, I thought then, and so I do now, it ware uncivell part of me to forbid him coming, but left it, you know, to himselfe" (Braybrooke 1842, 1–2). Bacon's parents, she writes to her intermediary, have assured her "that it was myselfe, and not my fortune, which they desiered; but, I confess, by several circumstances I maye justly feare that I shall find my fortune to be the chiefe motive which hath persuaded them to this" (2). Her letters justify the conditions she proposes with recourse to notions of the loyal wife and good mother: she has had no thought of remarriage since the death of her first husband, and she refuses to give away "the increase of my owne estate . . . for I would never have done my child so much wronge, though I might have had all the good of the world by it" (3). She and her prospective mother-in-law debate the conditions of the marriage with a clear sense of the material value of the exchange. While her mother-in-law, Lady Anne Bacon of Redgrave, writes to her professing that she loves her "unfainedly and most deerly in the Lorde," and asserts the spiritual value of a union based on love ("for a trewer husband, and on[e] that louved you better, shall you never have"; 12), she writes to their intermediary in other terms: "although the juell layd before us be never so riche, if we be not abill to buy it we must be content to forbeare it. We must not laye out all our stocke upon one purchas, having so many others to provide for" (15). Her letters construct her as a prudent and godly housewife, fully aware of the economics of an exchange which must not put her household at risk.

Lady Cornwallis's most frequent correspondent was Lucy Russell, Countess of Bedford (1581–1627), whose letters construct an identity primarily in relation to the court, where from 1603 until 1619 she held a favored position in the service of Queen Anne.[10] Rarely does she mention her husband in her letters to Cornwallis; and her housewifery provides the context only for a reference to a visit from the king. Her correspondence negotiates a friendship that is constantly interrupted by the court and its occasions. In or out of favor, the countess is always a courtier, much as Elizabeth is always a queen. Before 1619, the style of her letters is breathless, mirroring their assertions of a busy life where she writes "in haste," pressured by the demands of her royal mistress and court affairs:

"because I could not sett a sertaine day for my goeing with you, I deferred my wrighting to you till I cam into the contry, wheare within 8 days the K[ing] overtooke me. . . . Within 3 days after, my promis carried me to my Lo[rd] of Huntingdon's . . . ther I mett with a peremtory comandement from the Queene to wayte upon her at Woodstocke . . . within 2 days after my arrivall here I fell so extream sick as I was forced to take my bed" (Braybrooke 1842, 24–25).

Clauses linked by conjunctions and a loose association of ideas give the impression of spontaneity and light-hearted conversation. Excuses for deferred visits and an absence of communication expand into reports of the personal politics of the royal households and the latest London news. After 1619, however, her letters dwell increasingly on her ill health and the deaths of her closest friends and relatives, until, with the death of James I, her alienation from the court is complete. In 1625, she invites Lady Cornwallis and her husband to Moor Lodge, the estate that, in 1617, she was happily renovating, calling it "that place I am so much in love with, as, if I wear so fond of any man, I wear in hard case" (Braybrooke 1842, 47). Now, however, it has become a place of desolation: "I wish you would beare him companie to this solitarie place, whear I do not desier to see many now living, but yourselfe very much" (127).

A similar shift is evident in her attitude to the court itself. In 1617, she can lightly take on the persona of the court satirist, although her virtuous opposition does not alter the locus of her identity: "Of the Queen's court I can say litle good, for her resolution to part with [Lady] Roxbrough still continues, which makes her looke big upon all she thinkes loves that good woeman . . . but upon such an occasion [I] cannot be sorry for her frownes, which are now litle to me, all my court businesses being so dispatched as they will not much requier my attendance ther; and I am growne to love my ease and liberty" (Braybrooke 1842, 44–45). By 1625, she complains, after the death of the Marquis of Hamilton, that she is "a maimed body and worse, and so is my Lo[rd] Chamberlain, the last person left of power that I can relie on . . . and, to speake freely to you, the only honest harted man imployed that I know now left to God and his countrie" (119). Her letter figuratively marks her grief and her isolation from the court on her body itself, now "maimed" for good.

In the final years of her life, the Countess of Bedford's letters locate her alienation within a conventional religious framework. She becomes the pious Christian patiently awaiting her death, while her own misery is made analogous to that of the state: "God, I trust, will give mee thankfulnes to Him and patience till His apointed tyme of releasing mee from all misserie; of which wee are yett like to have in generall more and more, if this Parlement and the King part not upon better termes then yett they stand" (Braybrooke 1842, 146).[11]

Religion provides a more consistent framework for the articulation of identity in the letters of Lady Brilliana Harley. Lady Harley's letters represent her as a pious Christian woman and mother.[12] The third wife of the puritan and parliamentarian Sir Robert Harley, Lady Harley occupies a position in the class hierarchy less elevated than the positions of such women as the Countess of Bedford. Living her married life almost wholly on her husband's country estate, far removed from London and the Caroline court, and lacking an extensive humanist education, she constitutes her identity primarily in relation to the model of the effective family articulated in Protestant marriage guides. In her early letters to her husband and in her later letters to her son Edward, she regularly signs herself "your most faithfull affectionat wife" and "your most affectionat mother," and the cover directions preface their names with "my deare husband" and "my deare sonne." Her letters accord full authority to her husband, whether she is requesting permission from him to employ a gentlewoman to serve her, or advising her son. When Edward has apparently communicated to her his need for a piece of plate, she asks him to have his tutor confirm the request: "Tell Mr Pirkins rwit [sic] to your father that you did wante it, your father said he thought you had no neede of it" (Lewis 1854, 31). Never does she claim for herself the power of punishment: to Edward, for example, she writes a postscript recording Sir Robert's displeasure (28); and she leaves unspecified the agent of rebuke after the mention of her younger son's "stubborneness": "he has bine crost, when he desarved it" (12).

Lady Harley's correspondence displays her internalization of the model of the good wife articulated in humanist and Protestant literature; writing to her son of the "colericke" temper of one of her maids, she adds an afterthought, "I pray God, if ever you have a wife, she may be of a meeke and quiet spirit" (Lewis 1854, 85). A late letter of 1641 tells her son that she wishes she could "undergoo some of the paines" for her husband in London, but qualifies it with a proper respect for the male intellect: "but I would have him act the understanding part" (115). Likewise, her letters construct her as the loving wife and mother whose life is centered on the family. Responding to news from Edward, she writes: "I am sorry my lady Corbet takes no more care of her chillderen. Sr Andwe Corbet left two thousand pounds a year. Shee has a way that I should not take, by my good will with my chillderen, without it weare to correct some great fallt in them; but my deare ned, as longe as it pleases God, I have it, I shall willingly give what is in my power, for the beest advantage of you, and your brothers and sisters, as ocation offers itself" (33).

As the good mother, however, she acquires a degree of authority in her writing through her capacity as moral guide to her children. Whereas her letters to her husband are overtly submissive, asserting her affection and providing news of the children and household, her letters to her son participate in an exchange of news (domestic and political), offer moral and spiritual advice, and discuss books of various kinds. Her interest in current affairs is converted to a resource for educating her son, and repeatedly her letters interpret events as signs of the progress of Protestantism. "We heare that the kinge of Spaine begins to deale with the monestries in Spaine, as harry the 8 did in Ingland. My deare ned, let me upon this put you in minde that this year 1639, is the yeare in which maney are of the opinion that Antichrist [i.e., the episcopacy] must begine to falle" (Lewis 1854, 41).

Addressing her son in her letters as the comfort of her life, the child "next my oune hart," Lady Harley constitutes herself as loving mother whose reading and knowledge are directed to pious and familial ends. Within the confines of the gender roles she adopts, she finds the means to articulate a knowing self. Moreover, this "motherly" communication is extended to encompass other forms of writing. In one letter, Lady Harley sends Edward her own translation of Calvin's life of Luther, along with her opinions (which take issue with Erasmus) on the significance of Luther's actions. "Thus, my deare Ned, you may see how willingly I impart any thinge to you, in which I finde any good. I may truely say, I never injoy any thinge that is good but presently my thoughts reflect upon you" (Lewis 1854, 52). Even in this affectionate familial context, however, her translation is carefully represented as a profitable and solitary activity avoiding idleness. She prefaces her gift with a message about its origins: "Haveing bine offtin not well, and confined to so sollatary a place as my beed, I made choys of an entertainement for meself, which might be eassy and of some benifit to meself" (52).

Queen, courtier, widow, wife, mother—each of these gendered roles helps to shape the voices of the letter writers. The letters of Mary, Countess of Bath, to her sister-in-law Lady Cornwallis present a rather more unstable identity, and provide an illustration of the problems faced by a woman who is neither "maid, wife, or widow," drastically reducing the possibility of maneuver in a matrix of conflicting subject positions.[13]

Mary Cornwallis was married to the Earl of Bath in 1579; the marriage was later declared void in court, but it was upheld by her family throughout her life (Braybrooke 1842, xxi). Her letters represent her as an abandoned wife, a tragic victim whose suffering is registered on her body. Signing herself "your La[dyshi]ps lovyng unfortunat syster," she provides a detailed account of her ill health as she gives thanks for a gift of meat: "notwithstandying I was sike of a cheken yester night, yet I coold eat thys with desyre, and yet not sike of it, but my fitts never of mee." Repeatedly she begs Lady Cornwallis not to "loose so much of your presias tyme of entertaynyng" as to invite her for a visit when others are expected. Such an unfortunate, she suggests, could only be troublesome. She can write only "ragget lyns," and her letters themselves should be pocketed until such time as no other interests are at hand (54). Her writing, like the self she constructs, is impossibly marred by her situation. When an imposter claims he is her child by the Earl of Bath, her self-representation as tragic heroine seems complete: "so abject a woman, who hath ever syns not known what an howr's true content, but sorrowe and syknes, and such an aflykted mynde as shoold rather move . . . compacion then furder malles" (69). Body and writing mingle inextricably: "if my tears wooll wryt black, I need no inke" (70). There is little room left for rhetorical performance and flexible construction of the self as her letter becomes "unsensible wrytynge" (68).

The peculiar position of the letter as a form that occupies the borderline between private and public writing is shadowed by anxiety in the correspondence of these women. Often they register the potential of the written word to go astray, to be misplaced and read by prying eyes, to be misinterpreted. Elizabeth's concern for the privacy of her writing is clearly bound up with the politics of state. Her letters are often accompanied by an ambassador who is authorized to communicate information in private, and her repeated protestations of her own lack of deceit, along with her analytical responses to letters she has received, register a consciousness of textuality and the polysemic openness of language. Responding to a letter from Henry III, she can complain that she is "astonished to find no answer declared therein, as if paper and ink had been employed with no object, like ciphers signifying nothing" (Harrison 1935, 151). Her own attempts to maintain the privacy of the letter are preserved in a message to Sir Henry Sidney. The letter encodes its warning in abstract moral sentences and enigmatic generalizations which she calls "Gebourest" (gibberish): "If we still advise we shall never do; thus are we ever knitting a knot, never tied. Yea, and if our web be framed with rot-

ten hurdles, when our loom is wellnigh done, our work is new to begin.
God send the weaver true prentices again" (47). The letter concludes
with a demand that it be destroyed immediately, "only committed to
Vulcan's base keeping, without any longer abode than the leisure of the
reading thereof: yea, and with no mention made thereof to any other
wight" (50).

This anxiety about privacy is more mixed in character in the case of
Lady Harley, whose letters show an anxiety that extends to both political and domestic concerns. In a letter that comments on current attacks
"against Puretans," for example, she reminds her son of a method of
secret communication: "I have toold you if you remember of a paper that
some statemen make use of, when they would not have knowne what
they rwit of" (Lewis 1854, 40). Yet at times she also tells her son that
her letters communicate messages only for his eyes, or are sent secretly:
"Your father dous not knowe I send. Thearefore take no notis of it, to
him, nor to any. . . . Nobody in the howes knowes I send to you" (16).
Letter writing offers women a passage into literary life and self-expres-
sion, but it is a passage whose boundaries must be carefully guarded. As
Lady Harley comments, "it is an ease to me to tell you how I doo; it is a
thinge I cannot doo to every one" (74).

## Diaries and Autobiographical Writing

Like the letter, autobiographical writing is poised between public and private realms. In the Renaissance, the secular autobiography as we know it
today was only slowly emerging out of spiritual autobiography and con-
fession, and generic boundaries had not become hardened between forms
of writing such as letters, diaries, and memoirs.[14] Like the letter, the diary,
as Linda Anderson argues, "allows the woman to remain hidden while
providing her with a place to actualise her interiority, create herself for an
'other', even if that 'other' is also herself."[15] In its fragmented and apparently artless fashion, it moves toward the autobiographical narrative of
coherent selfhood. Yet little autobiographical writing by Renaissance
women, secular or spiritual, is now extant. The diaries of Lady Anne
Clifford and Lady Margaret Hoby, and the extended autobiographical
preface to Lady Grace Mildmay's as yet unpublished journal, are unusual
survivors from the period prior to the Civil War.[16]

Most overtly private of these three texts is Lady Hoby's diary, which
covers a six-year period from 1599 to 1605 and was apparently begun as
an exercise in piety that kept her "busie in [her] Clositt" (Meads 1930,

98, 182).[17] Probably a fragment of a larger whole since it begins with torn pages and ends without conclusion, the diary acts initially as a form of religious self-examination, a daily accounting of her spiritual self. On 10 September 1599, a month after the first entry, she comments on her neglect of prayer before dinner: "if I had not taken this Course of examenation, I think I had for gotten itt" (70). It is a course that is bounded equally by the privacy of her closet and that of her heart. In similar phrasing, she can say "I returned into my Closett unto privat examenation and praier" (91) and "I returned in to my hart, examenid my selfe, and Craved pardon for my severall ommitions and Comitions" (76). Her closet is identified as the place in which she can pray and write "for mine owne privat Conscience" (101).

In the first year or so, the diary examines "with what Integretie I had spent the day" (Meads 1930, 84) by outlining Hoby's periods of prayer, pious reading, and meditation before and after meals, and mentioning other activities, household duties, and acts of charity that occupied the remainder of her time. The entry for each day is effectively structured around the needs of the body and the soul. Tuesday 21 August 1599 is typical: "after I was readie I praied, and then I went awhile about the house and so to breakfast, and then to work, tell coveringe [a neighbor?] came: then I went to privat praier but was interrupted: after I had dined I went to work tell 6:, and walked a little abroad, and then Came to examenation and praier: after, I walked a litle, and so to supper: after which I went to praiers, and, Nut long after, accordinge to my wonted use, to bed, save only I did not so deligently think of that I had hard, which I be seech the Lord to pardon, for Christ sack Annen Amen" (65). Her entries are interspersed with brief prayers and allusions to spiritual temptations and assaults, which are rarely identified in any detail. Although at moments the diary points forward to later Puritan spiritual autobiography, with its drama of spiritual struggle and conversion, it predominantly records and enacts her avoidance of idleness in the pursuit of piety: "I did goe about to diverse places wher I find that buseneses hindereth wanderinge Coggetation . . . all the after none I was buseed about takinge of accountes and other thinges so that through Idlenes, distractions had no advantage" (109).[18] The industry of the good housewife is represented here as spiritual rather than economic profit. In the same way, her body becomes the site of a divine drama as periods of ill health are interpreted as God's "gentle corriction": "after dinner, it pleased, for a Just punishment to corricte my sinnes, to send me febelnis of stomak and paine of my head" (64).

Yet the emphasis of the diary shifts over time. In October 1600 she and her husband, Sir Thomas Hoby, travel to London for several months, and even as she packs for the journey, her spiritual exercises begin to take second place in her daily record: "All but the times of my ordenarie exercises of praier and readinge I was busie takinge order for my going to london, and packinge of thinges" (Meads 1930, 148). Once she is resident in London, her diary records visits, purchases, news of legal disputes, and current events as well as attendance at sermons and moments of prayer. Entries mentioning other kinds of pious writing activities—notes written into her Bible or sermon book, or copies of meditations, for example— dwindle from the prominent position they occupied before the trip.

This change of emphasis is maintained on her return to her Yorkshire estate. Instead of long entries built around meal and prayer times, each day is summarily disposed of: "As I was accustomed, I used my exercises, and was veseted by my Cosine Boucher, and Mr Gatt of Seamer" (Meads 1930, 178). Increasingly, the diary seems to be concerned with recording significant events rather than operating as a daily self-examination: "After prairs I went about, and was busie as I was accustomed, nether doinge nor receivinge any great matter of note" (179). Thus, in an unusually long entry, she can record a visit to a deformed calf, providing a detailed description of its anatomy (171). In another, she describes a surgical operation on a child "who had no fundement": "I was ernestly intreated to Cutt the place to se if any passhage Could be made, but, although I Cutt deepe and seearched, there was none to be found" (184). The events are recorded dispassionately, without spiritual framing or pious comment.

With her husband's increasing involvement in local administration, her diary takes more interest in his affairs and in county news, and no longer does she write daily entries, particularly when Sir Thomas is absent in London. Some of the events are interpreted in terms of divine justice, but such entries bear little resemblance to the early accounting of her own spiritual state. Four months before the diary ends, one entry suggests her recognition of the change. In the only explicit mention in the text of her diary writing, she calls herself back to her old course: "at Night I thought to writt my daies Journee as before, becaus, in the readinge over some of my former spent time, I funde some profitt might be made of that Course from which, thorow two much neccligence, I had a Longe time dissisted: but they are unworthye of godes benefittes and especiall favours that Can finde no time to make a thankfull recorde of them" (Meads 1930, 216).

The diary of one of God's chosen has been supplanted by the diary of a busy gentlewoman whose role is to support the public activities of her husband with her own domestic industry. The two exist in tension with each other, a tension that is found also in the ambivalent and shifting voice of the diary, which at times appears to address an audience other than the self. Why, for example, record a meeting with a "gentlewoman friend" (Meads 1930, 109) or a "kinswoman of mine" (110) without the specificity of a name? Or why record a conversation as a "privat Conference betwene Mr Rhodes and me of som thinges that Concerned us both nearly" (88) if no audience is imagined? At such moments, the diary moves beyond the enclosed privacy of the closet.

While Lady Hoby's diary is, ostensibly at least, addressed to her "privat Conscience," Lady Grace Mildmay's journal is explicitly directed to her family, in particular to her daughter and her grandchildren.[19] Her account of her life provides an extensive preface to a selection of her own meditations compiled for the use of her family, and in its emphasis on the godly education of children can be compared to the mother's-advice book.[20] Written toward the end of her life and after the death of her husband in 1617, the autobiography articulates her life as a spiritual journey. Her childhood education is displayed as an education that establishes the principles of religion and instills feminine virtue, and her adult life becomes a preparation for death. Every domestic crisis and property dispute is resolved with the assistance of God (Mildmay 1617, 58–59). In her account, it is women who bear the primary responsibility for religious education within the family. She describes her mother as an "Angell of God" who taught her prayers and meditations, and it is her mother who provides the young Grace and her two sisters with a governess, in the form of a niece she herself has raised.[21] Mildmay casts her writing as a continuation of that maternal teaching by heading her preface "experience I commend unto my children" (1).

Further, experience rather than learning is represented as the source of her authority; the autobiography makes no claim to the masculine world of the pedagogue. A recommendation for reading in the scriptures, history, and moral philosophy, for example, is framed as experiential observation: "I have found by observation this to be the best course to set ourselves in from the begining unto the end of our lyves" (Mildmay 1617, 1). Mildmay explicitly asks her "faithfull reader" to "accept my good meaning" without expecting "Eloquence, exact Method, or learning, which could not proceed from me who have not been trained up in universitie Learning" (31). Her "experience" of her parents and her governess, Mrs. Hamblyn, provides a model for childhood education to which she can attach more general observations. In this respect, her representation of Mrs. Hamblyn helps to construct her writing as an illustration of feminine virtue: "She proved very religious, wyse, and chaste, and all good vertues that might be in a woman very constantly settled in her, for, from her youth she made good use of all things that ever she did read, see or heare; and observed all companyes that ever she came in, good or badd: so that shee could give a right censure and true judgment of most things, and give wyse counsell upon any occasion" (9). Mildmay's journal offers her own "true judgment" and "wyse counsell" on a variety of matters, including "Myne owne observation of Sir Walter Mildmay," a "character" of her father-in-law.

Mrs. Hamblyn is likewise a useful touchstone for the act of writing itself: "she could . . . sett her mynd downe in wryting either by letters indited, or otherwyse as well as most men could have done. . . . And when shee did see me ydly disposed, shee would sett me to cipher with my penn, and to cast up and proove great summes and accomptes, and sometymes set me to wryte a supposed letter to this or that body concerning such and such things" (Mildmay 1617, 9–11).

Writing becomes a proper activity for avoiding idleness, as it was in Lady Hoby's diary, while at the same time writing skill is made the mark of a woman of exceptional virtue. In Mrs. Hamblyn's educational practices, writing is a means to chaste feminine virtue. A "monstruous spectacle" of wanton behavior provides the occasion for a joint composition by governess and child of moral verse put to music "for myne instruction to take heed of the lyke, and to abhorre and despise the same" (Mildmay 1617, 13). While Mrs. Hamblyn counsels her to "heare much and speake little" and to "avoyde the company of Servingmen, or any other of lyke disposition, whose ribald talke and ydle gestures and evill suggestions, were dangerous for our Chaste eares and eyes, to heare and behold" (10), observation and writing are nevertheless held up as virtuous modes of learning and judgment.

Mildmay's father, on the other hand, is represented as a careful teacher of a different kind, the pen replaced by the rod. The account of his concern for women's bodily behavior jumps uneasily to a description of a violent scene of punishment: "my father could not abyde to see a woman unstable or light in her caryage. . . . But he lyked a woman, well graced with a constant and setled countenance, and good behaviour thoroughout her whole partes, which presenteth unto all men a good hope of a stablished mynde, and vertuous disposition to be in her. . . . I have seene my father with his owne hands (for examples sake) scourge a young man naked from the girdle upwards, with fresh rodds, for making but a shewe, and countenance of a sawcie and unreverent behaviour towards us his children, and put him from his service" (Mildmay 1617, 13–14). Class and gender here operate in tandem to inscribe patriarchal law on the body itself, the young male servant acting as substitute for the transgressive female body. The material detail of the account, with its seminaked body and "fresh rodds," emphasizes the violence of an "example" which warns both male servants and female children at once. Mildmay's submissive acceptance of such patriarchal law is advertised in her conclusion that careful parenting would prevent much wickedness and misfortune in later years, yet her writing positions itself in a familial tradition which makes room for specifically female teaching.

The diary of Lady Anne Clifford, ostensibly written as a private record, is in a sense more of a "public" statement than either Hoby's diary or Mildmay's autobiography.[22] The diary, transcribed from a lost original, begins with an account of 1603 written at some later date and continues as a diary written in the years 1616, 1617, and 1619.[23] The text moves toward secular autobiography in its mingling of daily record and reminiscence, visibly engaging in the process of constructing a self. Unlike the writing of Mildmay or Hoby, the diary does not set out to map a spiritual journey. Instead, it is bound up with the family "chronicles," a history-in-the-making of an aristocratic woman. Her "chronicles"—diaries, reminiscences, records, and family papers—allow her to read over her life and self as object, helping her to shape her present self with reference to the past; she can "read over the Chronicles" and "compare things past with things present" (Sackville-West 1923, 56). The diary provides a space for constituting the story of her life.[24]

The identity Anne Clifford articulates in her diary is primarily that of an aristocrat, the wife of the Earl of Dorset, the child of the Earl and Countess of Cumberland. Running like a connecting thread through the whole is her struggle to regain the family estate and the conflict which that entails with husband, relatives, friends, and king. Her roles as wife and mother are prominent, but they appear repeatedly in relation to her cause. Her identity is constructed around a narrative of conflict and separation focused primarily on the Earl of Dorset and his attempts to make her give up her claim to the Westmoreland estate in return for a financial recompense from her uncle. When he is with her at Knole, the Sackville estate in Kent, the diary entries record their struggles as well as moments of harmony. When he is absent in London or elsewhere, the diary records verbal reports and letters that indicate his current opinion of her behavior, and marks time with an accounting of books and needlework that she has "made an end of."

A variety of domestic and material details come to signify the state of their relationship. A return to London that is greeted by her husband with "10 or 11 coaches" (Sackville-West 1923, 44) contrasts with the "cold welcome" she receives at Knole when her daughter "met me in the outermost gate and my Lord came to me in the Drawing Chamber" (24). The day after a "falling out about the land," the distance between the two is signaled by their physical separation: she visits her own closet and has a book read to her, "my Lord sitting the most part of the day reading in his closet" (47). Their sleeping arrangements act as signifiers in the same way. One entry records without comment that the Earl "lay in Leslie Chamber, I in my own" (29), while another specifies the disruption occasioned by the struggle: "This night my Lord should have lain with me but he and I fell out about matters" (65).

Frequently the diary comments on the Earl's courtly activities, his life of pleasure providing a contrast with her own isolation and solitude at Knole: "All this time my Lord was in London where he had all and infinite great resort coming to him. . . . I stayed in the country having many times a sorrowful and heavy heart, and being condemned by most folks because I would not consent to the agreements, so as I may truly say, I am like an owl in the desert" (Sackville-West 1923, 28). The sickness and death of her mother, whom she represents as model, confidante, and counselor throughout her life, become the emblem of her increasingly isolated position, with "God my only helper" (29). The diary, in recording her trials, participates in her resistance, and at moments of crisis she interprets her survival as a miraculous story of divine intervention. In an interview with the king himself and ten (male) nobles and lawyers, which is recorded in some detail, she alone refuses to submit to the king's judgment: "I would never agree to it without Westmoreland at which the King grew in a great chaff." Excluded from the final agreement, she can nevertheless reaffirm her position: "I may say I was led miraculously by God's Providence . . . for neither I nor anybody else thought I should have passed over this day so well as I have done" (50–51).

Clifford's diary is not only the record of a material struggle, it is also the record of a struggle for meaning. Is her behavior to be defined as "obstinacy" and disobedience, or is it "both just and honourable"? Her own belief in her position as rightful heir to the Earl of Cumberland sets aristocratic heir into conflict with aristocratic wife.[25] Her diary carefully records her obedience to her husband's commands, as she waits to be called to London or leaves for the country when she is "sent away upon half an hour's warning . . . about 8 o'clock at night so as it was 12 before we came to Knole" (Sackville-West 1923, 34). Such entries seem to be silent at crucial moments, following the advice given by her mother to "neither cross him in words but keep your resolutions with silence and what gentle persuasion you can, but alter not from your own wise course. . . . Dear heart be very wary what you say but most wary what you write for they desire to have advantage and to sever my Lord and you."[26]

Yet the diary also marks out Anne Clifford's insistence on her right to her own inheritance, and constitutes some of her actions as self-affirming rebellion. When a conveyance is brought to her, for example, she accounts for her refusal to sign "because my Lord had sent me down so suddenly 2 days before" (Sackville-West 1923, 35). At times, even her clothes are made to speak her resistance. On Easter day, 1617, the diary juxtaposes the record of a "great falling out" with the Earl against the statement that "All this time I wore my white satin gown and my white waistcoat," suggesting that these struggles do not impinge on her spiritual innocence (65). Her refusal to accede to the Earl's demands is represented at times as the refusal of the good mother (at odds with the good wife) who is anxious to prevent her daughter's disinheritance. At the end of June 1617, she writes that she is "still working and being extremely melancholy and sad to see things go so ill with me and fearing my Lord would give all his land away from the Child" (72). Yet she is prepared to let her daughter be removed from her care because of her refusal, a situation she works to represent as the proper action of submissive wife and good mother: "when I considered that it would both make my Lord more angry with me and be worse for the Child, I resolved to let her go" (25).

Throughout the diary, Anne Clifford's identity is constituted in relation to her family and rank through her acquaintance with the royal family and with other nobles, whether she is supported or condemned by them for her stance. Unlike Lady Mildmay and Lady Hoby, women of the lesser gentry who are actively engaged in the running of their households, she marks out a life of leisure rarely interrupted by the demands of the housewife.[27] Instead of figuring costs of wages and rents, like Lady Hoby, she lists the gambling wins and losses of both herself and her spendthrift husband without comment, as if such figures act as signifiers of their aristocratic means rather than as moral pointers. In the same way, she can report the cost of a New Year's gift to the queen, register the number of coaches in a retinue, or name the noblewoman she accompanies to a play without commenting on the play itself. While the diary vigorously asserts her right to Westmoreland even before the king, her resistance is never phrased as a rejection of the system itself; she cannot, in effect, subvert the very authority on which she bases her claim, though, as Lewalski argues, her life and writings "deliver a remarkable challenge to contemporary patriarchal ideology as she presses vigorously for her legal rights" (1993, 150).

Clifford's diary, in its provisional structuring of her life around a struggle to regain her rightful inheritance, reaches from a record of small daily happenings toward the self-constituting and self-justifying narrative of a woman whose conviction, supported by her mother, prompts her to write. The portrait she commissioned in later life, when Westmoreland was finally hers, provides a coherent visual statement of the self she begins to shape in these earlier years of strife, the self who is primarily the rightful heir to her parents and only secondarily a wife (see figure three). Pictured in the side panel on the left as a young woman of about 15 (at the time of her father's death), surrounded by signs of graceful accomplishment, and in the panel on the right as a mature woman of 56, her shelves piled with books in the disarray of constant use, she quite literally encompasses the central panel of her parents and the two brothers who died in their infancy. As Graham remarks, "the diminutive portraits of her two husbands hang behind Clifford in the right-hand panel of the triptych, almost as trophies of her past" (1989, 35), while her role as a mother is entirely excluded from her "Great Picture."[28]

In the early 20th century, Virginia Woolf envisaged for herself the nature of the diary she wanted to keep: "I should like it to resemble some deep old desk, or capacious hold-all, in which one flings a mass of odds and ends without looking them through. I should like to come back, after a year or two, and find that the collection had sorted itself and refined itself and coalesced, as such deposits so mysteriously do, into a mould, transparent enough to reflect the light of our life, and yet steady, tranquil compounds with the aloofness of a work of art."[29] Suspended between "life" and "art," the diary—or the letter— provides a space for the coalescing of experience and the self. Woolf's spatial figure of the deep old desk (or, for that matter, of a room of one's own) could be compared to the Renaissance figure of the closet. Each offers a private place in which a woman can collect and organize her thoughts,

LADY ANNE CLIFFORD'S "GREAT PICTURE" AT APPLEBY CASTLE IN CUMBRIA;
PROBABLY THE WORK OF JAN VAN BELCAMP.

*Reproduced courtesy of Abbot Hall Art Gallery, Kendal, Cumbria, England.*

her words, and herself, and can begin to affirm her own meaning. The diaries and letters of Renaissance women provide us with a valuable repository of women's writing which should not be ignored in favor of more conventionally "literary" material.

## Chapter Three

# Negotiating a Place in "Eruditions garden"[1]

The letters of Renaissance women offer us access to a variety of self-representations that provide an enlightening comparison with their more explicitly "literary" writing. Mary Ellen Lamb's contrast of the vigorous letters of the Cooke sisters (Mildred Cooke Cecil, Anne Cooke Bacon, and Elizabeth Cooke Hoby Russell) with the modest prefaces of their published translations acts as a reminder both of the cultural constraints on women that inevitably affected their writing practices and of the potential for finding a literary voice that existed despite such constraints.[2] Yet the Cooke sisters did find a way into print. In a literary tradition in which legitimate inheritance was a male prerogative, educated women were nevertheless able to make use of a range of authorizing strategies to create a place for themselves as writers.

## Translation

The Cooke sisters found their way into print through translation of religious texts, in a time when translation of religious and secular materials was an important activity for writers of both sexes, as humanism promoted the use of the vernacular.[3] A substantial proportion of women's writing in the Renaissance consisted of translation, predominantly of religious texts. Since translation was regularly described as a faithful reproduction of the (overwhelmingly male) author's original production, it could be figured as a feminized activity in which translator was humbly subordinate to author.[4] Such a representation had its advantages for women writers. Instead of the anxiety of a writer like Florio, who defends what he calls his "defective edition (since all translations are reputed femall)," the female translator can offer the assurance of propriety in her humble reproductive task.[5] In the case of religious prose texts, her selection of material allowed her to participate in religious controversy and godly teaching without transgressing the scriptural injunction against female preachers. In the few instances of translation of a literary and/or secular kind that have come down to us, it is clear that translation could operate as a form of appropriation that made a space for the woman writer even as it veiled her literary skill.

The potential challenge that translation could offer to male hegemony in literary discourse is exemplified by Margaret Tyler, whose prefatory comments to her translation of a Spanish romance are striking in their defense of "a woman's work." *The Mirrour of Princely deedes and Knighthood* (1578), which established a fashion for Spanish romance in England, engages with subject matter declared out of bounds by educational treatises and conduct books for women both as readers and writers.[6] The first installment of a multivolume Spanish text, the *Mirrour* opens with the marriage, marital rape, and abandonment of Princess Briana, and closes with reconciliation, as her husband, the Emperor Trebatio, returns from an adulterous liaison to carry her away from the monastery in which she has been secluded for the duration of the romance. This narrative frame encloses the birth and growth of her two sons, whose amorous and martial exploits make up the majority of the text. Tyler acknowledges the "boldnesse and rashnesse" (sig. A4v) of her translation in her address to the reader, describing the *Mirrour* as "a story prophane, and a matter more manlike then becommeth my sexe" (sig. A3). She highlights the "warlike" and effaces the amorous and licentious elements in her address: "to report of armes is not so odious but that it may be borne withal, not onely in you men which your selves are fighters, but in us women, to whom the benefit in equal part apperteineth of your victories" (sig. A3v). In both her address to the reader and her dedication to Lord Thomas Howard, Tyler constructs a readership of young gentlemen whose courage may be "set on fire . . . to the advauncement of their line" (sig. A3), while she herself writes from a position of "aged years" and "staied age," implicitly beyond sexual arousal (sigs. A4–A4v). She draws on the dedication of earlier romances to female readers as a way of defending her reading and translating of similar material: "it is all one for a woman to pen a story, as for a man to addresse his story to a woman" (sig. A4v). But there is no suggestion in her prefatory remarks that she is providing further "improper" reading for women.

Displacing agency onto the "importunity of my friends" who have allocated both task and text, so that "ther appeared lykewise little lybertie in my first yelding" (sig. A2), Tyler represents her translation as an exercise avoiding idleness, and alludes to the parable of the talents to turn her work to profitable virtue. Unlike the female translators of religious and moral texts, who identify themselves with the piety of their material, she distances herself from her subject matter by claiming only a minimal role: "The invention, disposition, trimming, and what els in this story, is wholy an other mans, my part none therein but the translation, as it were onely in giving entertainment to a stranger, before this time unacquainted with our country guise" (sig. A3v). The decorous role of English gentlewoman and housewife is called on in this metaphorical entertainment of a Spanish guest, an entertainment which cannot create scandal since the guest "might in good order acquaint it selfe with my years" (sig. A3v). The propriety of her "womans work" is similarly claimed as she tropes her translation with a display of housekeeping and with a "delivery." She reports her anxiety about a task that will "bewray every unswept corner in my house" (sig. A2), and suggests the greater virtues of the Spanish original: "seldome is the tale carried cleane from an others mouth. Such delivery as I have made I hope thou wilt friendly accept, the rather for that it is a womans work" (sig. A3). She becomes implicitly not mother but midwife to this verbal child, asserting her albeit limited claim to knowledge in a discursive field jealously guarded by men who "lay in their claim to be sole possessioners of knowledge" (sig. A4). Like the character Clandestria in the *Mirrour*, who attends on Princess Briana throughout her secret pregnancy, she assists in producing a child that hovers between legitimacy and illegitimacy, challenging the patriarchal order from within its confines. In the context of the new gender-conscious frame that Tyler provides, the *Mirrour* itself offers the possibility of a gender-conscious reading, its acceptance of double standards of moral behavior rendered visible by the female translator's public address to her male audience.

After the *Mirrour of . . . Knighthood* was published in 1578, it would be over 60 years before another romance would be translated by a woman. Tyler may have set in motion a vogue for Spanish romance, but her attempt to claim such territory for women bore little fruit. Her name is not among the list of female precursors that Judith Man cites in her translation of 1640, *An Epitome of the History of Faire Argenis and Polyarchus*.[7] Man's translation makes an interesting comparison with Tyler's work. Dedicated to a young gentlewoman (Lady Anne Wentworth, daughter of the Earl of Strafford) rather than to a young lord, the text translates a romance that revolves around the love and courtship of its eponymous hero and heroine. The plot has much in common with popular romantic tragicomedies of the early 17th century, with its focus less on martial exploits and chivalric adventure than on courtly lovemaking. Princess Argenis provides the inspiration for the heroic actions of the story, while she herself maintains a virtuous but passive constancy. Unlike Princess Briana in the *Mirrour*, Argenis is a central figure throughout the tale. Judith Man in her dedication makes use of this centrality to identify Wentworth as a pattern of the romance heroine: "making a Parallell of this Princesse with Your Honour I finde You very suteable; yea I can witnesse with truth, that You surpasse Her" (sigs. A3–A3v). In so doing, Man reproduces the model of the ideal woman, a woman who is not only virtuous and chaste, but who is "resolved, to be conformable unto the Will of God, and of my Lord Your Father" (sig. A4). In her address to the reader, moreover, Man is concerned to advertise both the virtue of her material and her own virtue as a young (and unmarried) gentlewoman. She describes herself as a young woman whose serious disposition inclines her to private reading ("in my Closet") of books "suteable to a Gentlewoman of my quality, and of eighteene yeeres of age" (sig. A5v). *Argenis and Polyarchus*, she asserts, has pleased her not only for its subject but also because she has heard the praise of its French translator, the Bishop of Marseilles, while "in France, in my Parents company" (sig. A6). Such parental framing of her viewpoint helps to confirm her, like Anne Wentworth, as obedient daughter. In this context, her protestation that her translation has been brought to light by "those who watch over my actions, and endeavour my diversion" (sig. A6) has little in common with Tyler's mention of importunate friends.

From this position of youthful and virtuous obedience, she makes the publication of her work an act of duty: "I have beene in a manner forc'd (least I should transgresse against the Law of God) to expose it to the publike view" (sigs. A6–A6v). Such public exposure is clearly marked as risky display. She acknowledges the ideal of female silence in terms reminiscent of Vives when she denies publishing her work "to be spoken of, knowing very well, that those of, my sexe, who are least spoken of, are the more to bee esteemed: But onely have I done it by meere obedience and duty" (sigs. A6v–A7). In a rare moment, Man inserts herself into a genealogy of women writers and translators of romance, which suggests the importance of locating a "tradition" of women's writing: "it is not without example, and [I] could produce thee many of my sexe, who have traced me the way, witnesse the translation into French of Sir *Philip Sidneys Arcadia*, the *New Amarantha*, and the *Urania*, with many others" (sig. A6v).[8] Man's translation becomes a part of her education in virtuous femininity in the accompanying address from "The Stationer to the Reader." This address advertises text, patron, and author in similar terms: Argenis, Wentworth, and Man herself are constructed as parallel models of ideal womanhood. Man's skill becomes the ornament of a marriageable young woman with birth, beauty, and good breeding, so that her own availability as a commodity functions to support the marketing of the text.

Man's *Argenis and Polyarchus* is suggestive of the courtly taste for refined romance in the Caroline period, far removed from the wandering exploits of Tyler's Spanish romance. Yet only a year earlier, Suzanne Du Verger had dedicated a translation of moral tales to Queen Henrietta Maria, denouncing romance and its narrative excesses.[9] *Admirable Events* (1639) is very different from both Tyler and Man in its didactic moralizing. It collects a number of exemplary tales, each with a moral conclusion which distributes appropriate rewards and punishments. Several of the tales show heroic female virtue (in the form of chastity and constancy) engaged with male vice. The tales make room for the exceptional ("manly") woman, but her virtue is inevitably based on chastity. More usually, they define exemplary female behavior in the roles of mother, wife, and daughter. The translated preface to the work announces the text as an attack on romance: "The enterprise which I have taken in hand, is to wrastle, or rather to encounter with those frivolous books, which may all be comprized under the name of Romants" (sig. A6). "Truth" becomes the mark of virtue in this didactic text, fiction the mark of vice. Du Verger makes use of this dichotomy in her Epistle Dedicatory to assert the virtue of her translation: "it is an extract of severall Histories . . . an argument not improper for a vertuous minde, whether profit or pleasure be aymed at, for Histories are the store-houses, where vertues are faithfully conserved to posterities veneration, and vices detestation: . . . in fine, they are the only monuments of truth, which they purely deliver, no way flattering or concealing any thing" (sigs. A4–A4v). The "truth" of the tales makes them morally pure, distancing them from duplicity, flattery, and vice. Given such pious representation of the text, Du Verger offers it to the queen as a mark of her own humility, virtue, and industry, inspired by the civilizing influence of royalty: "these first fruits of my small industry" (sig. A4v) are yet "no more then what the least and meanest in the ranke of subjects is owing to the source of Majesty, whose influence quickeneth, gives motion and being to all civill industries" (sig. A3v).

In these three secular translations alone, then, can be seen a range of authorizing strategies at work in the period to enable women to enter a discursive field conventionally reserved for male writers. Tyler's radical

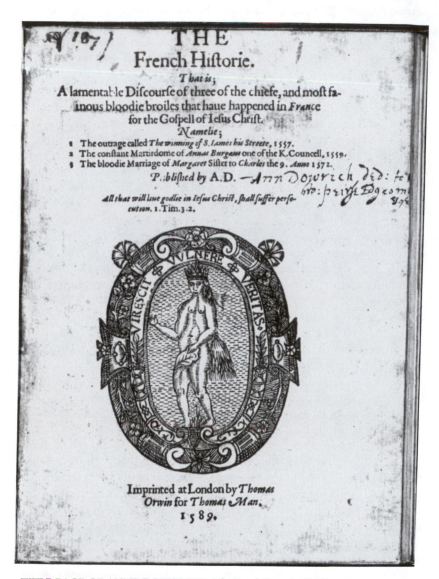

# THE
## French Hiftorie.

*That is;*

A lamentable Difcourfe of three of the chiefe, and moft famous bloodie broiles that haue happened in *France*
for the Gofpell of Iefus Chrift.

*Namelie;*

1. The outrage called *The winning of S. Iames his Streete,* 1557.
2. The conftant Martirdome of *Annas Burgæus* one of the K. Councell, 1559.
3. The bloodie Marriage of *Margaret* Sifter to *Charles* the 9. *Anno* 1572.

P:iblifhed by A.D. — *Ann Dowrich ded: te*
*bro: prieft Edgcom*

*All that will liue godlie in Iefus Chrift, fhall fuffer perfe-*
*cution.* 1. Tim. 3. 2.

Imprinted at London by *Thomas*
*Orwin* for *Thomas Man.*
1589.

**TITLE PAGE OF ANNE DOWRICHE,** *The French Historie* (1589).
*Reproduced by permission of the Huntington Library, San Marino, California.*

stance is not taken up by Man or Du Verger, each of whom attempts in her own way to construct herself as a model woman reproducing a text authored by model men. Yet translation offered all three women rudimentary access to literary writing. The work of Anne Dowriche suggests the way in which translation could mediate a more extensive access to literary writing. *The French Historie* (1589) is a verse narrative based on an English prose translation of a French work.[10] Written in the popular poulter's measure,[11] the poem describes "three of the chiefe, and most famous bloodie broiles" in which the Reformist church in France was attacked in the 16th century (see figure four). Dowriche, in both prefatory remarks and poem proper, lays emphasis on her subject matter rather than her poetry. She speaks of the writing of the text as an almost housewifely "collecting and disposing" of her material. In the address to the reader, she identifies her activity as "collecting and framing," "chusing and ordering," her sole purpose "to edifie, comfort, and stirre up the godlie mindes . . . in the cause of Gods truth" (sig. A3v). Her "framing" of the poem likewise structures the account to veil her own role as poet: in the 130–line equivalent of a dramatic prologue to the poem's three acts, Dowriche sets up two personae who function as substitutes for French (male) author and English (male) translator. The first-person speaker that opens the poem is an Englishman who encounters a grief-stricken French exile, and asks to hear his story: "Therefore my frend I praie, thy wit and tongue prepare, / The cause of all these bloodie broiles in verse for to declare" (f. 2v). It is the Frenchman, then, who is credited with the versification of the story, prompted by his English host. Dowriche's poetic skill is given no equivalent representation; her authorship is silently and modestly effaced within the text.

At the same time, however, Dowriche makes use of her edifying Reformist subject to authorize her poesy and draw attention to her own writing. In her prefatory address, she alerts her reader to the "picture of all the morall vertues most livelie described" in the narrative (sig. A3v), and explains her introduction of "the Divel brought in Poeticallie to make any oration" as an attempt "more lively to set them [cruelties] down in their colors, as if it came from the divels owne mouth, as no doubt it came from his spirite" (sig. A4). In the same way, she highlights the addition of other dramatic speeches "lively set downe" to illustrate the nature of both speaker and subject, and points to her amplification of the "just judgements of God" based on scriptural and secular histories. *The French Historie* has much in common with drama like John Bale's *King Johan*, with its morality play structure put to the use of Protestant propaganda.[12] God and Satan are the prime movers of the action, and the three discrete historical events are inserted into a providential scheme envisaged in the epigraph's scriptural quotation: "All that will live godlie in Jesus Christ, shall suffer persecution."[13] Dowriche concludes each section with a chorus-like addition of divine justice that places contemporary French evil-doers alongside past sinners and displays their fitting punishments.

The "punishment" of King Henry II following the martyrdom of Annas Burgaeus is a good example of the way that Dowriche turns poetic metaphor to dramatic and partisan use. Throughout the poem, sight and blindness are given a conventional spiritual parallel, but this imagery provides for a climactic moment of providential justice at the conclusion of Burgaeus's tale. A list of exemplary punishments builds to Zedekiah's blinding: "His eies that would not see Gods truth and shining light, / The King of Babel put them out as they deservde of right" (f. 17v). The account of Henry II's death that follows is turned into an analogous punishment for his imprisonment of Burgaeus. Participating in a joust to celebrate his marriage, "A splinter pierst the Princes eie, and ranne unto his braine. . . . / The King did often brag those eies of his should see / Burgaeus burnt; but loe the Lord did alter that decree" (ff. 17v–18). Henry's death, which preceded Burgaeus's martyrdom by several months, is transformed into a dramatic warning against persecution of the godly.

The orations that Dowriche develops from hints in the prose history complement such dramatization of the narrative. In the third account, for example, which tells of the St. Bartholomew Day Massacre in 1572, the massacre itself is made the immediate sequel of the marriage of Princess Margaret to the Prince of Navarre, a sequel long planned by a duplicitous king and council. Satan opens the section with a speech to his "mates," devising a "plaie" to be led by the king and the queen mother to deceive the Reformist nobles and trap them in a state of innocent trust: "The King as chiefest man this plaie must first begin, / By loving letters, words, and cheere at first to bring them in. . . . / The Mother Queene in this must also play her part, / That no suspect of treason maie remaine within their heart" (f. 18v–19). Satan's speech dictates the interpretation of the peace treaties that follow, and helps transform historical event into morality play. The queen mother's speeches are particularly forceful, and mark her as a "divelish sorceresse" (f. 23), demonized for her active engagement in public affairs and defined as a "good scholer of that divel of Florence, Machivel" (f. 23v), both by her own words and by the marginal annotation. A precursor of Lady Macbeth, she abuses the rules of hospitality and urges the council to action by challenging their masculinity: "What shame is this that I (a woman by my kinde) / Neede thus to speake, or passe you men in valure of the minde? / For heere I doo protest, if I had bene a man; / I had my selfe before this time this murder long began" (f. 24). Dramatic monologues such as these enliven the action of the poem, while the speeches given to imprisoned and dying martyrs function as sermons on the "true faith" and the art of dying.[14] Placed in the mouths of historical characters, such speeches evade the accusation of female preaching.

Dowriche implicitly locates her writing in the tradition of John Foxe's famous Book of Martyrs when she compares the relative unfamiliarity of these French events with the "noble Martirs of England . . . knowen sufficientlie almost to all" (sig. A4). Given this venerable precursor and her stated aim of restoring credit to a Poetry defaced by "wanton vanities" and "vaine devises," she concludes her preface with a remarkably strong assertion of the value and novelty of her work: "To speake trulie without vaine glorie, I thinke assuredlie, that there is not in this forme anie thing extant which is more forceable to procure comfort to the afflicted, strength to the weake, courage to the faint hearted, and patience unto them that are persecuted, than this little worke, if it be diligentlie read and well considered" (sig. A4). In *The French Historie*, Dowriche's signature appears seven times: she is "A. D.," "A. Dowriche," "Anne Dowriche," and "Anna Dowriche," and her name also reappears in the anagram that precedes her acrostic verse to her brother ("AN . . . DOWT . . . RICHE"). The poem is firmly claimed as her own, even as she offers praise for "this worke of mine" to God (f. 37v). Dowriche's claims for her poetry are reinforced by the associations that accrue in the poem itself. When, for example, her French exile laments that France has "for wooden Gods, Gods livelie Image spilde" (f. 2), spiritual truth is linked to her own "lively" image of events. The adjective recurs in the poem, in the "livelie bread" of the Gospel (f. 4), for example, or the "livelie spring" of the Word (f. 10v), and the "livelie faith" of the godly (ff. 11, 16). Dowriche's poetic dramatization and description become by association the manifestation and encouragement of godliness.

## Piety

Poetry with a religious focus offered an important outlet for women writers, since, like translation of religious texts, it offered the possibility of identification of the author with her pious subject matter. As Elaine

Beilin has remarked, "the Reformation authorized the English woman writer by giving her both a language and a role" (1987, 50). Religious poetry could function as a witness both to the writer's faith and to her appropriately pious reading, marking the erudition of the "wise virgin." While here I give only a brief account of some early writers who find their way into print through the authority of religion, the chapters that follow will draw out the vital significance of such authority for other Renaissance women, such as Mary Sidney and Aemilia Lanyer.

Thomas Bentley's introduction to his *Monument of Matrones* (1582) is a pertinent example of the limited permission given to women to exercise their writing skills in the cause of their faith, making devotional meditations the exception to the rule of female silence. In "A praier upon the posie prefixed," the written "lamps of virginitie" he has collected bear witness to wise preparation for the coming of "our spirituall Spouse." It is God's command that his "chosen virgins . . . watch full warilie," directing their "thoughts, words, and works . . . to doo [his] holie will." The "words, and works" that Bentley gathers from godly women become lamps in his dedicatory address to Queen Elizabeth—lamps that are to "remaine unto women as one entire and goodlie monument of praier, precepts, and examples." This is a monument both by and for matrons, its writers and readers identified with the daughters of Jerusalem. In Bentley's address to the "Christian Reader," publication itself becomes a religious duty: the *Monument* is to provide a "domesticall librarie" which will not only store precepts and stir up devotion, but also "encourage others (which as yet of anie singular affection for their private use conceale or deteine the woorks of anie godlie authors men or women) to take good opportunitie by this occasion offered even for the common benefit of Christs congregation, to publish the same abroad" (sig. B2v). The authors he includes are correspondingly praised as "paternes of all pietie, godlinesse, and religion to their sex" (sig. B1), their learning and painful industry a mark of their virtue.

The *Monument of Matrones* is largely composed of prose meditations and prayers, but in the "Second Lampe of Virginitie" are scattered several verse prayers. Lady Elizabeth Tyrwhit, in particular, intersperses her prose writing with a number of hymns in a variety of forms.[15] The hymns do not attempt to convey a personal voice; rather, they speak for a community of believers, as many medieval lyrics do. Simplicity of diction and form aim to communicate central spiritual concerns and doctrine. The artful compression of the "Hymne to God the Creator" (114) is a good example. One six-line stanza of iambic tetrameter lines makes use of sound devices, grammatical parallelism, and predominantly monosyllabic diction to construct a poignant call for grace:

> O Creator, to thee thy creature I call,
>
> Who made of mould do live in paine,
>
> And sicke in soule, my flesh is thrall,
>
> O wo is me, my daies be vaine:
>
> Yet unto God I call for grace,
>
> My soule in heaven to have a place.

Tyrwhit's "Hymne of the passion of Christ" (112–13) is more elaborate, dividing the narrative of the passion into five six-line stanzas each followed by a refrain of collective praise. The narrative is structured around the time of day, moving from midnight and Judas's betrayal to dawn and the false witness of the Jews, to Pilate's sentencing "When three houres were past," the Crucifixion at the sixth hour, and finally to Christ's death, implicitly at the ninth hour pinpointed by the Gospel. The sequence focuses on Christ's isolation, and builds to a climactic moment when heaven and earth respond to the impact of Christ's death: "The heavens were darkned, asunder the stones where shaken. / Bloud and water then sprang from this blessed lamb, / Then graves opened, the dead alive foorth came" (113). The poem is organized in much the same way as the Stations of the Cross in Catholic ritual, providing a series of discrete moments for meditation and collective celebration.

The two verses by Lady Frances Aburgavenny (?–1576) that appear later in the "Second Lampe" are suggestive in their identification with the model of the godly woman that Bentley constructs for his authors.[16] In "A necessarie praier in Meeter against vices," such vices as lust, pride, idleness, and disobedience are rejected in a series of precepts for daily living reminiscent of the mother's-advice book.[17] In their place is the ideal woman, meek, obedient, charitable, and chaste. Silent, though, she is not, despite the casting out of backbiting, slander, and blasphemy. In the acrostic verse that concludes her writing, Aburgavenny attaches the generalized persona of the speaker to her own name, shaping herself as a pious Christian through her poetry. Body and soul are ordered by her verse prayer to compose a whole of virtue that is equal to FRAUNCES ABURGAVENNY.

Neither Aburgavenny nor Tyrwhit wrote for publication, and the work of both comes down to us as a result of Bentley's avid prayer gathering. The pious verse of Anne Locke Prowse finds its way into print through her published translations of Calvinist texts.[18] Appended to her *Sermons of John Calvin* (1560) and her translation of John Taffin's *Of the markes of the children of God* (1590), her poems stand as complementary texts that "well agreeth with the same argument" (1560, sig. Aa1), while they remain modestly absent from the title pages of each work.[19] The verse "Meditation of a Penitent Sinner: written in maner of a Paraphrase upon the 51. Psalme of David" follows the *Sermons*, while a brief poem entitled "The necessitie and benefite of affliction" follows her translation of Taffin.

Prowse dedicates both of her translations to a female patron with Reformist sympathies. The *Sermons*, printed soon after Elizabeth's succession, and explicitly "set fourth and allowed" by the Queen, are dedicated to Katharine Bertie, Duchess of Suffolk, whose troubles during the Marian persecution were included in Foxe's Book of Martyrs. Anne Prowse, encouraged by John Knox, had left her first husband Henry Locke to join a Reformist circle exiled in Geneva (Collinson, 280), and her dedication helps to position her among the elect. *Of the markes of the children of God* looks back almost nostalgically to a time 30 years earlier, the days of religious struggle before the Elizabethan settlement. Dedicating the work to Anne Dudley, Countess of Warwick, Prowse represents the text as a preparation for the struggle when it is renewed. The dedications of both texts stress the Christian community that provides an authorizing context for Prowse's dutiful writing. The address to the Duchess of Suffolk makes use of an extended metaphor of sermons as medicine for the soul; the recipe, she declares, derives from "God the heavenly Physitian." What God has taught, "his most excellent Apothecarie master John Calvine hath compounded, and I your graces most bounden and humble have put into an Englishe box, and do present unto you" (1560, sig. A3). The work of her translation is reduced to the packaging of a humble assistant. Yet the "remedye" is one that "resteth onely amonge trewe belevyng Christians"; "no Philosopher, no Infidele, no Papist" can administer it (sigs. A3v–A4). Prowse's translation, however humble, marks her out as a believer. In the later text, it is gender that Prowse calls on to justify her writing. She turns the limitations on women's public action to her advantage by setting them against religious duty: "Everie one in his calling is bound to doo somewhat to the furtherance of the holie building; but because great things by reason of my sex, I may not doo, and that which I may, I ought to doo, I have according to my duetie, brought my poore basket of stones to the strengthning of the walles of

that Jerusalem, whereof (by grace) wee are all both Citizens and members" (1590; sigs. A3v–A4). Publication becomes a Christian duty in this
context, as it does in Bentley's *Monument of Matrones*.

"The necessitie and benefite of affliction," like the dedication to
Prowse's translation of Taffin, help to justify the need for Prowse's "basket of stones." The poem, 31 fourteener couplets typographically divided
on the page, complements her dedication in its meditation on the afflictions of the righteous, sent by God to combat "worldly pleasures" and
draw humanity toward heaven. "Then dooth the holie word of God /
most comfortable seeme: / Which we (before we felt the rod) / mere follie did esteeme" (sig. S2v). The poem attempts to create a desire for
affliction to sustain the religious mind. Affliction is perhaps even more
prominent in the verses appended to the *Sermons*, which build on Psalm
51 to voice an ungendered sinner's anguished plea for mercy.
Remarkable in its status as the first sonnet sequence in English, the
"Meditation of a Penitent Sinner" is composed of six prefatory sonnets
that establish a context for the prayer ("expressing the passioned minde
of the penitent sinner"), and a series of 21 sonnets developing the psalm
text. The Psalms were an integral part of congregational and individual
worship during the Reformation, and Prowse's "Meditation" can take on
the voice of David without impropriety. Prowse not only takes advantage of the universalized cry for mercy of a Christian sinner, she also
chooses a psalm which promises to teach the wicked and voice God's
praise if that mercy is granted.

> Lord, of thy mercy if thou me withdraw
> From gaping throte of depe devouring hell,
> Loe, I shall preach the justice of thy law . . .
>                                     I saved so
> Shall spred thy prayse for all the world to know. (sigs. A6v–A7)

In the process, her published poem becomes the sign of God's grace, and
her work as a poet can be framed as the "sacrifice" of a "thankfull
minde" (sig. A7). Moreover, the psalm concludes by extending the
prayer for mercy to Sion, and Prowse's sequence can thus open out from
the penitent sinner to the community of believers which she inhabits:

> Shew mercie, Lord, not unto me alone . . .
> Defend thy church, Lord, and advaunce it soe,

So in despite of tyrannie to stand . . .

That Sion and Jierusalem may be

A safe abode for them that honor thee. (sigs. A7v–A8)

Unannounced by the title page of the translation, ungendered in its penitent sinner's voice, and inscribed in the company of the elect, Prowse's "Meditation," like Dowriche's *French Historie* and the verses of Bentley's *Monument*, speaks with the authority of piety.

## Elegiac Writing

The somber subject of death provided an enabling context not only for meditations on affliction like Prowse's, but also for elegiac women's writing. Epitaphs and elegies by women have survived in various media, from manuscript to funereal monument. They differ from the male elegiac tradition which, in Celeste Schenck's view, is a "resolutely patriarchal genre" functioning as a "ritual hymn of poetic consecration during the course of which a new poet presents himself as heir to the tradition."[20] The elegy, in the hands of the woman writer, was not (overtly at least) a "vocational poem" (Schenck 1986, 13). Largely addressed to members of the family, these poems act as guarantees of domesticity and embed their writer's learning in a reassuring private context that can be represented as the spontaneous and feminine expression of personal grief rather than as literary ambition. As Lamb remarks, the acceptance of elegiac writing by women clearly reveals the "force of the paternalistic power structure controlling women's learning" (in Hannay 1985, 119).

The erudition of elegy writers is particularly marked in the tombstone poems of Elizabeth Cooke Russell (1528–1609). Several of her epitaphs and elegies, in poetry and prose, are written in Latin and Greek as well as in English. Addressed to two husbands as well as to other family members, her writing is made public in a limited way on tombs in Bisham Church, Shottesbrooke Church, and Westminster Abbey.[21] An elegy to her second husband, Lord John Russell, emphasizes the loss of a patriarch, and represents the speaker as a "hapless woman," a powerless widow socially isolated by the death of her husband.[22] The poem is built around the breakdown of house, family, and estate that this death entails. As heir of his father, as the glory of his house, as the key figure of a large estate, Lord Russell is represented as the center of family and household. His death consequently brings decay; widow and "orphans" mourn their wretched state without husband and father. The formal control of the elegy, with its heroic couplets, is paralleled by its figurative containment: The poem begins and ends with the image of a feast. The opening is abrupt, highlighting the sudden alteration in the speaker's life: "How was I startled at the cruel feast, / By Death's rude hands in horrid manner drest" (ll. 1–2). The feast recalls the biblical parable, here attended not by the bridegroom but by Death, yet by the end of the poem, the dead lord becomes analogous to Christ himself, the godly rule of a large estate owner manifested in his properly distributed hospitality: "He made no flatt'ring parasite his guest, / But ask'd the good companions to the feast" (ll. 19–20). The image of the feast points toward spiritual transcendence of death. Only "chaste lovely faith" is guaranteed to last, against other virtues and against learning itself. Faith, however, is generalized, not attributed to the dead lord alone. It is as if the poem suggests that any lasting qualities of the verse itself must be attributed to the faith of the chaste wife who mourns her husband, rather than to any learning she may possess.

The learning of Elizabeth Cooke Russell's niece, Anne de Vere, Countess of Oxford, is made visible in her sonnets on the death of her son.[23] Rather than drawing on Christian ideology, however, de Vere makes extensive use of classical mythology, and in particular of Ovidian tales of transformation. The speaker asserts her maternal grief with both pathos and rebellious anger, her "voice inflamed" like Venus in the first sonnet. Mother and son make up a symbiotic dyad in de Vere's sonnets, in an exclusive relationship in which maternal love surpasses other kinds of love: "Idall, for Adon, nev'r shed so many teares: / Nor Thet', for Pelid: nor Phoebus, for Hyacinthus" (sonnet 4, sig. C4). The verses emphasize the deprivation that ensues for the mother of this dead child ("Destins, Gods, and worlds, are all in my losse," sonnet 2, sig. C4), repeat the desire to revive the child, and articulate a desire to join the child in death since the speaker is "no more now, but a shadow" (unfinished sonnet, sig. C4v). The Countess of Oxford's elegies refuse apotheosis; the sonnets insistently gesture toward an epitaph that cannot be written, in which the body of the mother, in one more Ovidian transformation, itself becomes both monument and epitaph:

> Amphions wife was turned to a rocke. O
> How well I had beene, had I had such adventure,
> For then I might againe have beene the Sepulcure,
> Of him that I bare in mee, so long ago. (fragment, sig. C4v)

The rough metrics of the sonnets, which Ellen Moody (161–62) links with other experimental English verse of the 1570s and 1580s, contribute to the effect of emotional resistance in their jarring rhythms. This is pronounced in the first sonnet:

> Had with moorning the Gods, left their willes undon,
> They had not so soone herited such a soule:
> Or if the mouth, tyme dyd not glotton up all.
> Nor I, nor the world, were depriv'd of my Sonne. (sig. C3v)

The death of the child is here represented as an arbitrary and excessive act perpetrated by the willfulness of the gods and the gluttony of Time, a time starkly imaged as a mouth alone. The rebellious note is further heightened by the negative construction of the quatrain, and the forceful transformation of noun to verb in "glotton up all." Yet at the point where the speaker announces the loss of "my Sonne," the sonnet shifts to envisage Venus "inveying the skies" and weeping over the body of the child. Maternal grief and accusation are displaced onto the classical goddess, whose presence transforms a mother's mourning into a scene of ideal beauty and love, just as her "golden teares" "almost" enact a transformation of the child, so that she "Makes almost alive, the Marble, of my Childe." The speaker's desire is poignantly located in this near-revival as she repeats her claim to the body of "my Childe." Venus's mourning does not fully veil the mourning of the child's mother, but rather interacts with it in a doubling that slides toward a merging of voices in the final couplet. With a "voice inflamed" in bitter "venime," Venus identifies the child as her own: "As I was of Cupid, even so of it mother: / 'And a womans last chylde, is the most beloved'" (sig. C3v). The proverbial quotation of the concluding line opens to include the speaker, both mothers conflated in a challenging statement of maternal love. In the context of de Vere's own life, the ambiguity of this statement takes on particular resonance: the son and heir who might have given her social standing and acted (like Cupid) to confirm the reconciliation between herself and her estranged husband may be both her most recent child and her last or final child.[24] The publication of the sonnets among other verses in John Soowthern's *Pandora*, a collection dedicated to the Earl of Oxford, suggests that de Vere's poetry is engaging on various levels with domestic politics.

Different again is the four-stanza poem found on the cover of a letter in the hand of Anne Howard, Countess of Arundel.[25] The poem specifies neither the gender of the speaker nor the relation of speaker to dead (male) subject. Howard's poem is a pastoral elegy that shows her ability and her knowledge of pastoral convention. The first stanza sets the scene with an assured lightness of touch:

> In sad and ashy weeds I sigh,
> I groan, I pine, I mourn;
> My oaten yellow reeds
> I all to jet and ebon turn.
> My watery eyes, like winter's skies,
> My furrowed cheeks o'erflow.
> All heaven know why, men mourn as I,
> And who can blame my woe? (ll. 1–8)

The stanza sketches the speaker's emotional state through an analogy with the seasonal changes in a pastoral landscape, while aural and verbal patterning soften the note of complaint. In the second stanza, the poem shifts from seasonal to diurnal parallel: the "sad and ashy weeds" that the mourner wears become the "sable robes of night" that consume their "days / Of joy." The cause of the all-consuming transformation is elucidated by extending the image:

> For now my sun his course hath run,
> And from his sphere doth go,
> To endless bed of folded lead,
> And who can blame my woe? (ll. 13–16)

In the third stanza, the speaker's emotional state is elaborated in terms of a relation to the pastoral world: sheep are forsaken, lilies left untouched, air and earth reviled. The idyllic pastoral world is disrupted by the loss of the "youth," and the final stanza extends this disruption out from the speaker to the numerous inhabitants of this landscape, who "all condole my woe" (I. 32). In its artful simplicity, Howard's poem recalls Spenserian pastoral. The condolence of the pastoral inhabitants gestures toward a poetic inheritance which the speaker's imitative and ungendered voice can never fully claim.

Perhaps the best example of elegiac writing by women is a poem by Lucy Russell, Countess of Bedford, which was long attributed to John Donne. Part of a more extensive poetic dialogue between Donne and the Countess, the elegy seems to have been written in response to a poem by

Donne on the death of Russell's friend, Cecilia Bulstrode.[26] The poem incorporates a strong argument for the locating of Bulstrode among the "just," in an implicit rebuke of court gossip that had circulated about her prior to her sudden death in 1609.[27] Opening with a quotation from one of Donne's holy sonnets which highlights the poetic exchange, the initial stanza makes a series of contrasts between the violence of Death as "executioner" of divine wrath and the quiet death of Bulstrode to provide evidence of her regenerate soul.

> Death be not proud, thy hand gave not this blow,
> Sin was her captive, whence thy power doth flow;
> The executioner of wrath thou art,
> But to destroy the just is not thy part.
> Thy coming, terror, anguish, grief denounce;
> Her happy state, courage, ease, joy pronounce. (ll. 1–6)

Russell argues that Bulstrode's "clearer soul" is not given up to death's destructive force but called gently "home" by God. Heaven is imaged here as a safe and welcoming haven, not a fortress; here is no gate to be battered, but a door to be quietly opened: "The key of mercy gently did unlock / The doors 'twixt heaven and it, when life did knock" (ll. 13–14). The second stanza continues its address to Death, turning to the misinterpretation of bodily decay as a sign of sin. Such misreading of the mortal body is blamed on "mortal eyes," and Death is urged to win the spoils of conquest from the reprobate, "people cursed before they were" (l. 21). Those who do not mourn Bulstrode's death are excluded from the circle of grace and virtue, castigated as blind and deaf, unable to see past the "misty veil" of the decaying body to the virtuous spirit within. The third stanza concludes with an address to her mourners, "all souls not by corruption choked" (l. 37), who are called on to sing her to rest in heaven in a hymn which celebrates the destruction of Death's power, a destruction reinforced by scriptural allusion: "And teach this hymn of her with joy, and sing, / *The grave no conquest gets, Death hath no sting*" (ll. 41–42). In this imagined apotheosis of a female friend, collective hymn, biblical text, and poetic allusion merge to empower the voice of the speaker.

## Manuscript Collections

Lewalski argues that the Countess of Bedford's elegy "shows her claiming the status of [a] coterie poet . . . [who] evidently regarded writing poetry as a social grace rather than a serious endeavor" (1993, 120).[28] While the two terms need not be as exclusive as Lewalski suggests, it is clear that Lucy Russell's poetry was merely one among many activities that supported her self-representation as the successful courtier. Other women, too, took advantage of their social circles to circulate their writing in manuscript. The papers of the Aston family of Tixall in Staffordshire, for example, contain a number of occasional poems written by Gertrude Aston Thimelby (fl. 1630s–90) and her sister-in-law Catherine Thimelby Aston (fl.1630s–58), most of which belong to the period after 1640.[29] Gertrude Thimelby's manuscript book of poems includes an elegy on the death of Sir Walter Aston in 1639, "Upon A Command to Write on My Father" (Clifford 1813, 92–93). The first half of the poem, written in heroic couplets, addresses an unidentified "you" who has given the speaker the command to write. The poem is represented as an act of obedience, guided and instructed by a superior other who also wills her to live after the death of her "author":

> Teares I could soone have brought unto this hearse,
> And thoughts, and sighs, but you command a verse . . .
> If you will be obay'd, Ile hold the pen,
> But you must guide my hand, instruct me then. (ll. 1–8)

The poem anxiously displaces the authority of authorship onto first father and then guide before moving on to praise the worth of the dead man and assert the collective need to meditate on and accept his death.

Thimelby's poetry is circumscribed by its familial context; the poetry of Lady Anne Southwell indicates a social circle of friends and acquaintances who provide a more varied context for manuscript circulation. Lady Southwell's writing exists in an unpublished commonplace book, which has as yet received little critical attention; it encompasses letters and inventories (including a list of books) as well as poems in various states of completion.[30] The commonplace book concludes with verses by her second husband, Sir Henry Sibthorpe. Included is his memorial in praise of his wife written after her death, in which he calls her "The patterne of conjugall love and obedience" and "the compleate Character of Female perfection" (f. 74). Lady Southwell's own poetry exhibits a similar insistence on her virtue.

Much of the manuscript is devoted to verse meditations on specific biblical commandments, such as "Thou shalt have noe other gods before mee." In the prefatory stanzas of this poem, the speaker calls on her soul to rise up to the heavens to enable her to write on her godly subject: "And being dipt in heavens Selestiall Springes / My penn shall portrait Supernaturall thinges" (f. 28). Yet she is careful to assert the modesty of her enterprise, and to contrast her pious concerns with the wantonness of Ovid:

> And ere I further goe, I heavens Implore
>
> that with artes grande careere I doe not mount . . .
>
> nor for vayne glorye of historian fame,
>
> crowne Ovids Idolls with with [sic] Jehovaes name. (f. 28)

Aristotle and Seneca are likewise dismissed in favor of "wise Solomon" and Paul.[31] These lines appear again in the manuscript, barely altered, toward the end of a poem entitled "Thou shalt keepe holy the saboth daye" (ff. 42v–43). Here, Southwell reins herself back to her topic:

> But stay weake female whether doest thou wander
>
> how dares thy waxen phewmes approtch the soonne
>
> thy better sex are lost in this meander
>
> in which thy ignorance presumes to roome. (f. 43v)

Having drawn attention to her sex, she goes on to compare herself to Deborah and turns her voice into an innocent vessel for God's word: "Weakelings and babes gods woonder shall reveale / to give the greater looster to his deede" (f. 44). Her subject here, however (as elsewhere), has allowed her to "meander" over much broader material. From a discussion of the Christian man's duty "to bring thy famyly" to work in "gods vynyarde" (f. 38), the poem digresses to a lengthy discussion of the education of (male) children who "like blanck paper to thy scribling yeeld" (f. 38v). In this context, the poem explores the uses of such studies as philosophy, mathematics, music, astronomy, and rhetoric. In much the same way, the poem on adultery is focused largely on marriage and the complementary duties of husband and wife (ff. 46v–51v). While Southwell does not challenge accepted notions of female virtue, she makes "devine poesye," like her own pious virtue, the framework for a poetic exploration of topics usually the province of male writers.[32] While the poems that overtly address friends and acquaintances consist of more contained piety or elegiac writing, Southwell's poetry, in its variety of form and subject matter, suggests that her familial and social milieu provided an enabling context for her writing; indeed, the first page of the manuscript claims a place for her as an author in identifying the text as "The Workes of the Lady Ann Sothwell."[33]

## The Authority of Royalty

The poems and verse translations written by Queen Elizabeth during her reign function even more clearly as a courtly display of erudition and art.[34] Many of the poems attributed to Elizabeth are of doubtful authorship, but the occasional poems written "On Monsieur's Departure" and on the circumstances relating to the exile of Mary Queen of Scots are more certainly hers. Remarkable for their subject matter and voice, the poems diverge from the topics addressed by the majority of women writers with an authority that derives from Elizabeth's inherited position as patriarch and sovereign. "The doubt of future foes" is particularly striking in this respect. The poem is constructed as a confidential yet powerful exchange between an ungendered speaker who assumes control of wit, wisdom, reason, and command, and an unspecified "ye," an audience who functions as the passive observer of the action. The "foes" and "snares" that "threaten mine annoy" are associated with falsehood, ambition, pride, and guile. After a brief exposition, the consequences of such threats are outlined forcefully, couched in the repeated imperative of the future auxiliary "shall" and the negating of seditious attempts:

> The daughter of debate that discord aye doth sow
> Shall reap no gain where former rule still peace hath taught to know.
> No foreign banished wight shall anchor in this port;
> Our realm brooks not seditious sects, let them elsewhere resort.

> (ll. 11–14)

The ebbing of "subjects' faith" is countered by the "former rule" of peace and by an overt threat of punishment which inscribes both the speaker's habitual mildness and her potential violence: "My rusty sword through rest shall first his edge employ / To poll their tops that seek such change or gape for future joy" (ll. 15–16). The authoritative voice of the speaker reaches its apogee here, where the oblique references to subjects, former rule, and realm coalesce in the personalized threat of "My rusty sword." The poem closes with an imagined beheading and a neat turn

that inverts the situation of the opening line, the "future joys" of gaping
foes cut off to recall the speaker's "present joy."

"On Monsieur's Departure" lays claim to the territory of love poetry
in another departure from the acceptable in women's writing. The poem
is constructed less as a public statement whose political allusion is made
available to those "in the know" than as a private expression of hidden
conflict. This love poem is addressed only belatedly to love itself and
includes the beloved only obliquely, similarly to the way in which the
third person enemies are brought into "the doubt of future foes." "On
Monsieur's Departure" draws on the conventions of Petrarchanism to
articulate a disrupted courtship. The contraries of the Petrarchan lover's
emotional state are appropriated to render a self split by the divergent
demands of love and public behavior:

> I grieve and dare not show my discontent,
> I love and yet am forced to seem to hate,
> I do, yet dare not say I ever meant,
> I seem stark mute but inwardly do prate.
> I am and not, I freeze and yet am burned. (ll. 1–5)

While the poem seems at one level to take up an appropriately feminine
passivity ("For I am soft and made of melting snow," l. 14), the agency
of the speaker appears in the final line of the first stanza, "Since from
myself another self I turned" (l. 6). A direct plea to love concludes the
poem: "Or let me live with some more sweet content, / Or die and so
forget what love ere meant" (ll. 17–18).

The royal birth that gave Elizabeth I access to an outstanding education and to poetic materials beyond the range of the majority of women
writers provided a more limited access to Princess Elizabeth, daughter of
James I and later Queen of Bohemia. In what appears to be an early
exercise, written in monorhymed tetrameter quatrains, the young
Elizabeth dedicates a morally conventional poem in the *contemptus mundi*
tradition to the Countess of Bedford's father, Lord Harington of Exton.[35]
Princess Elizabeth's simple exercise preserves the evidence of both her
own royal virtue and the virtuous teaching her "preceptor" provides.

It is likewise royal virtue that facilitates the writing of Diana Primrose,
whose *A Chaine of Pearle* (1630) is written in praise of the long-dead
Queen Elizabeth.[36] Written by a woman on the subject of a female
monarch, dedicated to "All Noble Ladies, and Gentle-women," and pref-

aced by a woman's commendatory verse, *A Chaine of Pearle* advertises itself as a specifically female text. The very title marks it as an ornament to the sex, and Dorothy Berry's prefatory verse figures the poem as a "precious Ornament" to Primrose herself. Both Berry and Primrose invoke nationalism as well as an all-female audience to authorize the verse. Queen Elizabeth is emphatically an English queen, a queen who raised "the English Name to Heaven." In Primrose's "Induction," Elizabeth, as "England's brightest Sun," aquires the masculine qualities of Phoebus, whose gender is reiterated in phrases such as "his radiant face," "his Imperiall Scepter," and "his Starry Monarchy." The author's name itself takes on mixed gender attributes in Berry's poem. An allusion in the commendatory verse to the goddess Diana, associated with the moon and with chastity (and with Elizabeth herself), gives her the "Golden Raies" more commonly attributed to the sun, as they are in the Induction's "Golden Phoebus." Diana Primrose, like Elizabeth, seems to acquire the attributes of the masculine sun without any incursion on her chastity.

The ten "pearls" that make up the *Chaine*, each identifying a particular virtue, similarly grant a mixture of masculine and feminine attributes to Elizabeth. As in the "Induction," power is figured as masculine, and Elizabeth's acquisition of power is rendered acceptable by marking her as exceptional. She is a woman beyond her sex, her female body combined with the masculine authority of the monarch; her apparent androgyny is unimpeachably grounded in her role. In the third pearl, for example, Elizabeth's "prudence" is held up as a heroic (implicitly masculine) virtue which the majority of women cannot hope to emulate: "This Gift in her was much more emminent, / In that it is so rarely incident / To our weake Sex . . . / For Kings are Gods, and Queenes are Goddesses" (5). Elizabeth's "fortitude" is likewise made the attribute of her "Great Majestie" in the seventh pearl. Primrose's verse is cautious in its acknowledgement of the gendered ideology of virtue. The second pearl, "Chastity," extends its praise of Elizabeth into a moral warning to all (female) readers:

> And this may be a Document to all,
> The Pearle of Chastity not to let fall . . .
> For whether it be termed Virginall
> In Virgins, or in Wives stil'd Conjugall,
> Or Viduall in Widdowes, God respects
> All equally, and all alike affects. (4)

No sense of a male audience is present in this expansion from "all" to virgins, wives, and widows; nor is it apparent in the fourth pearl, where the
verse on temperance opens with another message to women:

> The Golden Bridle of Bellerophon
>
> Is Temperance, by which our Passion,
>
> And Appetite we conquer and subdue
>
> To Reasons Regiment: else may we rue
>
> Our yeelding to Mens Syren-blandishments,
>
> Which are attended with so foule Events. (6)

Once again, "our Passion" assumes a specifically female audience who
may yield to male seduction. The term "Syren" here is conspicuous in its
prejudicial gendering of seduction.

The problematic nature of women's speech and writing in this period
is illustrated in the figuration of the eighth pearl, "Science," defined as
chief of the "Vertues Intellectual." The verse begins with an evaluative
comparison:

> A Pearle more precious then th' Aegyptian Queene,
>
> Quaft off to Anthony; of more Esteeme
>
> Then Indian Gold, or most resplendent Gemmes,
>
> Which ravish us with their translucent Beames. (10)

The "Arts and Sciences" that deck the queen are linked to both erotic
seduction (through the reference to Cleopatra) and ravishment.
Elizabeth's eloquence, grounded in her learning, is similarly figured in
terms that eroticize her female voice:

> Then might you see her Nectar-flowing Veine
>
> Surround the Hearers; in which sugred Streame,
>
> SHEE able was to drowne a World of men,
>
> And drown'd, with Sweetnes to revive agen . . .
>
> But with what Oratory-ravishments,
>
> Did Shee imparadise Her Parliaments? (10–11)

Even in this celebratory and elegiac context, in which Elizabeth's heroic
sovereignty validates her "Sacred Lips," female speech is figured as pow-

erfully sexual, dangerously phallic in its capacity to ravish, drown, and revive men. Yet Primrose, like the other women writers surveyed in this chapter, is not silenced by the dangerous display inherent in her woman's voice. In the sixth pearl, "Justice," the speaker asserts her own feminine inability to write of the just punishments executed in Elizabeth's reign, "a Taske / Unfit for Feminine hands, which rather love / To write of pleasing subjects" (8). The decorous denial, however, implicitly asserts that writing on "pleasing subjects" is an acceptable activity for women. Elizabeth's (female) authority provides Primrose with room to maneuver, as her epideictic verse celebrates the queen's virtues as woman and sovereign, just as translation, piety, elegiac writing, and manuscript circulation offered other women writers access to "Eruditions garden."

## Chapter Four

# "Some inspired stile": Mary Sidney, Countess of Pembroke[1]

The writing of Mary Sidney, Countess of Pembroke (1561–1621), epitomizes the complex negotiations that women writers of the English Renaissance inevitably faced in their encounters with contemporary gender ideology. Sidney's work encapsulates several of the strategies adopted by writers discussed in the previous chapter. In apparent conformity to the discourse of gender difference, Sidney locates herself as a writer within the context of the family, while employing translation, piety, and a focus on death to counter the constraints of that discourse. Her work is a remarkable testament to the maneuvers of women writers within the narrow space available to them. Sidney is now recognized as one of the most outstanding women writers of her time, and her writing is being reassessed both in terms of its own merits and in relation to its significant influence on 17th-century poetry.

Until recently, critics have often considered Sidney's work merely a subsidiary offshoot to the writing of her brother, Sir Philip Sidney.[2] Known primarily as literary patron, as editor of Philip Sidney's works, and as primary reader/recipient of his *Arcadia*, the countess has been effaced as writer.[3] Even Gary Waller's *Mary Sidney, Countess of Pembroke* (1979), the first book-length study to focus on Mary Sidney's writing, argued that she was continuing cultural and literary projects begun by her brother; according to Waller, this was true in her patronage, in her prose and dramatic translation, and in her versification of the Psalms.[4] The critical focus on Philip Sidney—a focus, indeed, that has its origins in Mary Sidney's own writing—is bound up with representations of her implicitly dependent and derivative status as student-sister of master-brother. Such criticism has not escaped gender assumptions privileging the masculine.

Yet Philip Sidney, during his lifetime and immediately after his early death, was known primarily as courtier and soldier; his friends attempted to highlight not his literary writing but his political and social concerns as

Protestant humanist.[5] Even Fulke Greville, who prepared the first edition
of the *Arcadia* (1590), was concerned to focus attention on Philip Sidney's
epic and religious writing alone, as Victor Skretcowicz argues.[6] Few of the
tributes to him in the first few years after his death mentioned his poetry;
yet by the end of the 16th century, his reputation had been transformed.
Largely owing to Mary Sidney's editing and publication of his writings,
he had become the model Elizabethan poet. Mary Sidney, as Hannay suggests, "became the primary agent in the refashioning of Philip Sidney's
life into a 'notable image of virtue,'" and, more specifically, of Sidney
himself into a virtuous man of letters.[7] It is possible to interpret her activity in promoting her brother's reputation as a poet not as an emotional
tribute to a much-loved sibling (though such emotion may well have
played a part), but as a contribution to the myth of Philip Sidney which
allowed her to locate her own voice as a writer in a familial context. Her
brother's reputation as a courtier-soldier would have provided little protection for her writing; however, his reputation as a courtier-poet guaranteed her a space for maneuvering within the domestic realm allotted to
women. Interpreted as strategic manipulation (conscious or unconscious)
of gender ideology rather than as derivative dependency, Mary Sidney's
work may suggest that the reception of Philip Sidney's writing says as
much about her "cultural projects" as about his own.

## Exemplary Elegiacs

Mary Sidney's writing directly draws on her brother's reputation in three
of the four original poems that have come down to us.[8] The first is an
elegy commonly known as the "Dolefull Lay of Clorinda"; the poem was
published in 1595 in *Astrophel*, Edmund Spenser's collection of elegies to
Sir Philip.[9] Two dedicatory poems by Mary Sidney are also prefaced to a
royal presentation copy of the Sidney Psalms dated 1599; the poems
include a poem addressed to Queen Elizabeth, "Even now that Care," 
and a second elegy beginning "To thee pure sprite."[10] The death of a relative offers Mary Sidney one avenue for expression within the acceptable
confines of the family, by means of which she can display the apparently
spontaneous overflow of feeling that corresponds to contemporary
notions of femininity. All three of these poems have a female speaker;
each visibly works with the discourse of gender difference to produce a
female voice.

The difficulty of that task is marked not only within the text of the
poems, but also in their subsequent history: both of the elegies have

been attributed to male writers since Mary Sidney's death. "To thee pure sprite" was long thought to be the work of Samuel Daniel, since an early version of the poem was printed among his collected works in 1623.[11] "The Dolefull Lay of Clorinda," identified by Spenser as the work of Mary Sidney in his allusion to the writer as "sister" to Astrophel, was in the early 20th century attributed to Spenser himself on the evidence of its quality and its Spenserian effects. Gender ideology suffuses the authorship debate. Charles Osgood, for example, suggests that Spenser is "impersonating the Countess of Pembroke" by the "cloaking of his natural tone to something more feminine and tenuous"; while A. A. Jack supports Mary Sidney's authorship on the grounds that the poem is an "outpouring of a personal grief," a "pretty and a skilful Spenserian exercise" in which, however, the "prettiness is a minor prettiness." H. D. Rix argues that Mary Sidney's authorship is "not only improbable but impossible" because the mastery of rhetorical figures displayed in the poem would have required "a severe discipline in the schools."[12] Implicit in this debate is a circular argument: if the "Lay" is seen as a highly crafted and skillful poem, it is attributed to Spenser, while any suggestion that it lacks such quality is held to guarantee Mary Sidney's authorship.[13] The debate is not helped by the isolated comparison with Mary Sidney's fourth original poem, a relatively conventional pastoral poem of praise written for the projected visit of Queen Elizabeth in 1599; by excluding any reference to other original poems and to the highly skilled Psalms, it is relatively easy to suggest that the "Dolefull Lay" has more connections with Spenser's poetry than with Mary Sidney's own work.[14] Yet as Gary Waller (1979, 91) points out, many of the Spenserian effects identified by critics are common in Elizabethan poetry.[15]

The "Dolefull Lay" was probably written between 1586 and 1589, and may have been revised before its publication in *Astrophel*.[16] It is a pastoral elegy that follows classical tradition in its incorporation of complaint and consolation; its speaker is gendered by the lines that precede and introduce the poem:

> But first his sister that *Clorinda* hight,
> The gentlest shepheardesse that lives this day:
> And most resembling both in shape and spright
> Her brother deare, began this dolefull lay. (ll. 211–14)[17]

In the four opening stanzas, that speaker debates the nature of the audience to be addressed, dismissing first "heavenly powres" and then "earthly men" as potential addressee and concluding with a decision to turn the complaint in on the speaker's self: "Then to my selfe will I my sorrow mourne, / Sith none alive like sorrowfull remaines" (ll. 19–20). The lament, boldly published among the poems of eminent men such as Edmund Spenser and Sir Walter Raleigh, nevertheless represents itself as an introverted, isolated, and spontaneous cry of grief which aims to "unfold my inward paine / That my enriven heart may find reliefe" (ll. 3–4). As Mary Ellen Lamb points out, the solitary mourner is not uncommon in pastoral elegy, but none of the other poems in Spenser's collection employs this convention. "Clorinda is the only author who denies the presence or possibility of an audience" (1990, 63). That denial simultaneously allows her to claim priority of feeling and to divert any suggestion that her poetic tribute is a claim to the artistic inheritance of the dead poet-shepherd. Clorinda becomes implicitly analogous to Echo (a female figure with an accepted place in pastoral elegy), repeating back words of mourning. Mourning to her self, she becomes both mourner and echo at once: "And to my selfe my plaints shall back retourne, / To pay their usury with doubled paines" (ll. 21–22). With her self split into speaker and auditor, her voice doubles back on itself, finding not "reliefe" but "doubled paines." Troping her grief with the economics of usury, the speaker suggests that any plaints she makes are only lent out, can never be fully "owned" or located elsewhere, and must return to their original owner with interest. Through Clorinda's denial of an audience outside herself, the "Dolefull Lay" is distanced from its companion poems in Spenser's *Astrophel*, a poem "lent out" yet not properly "owned" by the collection.

With similar reflexivity, the traditional use of the pathetic fallacy in which all nature mourns with the speaker is made to double back on itself: "The woods, the hills, the rivers shall resound / The mournful accent of my sorrowes ground" (ll. 23–24). Punning on the connotations of "ground" (as both legal basis and musical bass line), Clorinda turns the resounding landscape into both a mourning of nature and a reflection (re-sounding) of her own sorrow. This "doubling" provides a frame for the following stanzas, in which the land is made desolate by the death of "their fairest flowre." Clorinda's specular sorrow is effectively centered, supporting her claim that the loss of Astrophel is "greatest losse to mee" (l. 36). Even when she begins to address the "shepheards lasses" in stanza seven, the introversion of the complaint is continued in its verbal repetitions and schemes of inversion.[18] The speaker's voice echoes itself, in word and phrase. Variants of "their fairest flowre" (l. 28) recur, for example (ll. 29, 32, 38), while several phrases echo and build on each other: "Sith the faire flowre, which them adornd, is gon: / The flowre, which them adornd, is gone to ashes" (ll. 38–39).[19]

This verbal doubling is left behind when the speaker turns from complaint to consolation. Just as Clorinda soothes her "doubled paines" with a vision of Astrophel's apotheosis, his "immortall spirit" removed to "everlasting blis," her echoing voice is replaced by the firmer tones of heavenly consolation. With attention redirected from body to soul, from this world to the heavens, the speaker is now able to answer her own questions rather than merely echo them: "Ay me, can so divine a thing be dead? / Ah no: it is not dead, ne can it die" (ll. 66–67). Clorinda's description of the soul's blessed state concludes with a direct address not to her self but to the "happie spirit" of Astrophel, an address which moves away from personal loss to a communal lament for the human condition: "Thus do we weep and waile, and wear our eies, / Mourning in others, our owne miseries" (ll. 95–96). The final couplet summarizes the entire elegiac tradition as a projection of human misery onto the lamented dead, a misdirected doubling which, untangled, points toward a pious disregard for things of the world.

The "Dolefull Lay," then, can be read as a skilful encounter with the expectations of gender in its representations of the speaker's voice, echoing in introverted grief in this world, piously firm in its otherworldly vision. It is perhaps ironic that the speculations of 20th-century critics have suggested that Clorinda's doubling poem is the doubling poem of Spenser, "impersonating" Mary Sidney.

The two dedicatory poems prefaced to the presentation copy of the joint Sidney Psalms have much in common with the "Dolefull Lay" in their construction of the voice of the female speaker. They work to represent Mary Sidney's writing as a humble and emotional outpouring of "love and zeal," and to locate its origins elsewhere—in the queen, in God, in Philip Sidney himself. Margaret Hannay has persuasively argued that the dedication poems function as admonitory flattery, reminding Elizabeth of Sir Philip's death in her service, and encouraging her to fulfil her godly duties as the new David of England and Europe.[20] Such public political concerns only intensify the politics of gender at work in the poems. While the analogy of Elizabeth and the psalmist King David is clearly outlined in "Even now that Care," for example, the poem emphasises the monarch's sex, her status as a woman and as queen, and her difference from David. The poem draws attention to the exceptional nature of the female sovereign; in the process, her female subject makes room for her own "handmaids taske." As Elaine Beilin suggests, "the poet's legitimacy as a divine maker comes . . . because she provides a song for the chosen, for God's new David, Elizabeth" (1987, 143). Yet rather than simply identifying Elizabeth with David, the poem draws on the metaphors of love and courtship to indicate their likeness-in-difference. The gift of the Psalms, for example, is represented as the decorous matching of king and queen: "A King should onely to a Queene bee sent, / Gods loved choise unto his chosen love" (ll. 53–54). After sketching the likeness of the two reigns ("For ev'n thy Rule is painted in his Raigne," l. 65), the poem describes their harmonious union: "Thus hand in hand with him thy glories walke" (l. 73). For this exceptional queen, the "natural order" of things is reversed:

> Kings on a Queene enforst their states to lay;
>
> Main-lands for Empire waiting on an Ile;
>
> Men drawne by worth a woman to obay;
>
> one moving all, herselfe unmov'd the while. (ll. 81–84)

To her still center kings, nations, and men are subjected.

Overtly conforming to gender ideology in this representation of Elizabeth as exceptional woman and "thrise sacred Queene," the poem likewise suggests Sidney's personal conformity. It raises only to reject the possibility of an epic poem written in praise of Elizabeth's trials and triumphs. The speaker interrupts her outline of Elizabeth's conquests to rein herself back from the privileged territory of epic: "But soft my muse, Thy pitch is earthly lowe; / forbeare this heav'n, where onely Eagles flie" (ll. 79–80). Denying any claim to "some inspired stile," she belittles her own gift: "Thy utmost can but offer to hir sight / Her handmaids taske, which most her will endeeres" (ll. 89–90). In the final line, Sidney's singing is erased in the wish that Elizabeth may "Sing what God doth, and doo What men may sing" (l. 96).

Earlier in the poem Sidney makes use of both the queen's sovereignty and her brother's part in the versifying of the Psalms to trivialize her own activity. The queen is made not only the perfect reader, recipient, and patron of such writing, but also both origin and rightful owner of the work: "For in our worke what bring wee but thine owne? / What English is, by many names is thine" (ll. 41–42). The vocabulary of land ownership is employed ("undischarged rent," "paiments," sown "feelds") in suggesting that the Psalms are a small parcel of cloth woven by the Sidneys, which pays back what is owed to (and owned by) the queen.

With the cloth they compose a "livery robe," a sign of service that it is nevertheless the queen's right to confer. Moreover, the joint act of making this verbal cloth is in itself distanced from any originating authority of authorship: "but hee did warpe, I weav'd this webb to end; / the stuffe not ours, our worke no curious thing" (ll. 27–28). The substance of the Psalms, the "stuffe" they work with, the speaker asserts, is not theirs: their artless "translation" merely provides an "English denizen" for the psalmist king. Mary Sidney's activity is reduced in the poem to the appropriately feminine task of weaving a cloth from a framework established by her brother in the "warp" of the web, an activity that is represented as an inferior "defrayment" of debts, a familial payment of a dead man's dues.

Philip Sidney's primary role in the versification of the Psalms is given even greater emphasis in the accompanying poem, "To thee pure sprite." Lamb points out that the speaker of this poem, like Clorinda, "creates her authorship as a form of mourning. Not only is Philip the countess's only meaningful audience, but he is also her poetry's real author, inspiring her after his death. . . . Merely completing what her brother would have finished had 'heav'n spared' (74) his life, she is not a 'real' poet asserting the independent subjectivity of an author" (1990, 116). "To thee pure sprite," unlike "Even now that Care," removes the work from the public eye, as if it is addressed not just to her brother, a private familial affair, but specifically to a dead brother, a "pure sprite" totally removed from the world. The opening stanzas recall the "Dolefull Lay of Clorinda" in their use of the notion of doubling. Here, it is not the speaker's voice that doubles back on itself, but rather the writing that doubles back on the spirit of Philip Sidney as "primary" author: "To thee pure sprite, to thee alones addres't / this coupled worke, by double int'rest thine" (ll. 1–2). The differences between the opening stanzas of the revised version and those of the early version addressed "To the Angell Spirit of Sir Philip Sidney" ("Spirit") show Mary Sidney developing the analogy of the creative act of writing with childbirth. Yet rather than using this analogy to argue that creativity belongs "naturally" to women as well as to men, Sidney draws on the phallocentric discourses of medicine and theology to erase her own significance in the versification of the Psalms. The analogy is set in motion when Sidney revises "this joynt worke" ("Spirit," l. 2) to "this coupled worke" (l. 2) with its suggestive sexual connotations. The "work" of this "coupling" belongs to Philip Sidney alone, in both versions. But where the early version reads "Thine by his owne" ("Spirit," l. 3), clumsily identifying Philip Sidney's own writing, the revision implicitly extends the analogy with childbirth in its "First rais'd by thy blest hand" (l. 3). In this context, the inspiration that her brother provides for her own work in both versions ("what is mine / inspird by thee, thy secrett power imprest," ll. 3–4) is simultaneously a sexualization and an erasure of Mary Sidney's creative activity. Like the Aristotelian view of reproduction, which still held currency in contemporary discourses of medicine, the woman becomes a passive vessel for the man's active seed; as the royal physician William Harvey wrote in the early 17th century, "the semen arising from the male is the efficient or instrumental cause of the foetus."[21] Philip Sidney, like the Aristotelian father, becomes the sole creator of the "coupled worke."

This sexualization of the writing act is at the same time emptied of dangerous erotic implications by representing it as the nonphysical coupling of two "Muses," one divine, the other earth-bound: "So dar'd my Muse with thine it selfe combine, / as mortall stuffe with that which is divine" (ll. 5–6). The activity takes on overtones here of the Annunciation; "imprest" by the "lightning beames" of a "secrett power" (ll. 4–7), Mary Sidney becomes a second Virgin Mary, the passive vessel extraordinary, her chastity unimpeachable. The revision of the early version's "faire beames" ("Spirit," l. 7) to "lightning beames" extends the force of the parallel, as does the substitution of "heavens King" for "Israels King" ("Spirit," l. 8): "That heavens King may daigne his owne transform'd / in substance no, but superficiall tire / by thee put on" (ll. 8–10). "Israels King" is displaced to the final line of the stanza, reappearing as "thy Kinglie Prophet" (l. 14).

Like Christ made man, the word made flesh, this transformation operates at once as a further sanctification of Philip Sidney (as if it is he who has temporarily put on the garments of flesh) and as a statement of the divine origins of the "coupled worke" changed only in its "superficiall tire" by the English translation of the Psalms attributed to Philip Sidney. The revised stanza, having extended its claims both for Philip Sidney and for the origins of the Sidney Psalms, goes on to cut the early version's reference to the aspiration of this "English guis'd" work to outdo more popular versifications, to "better grace thee what the vulgar form'd" ("Spirit," ll. 10–11). Instead, it insists on the humility of the endeavour: "to praise, not to aspire / To, those high Tons, so in themselves adorn'd, / which Angells sing in their coelestiall Quire" (ll. 10–12). Any suggestion that there might be some active artistic project at work in the versification of the Psalms is rejected for the pious claim that praise of God is the only aim, in the same way that Mary Sidney rejects any active role for

her own creativity. The revised version repeatedly extends and intensifies
the distance posited between Philip Sidney's idealized significance as
man and poet and Mary Sidney's minimal contribution. Philip Sidney's
status, even in heaven, is represented as that of the poet—blessedly singing "thy Makers praise" among the angels, while "here thy workes [are] so
worthilie embrac't / By all of worth, where never Envie bites" (ll. 62–63).
His "workes" are his literary works, "Immortall Monuments" despite
their lack of completion: "Yet so much done, as Art could not amende; /
So thy rare workes to which no witt can adde" (ll. 67–68). Art, wit, and
thought are all helpless to "frame the rest" after the death of this
paragon of perfection, but it is specifically *not* art, wit, or thought that
Mary Sidney claims for herself in completing the versification of the
Psalms.[22] Instead, she puts to work the dichotomy of reason and emotion, thought and feeling, to make her female voice acceptable:

> these wounding lynes of smart
> sadd Characters indeed of simple love
> not Art nor skill which abler wits doe prove,
> Of my full soule receive the meanest part. (ll. 81–84)

As Lamb argues, she represents her writing as a "physical rather than an
intellectual act, literally writing from the heart's feelings rather than
from the head's thoughts" (1990, 117): "theise dearest offrings of my
hart / dissolv'd to Inke, while penns impressions move / the bleeding
veines of never dying love: / I render here" (ll. 78–81). In the additional
stanzas of the revised poem, the ink with which she writes is merely secondary, a material emptied of its primary meaning, a poor substitute for
her heart's blood. The "real" is located elsewhere, unable to be unfolded
in a "world of words," while her writing comprises dissolved "offrings"
and mere "impressions."

   The revision returns to the analogy with childbearing in the final stanza of the poem, with a neat framing effect: "Receive theise Hymnes,
theise obsequies receive; / if any marke of thy sweet sprite appeare, / well
are they borne, no title else shall beare" (ll. 85–87). The early "Made only
thine, and no name els must weare" ("Spirit," l. 73) is revised to allow the
punning on "borne," as marks that are both carried and given birth. It is
perhaps significant too that the revision replaces "name" with "title"—for
the "Sidney Psalms," whether attributed to Philip Sidney alone or to both
brother and sister, carry the names of both authors, whereas the "title" of

the Countess of Pembroke is suppressed in her representation of the "coupled worke, by double int'rest thine." As if to confirm the properly unambitious and unworldly focus of this representation of her writing, the poem ends with a final couplet added in revision. Where the early version ends "My sorrow strives to mount the highest Sphere" ("Spirit," l. 75), the revised poem concludes with an assertion of the speaker's desire to join her brother in death:

> I can no more: Deare Soule I take my leave;
> Sorrowe still strives, would mount thy highest sphere
> presuming so just cause might meet thee there,
> Oh happie chaunge! could I so take my leave. (ll. 88–91)

Beth Fisken argues that Sidney has fashioned, in "To thee pure sprite," an "elaborate Chinese box of obligations" to escape criticism: "Mary Sidney was inspired by her brother, who emulated David, 'thy Kinglie Prophet,' in re-creating the 'high Tons . . . which Angells sing in their caelestiall Quire' in praise of 'heaven's King' (ll. 14, 11, 8)."[23] Yet even this strategic positioning of her writing has not succeeded in avoiding the eroticization so often attendant on women's words. Sidney's very insistence on her writing as the product of love for her brother, on the private intimacy of the familial relation, seems to have provided fuel for sexualized commentary. Such commentary includes the salacious gossip of Aubrey, who, alongside his account of Sidney's literary activities at her Wilton estate, repeats rumors of her lasciviousness and her sexual relations with her brother. It extends to interpretation of Breton's account of his loss of favor at Wilton as the dismissal of a man whose intimacy with the Countess "passed beyond the bounds of poet and patron,"[24] to Holzapfel's suggestion that Sidney was Shakespeare's dark mistress, and even to Garry Waller's cautious interpretation of a reference to "strange passions" (l. 45) in "To thee pure sprite": "It is as if a veil is being lifted very briefly, unwillingly, even unconsciously. Her love for her brother passes even her own understanding" (1979, 100). Interestingly, this reference to "strange passions" revises the early version's "swelling passions" ("Spirit," l. 59); it may be more relevant to note the constraints on female pride and ambition that operate in the poem as a whole, and to read the "strangeness" of the speaker's passions not in terms of some impossible love for her brother but rather as an attempt to assert a normative moderation and proper rule of the emotions in a woman who was cast by her gender as "more prone to all weak affections and dispositions of mind."[25]

## Inspired Translation

"The Dolefull Lay" and the two dedicatory poems are three of only four original poems by Sidney that have survived, and represent only a small proportion of her writing. The majority of her work follows the formula established by other women writers in translating texts by male writers. In Sidney's work, the distinction between original and translation becomes particularly questionable. Her "translations" encompass the idiomatic but relatively literal renderings from the French of a prose tract on dying by Philippe de Mornay and a Senecan play by Robert Garnier on the deaths of Antony and Cleopatra, a brilliant and sensitive version of Petrarch's Italian *Triumph of Death*, and the markedly nonliteral versification of the Psalms that "completes" work begun by her brother.[26] With the translation of Petrarch and the Psalms, moreover, Sidney chooses to work with two of the most popular and influential texts of the Renaissance and the Reformation.[27] Her translations of the two French texts were published jointly under her own name in 1592. *Antonie*, her verse translation of Garnier's play, initiated a number of Roman tragedies written in imitation of French Senecanism, and has sometimes been considered her most important work "from the point of view of literary history and literary influence" (Young 1912, 144).[28] While the *Triumph of Death* and the Psalms remained in manuscript for centuries, the Psalms, at least, circulated widely before 1630 and acquired both reputation and influence among Sidney's contemporaries; today it is the Psalms that guarantee Mary Sidney's significance as a writer.[29]

Mary Ellen Lamb has argued that the translations of Mornay's *Discourse of Life and Death*, Garnier's *Antonie*, and Petrarch's *Triumph of Death* demonstrate Sidney's response to the tradition of the *ars moriendi* (the art of dying) and her attempt to relate that tradition to the particular situation of women (1990, 119). The art of dying not only makes available a model of female heroism that does not violate gender ideology; it also, Lamb suggests, cleanses Sidney's writing from the contamination of illicit sexuality inherent in female authorship (119–20). Both the Cleopatra of Garnier's *Antonie* and Petrarch's Laura define themselves in relation to men in their heroic deaths; both are models of female self-effacement. Sidney's translations, Lamb concludes, literally and figuratively translate male perspectives on women (141). The juxtaposition of

Mornay's tract on dying with Garnier's *Antonie* in the 1592 edition is certainly provocative in this respect. Completed by Sidney in 1590, the two texts are notably Stoic in emphasis.[30] The Choruses of Garnier's play repeatedly echo Mornay's focus on mutability and the trials of human life, and both texts praise death as an escape from the torments of this world. The passion of the two protagonists is less in tune with Mornay's tract; yet it is Antony who is singled out for blame in the preliminary argument of the play, while Cleopatra is sympathetically represented in terms of her wifely constancy and loyalty, contradicting Antony's appraisal of her in Act I:

> And didst thou then suppose my royall heart
>
> Had hatcht, thee to ensnare, a faithles love? . . .
>
> And did not I sufficient losse sustaine
>
> Loosing my Realme, loosing my libertie,
>
> My tender of-spring, and the joyfull light
>
> Of beamy Sunne, and yet, yet loosing more
>
> Thee Antony my care, if I loose not
>
> What yet remain'd? thy love alas! thy love,
>
> More deare then Scepter, children, freedome, light. (ll. 399–410)[31]

Cleopatra's lament rejects the conclusion that fate, the "rigour of your desteny" (l. 467), rules her life. The rejection makes an interesting parallel with one of the few "errors" of translation in the *Discourse*. Where Mornay recommends that one should not hold back from the necessity of one's destiny (*"et non se laissant trainer à la necessité de son destin";* Bornstein 1983, 96), Sidney's *Discourse* recommends the opposite, "not suffering us to be drawen by the necessitie of destenie" (68–69). The significance of human agency is reclaimed, as it is in one other mistranslation in the *Discourse:* where Mornay's biting remarks reject the worldly excuses of devotion to court and palace, country and God (*"Ne me di point que tu plains la Cour ni le Palais, que tu desidererois plus longuement servir à la Republique, à ta patrie, à Dieu mesme";* 95), Sidney separates court from country to allow for service to the state and to God: "Say not thou findest fault with the Court, or the Pallace: but that thou desirest longer to serve the common wealth, to serve thy countrie, to serve God" (67).

Such mistranslations of the *Discourse* are suggestive in the light of Cleopatra's claim to personal responsibility and her dedication to Antony even in death, and in relation to the Chorus's critique of the public impact of her private actions.[32] The play's mingled sympathy and criticism combine a humanist concern for human agency with a Protestant preoccupation with death. Cleopatra's choice of death marks her out as heroic in constancy; but it also distinguishes her in her rejection of a more traditional form of female mourning outlined by Charmian:

> Then let your love be like the love of olde
> . . . builde for him a tombe
> Whose statelinesse a wonder new may make.
> Let him, let him have sumptuous funeralls . . .
> And yearely plaies to his praise institute. (ll. 603–14)

Cleopatra draws attention to the heroism of her self-effacement in rejecting this model. Mary Sidney, in contrast, adopts a posture very close to that of Charmian's "olde" model to efface the boldness of her writing.

Sidney's translation of Petrarch's *Triumph of Death*, as Lamb suggests, may provide another model of negation—one that offers at the same time the active role of spiritual guide, a role that once again does not overstep the boundaries of gender ideology (1990, 139). In this triumph, Laura returns after her death to assert her love and explain her course of action to her troubled lover, encouraging him to follow in the path of virtue she has established. Perhaps even more significant is Sidney's choice of a poem so central to the Renaissance. Her translation has been hailed as the "finest translation of this triumph in the English language" (Coogan, 324), and it is the only version to retain Petrarch's terza rima. The *Triumph*, like the translations of the *Discourse* and *Antonie*, maintains both rhetorical effect and accuracy. Moving away from the line-by-line translation of *Antonie*, Sidney uses the three-line *terzina* as the unit of translation, which gives her more room for idiomatic and syntactically smooth expression, despite the constraints of the shorter pentameter line that replaces the Italian 11-syllable line. It is her very "faithfullness" to the original that marks out the superiority of her craft (as reader and writer), the artful poetry of her version far exceeding that of previous attempts by Henry Parker, Lord Morley (1554) and William Fowler (1587–88). The secular poet thus preserves her chaste reputation in the guise of the translator.

Sidney's translation pays attention to style as well as content in her concise expression and carefully chosen diction. Balance and syntactic parallelism, aural effects, and vivid metaphor are exploited to render the poetry of Petrarch into English. Compare, for example, Petrarch's description of Laura in death (*"Pallida no ma più che neve bianca / che senza venti in un bel colle fiocchi";* I.166–67)[33] with Sidney's haunting translation: "Pale? no, but whitelie; and more whitelie pure, / Then snow on wyndless hill, that flaking falles" (I.166–67).[34] Hill and snowflakes are given concrete edge and clarity, while the lines effect a strong rhythmic balance by means of the three paired phrases, "whitelie pure," "wyndless hill," "flaking falles." Contrast this with Lord Morley's version of the lines, which not only diverges from the sense of Petrarch but also has none of the evocative phrasing of Sidney: "Not pale she laye, but whyter then the snow / That the wynde agaynst the hyl doth blowe."[35] Sidney sometimes expands Petrarch's wording into the balance of the doublet (e.g. *"dal publico viaggio"* becomes "The vulgar path, and ordinarie trade," II.14) or, more often still, turns his doublets into the compound epithets that Philip Sidney called one of the "greatest beauties" of language (e.g., *"cieca e dura"* becomes "obscurelie blynde," II.32).[36] At times, she extends the figurative hints of Petrarch's lines, as when the unexpected arrival of death is turned into the stealthy action of a thief "stealing on with unexpected wound" (I.44; cf. *"e guignendo quand' altri non m'aspetta"*), or when she adds a paradoxical image to the original: "Therefore thy words in times short limits binde" (II.182; cf. *"e col tempo dispensa le parole"*). Often she chooses her words for strength of phrasing and aural effect, as when she translates Petrarch's *"arse ed alse"* (burning and shivering) as "frye and freese" (I.128).

Succinct and ornamented phrasing is evident too in her compression of Petrarch: "On pleasing bank in bay, and beeches shade" (II.18) renders *"in una riva / la qual ombrava un bel lauro ed un faggio,"* which Lord Morley translates loosely and wordily: "Apon a bancke me thought we twayne were / Whiche was shadowed with the Lawrell tree; / A greate beche therby well myght I see" (123). At times Sidney's compression leads to obscurity, as when she leaves out phrases identifying who is speaking, or awkwardly rearranges the Italian, as in II.178–80, where Petrarch's image of the sun rising breast-high above the horizon (*"Vedi l'Aurora de l'aurato letto / rimenar ai mortali il giorno, e 'l sole / già fuor de l'oceano infin al petto"*) is conflated with the preceding image of dawn, with confusing effect: "See from hir golden bed Aurora bright / To mortall eyes returning sunne and daye / Breast-high above the Ocean bare to sight." Despite such occasional lapses, Sidney's translation is a highly successful transformation into the vernacular of one of the most important lyric poems of the Renaissance.

In translating the *Triumph of Death*, Sidney chooses a poem that asserts the importance of female chastity and offers death as a model for female heroism; however, it also reinscribes women as the objects of male writing rather than as writing subjects. Laura is the inspiration for the speaker as poet, just as the group of women who are "hir chosen mates" are praised as the fitting objects for story and verse. Sidney's translation of these passages is particularly interesting in the light of her own writing activity. For example, where Petrarch talks of Laura's women friends as each worthy of a famous poem and story (*"degna / di poema chiarissimo e d'istoria"*), Sidney emphasises their claim, making them worthy of total attention: "But eache alone (so eache alone did shine) / Claym'd whole Historian's, whole Poete's care" (I.17–18). While the hypothetical writer in Petrarch's version is not identified or gendered, the lines suggest that it is the male poet/speaker who offers the possibility of such commemoration. In Sidney's version, however, the shift to the writers themselves perhaps leaves the question of gender more open. Similarly, in Petrarch's poem Laura provides as the primary evidence of her love a reminder of an occasion when she sang her lover's verses back to him (II.148–50). Sidney's translation of Laura's account, however, makes it possible that Laura is singing her own song and not the "ditties" of her lover: "But clear'd I not the darkest mists of yore? / when I thy words alone did entretaine / Singing for thee? my love dares speake no more." The punctuation, in particular, separates the act of singing from the statement concerning the fear of speaking. Petrarch reads *"dir più non osa il nostro amor' cantando"* (II.150; "singing 'our love dares not say more than this'"), suggesting that the statement of love is the line of a poem; editors have assumed that this is the line of a lost poem by Petrarch himself.[37] Sidney's version, on the other hand, turns the statement into an afterthought that expresses Laura's own fear of saying more as she speaks to her lover after her death. Moreover, in translating *detti* not as verse or song but as "words," and dropping the reference to such words being "presented" to Laura, Sidney allows for the possibility that the lover's words have no direct relation to Laura's singing. Ironically, given Sidney's "impersonation" of Petrarch (through the art of translation), a space is opened for Laura as singer in her own right.

It is worth noting, in this context, that Laura is at several points made a more active and powerful figure in Sidney's translation. Thus, for example, in the opening lines of the poem, she returns from her wars "a joyfull Conqueresse" (I.4), rather than simply with honour (*"con onor"*). At I.10–12, Sidney rearranges Petrarch's lines so that it is "love's new plight to see strange wonders wrought" by Laura, rather than the more general statement that it was a wonder to see Love's arms broken (*"Era miracol novo a veder ivi | rotte l'arme d'Amore, arco e saette"*). It is Laura who appears to have appropriated Cupid's traditional weapons; as conqueress it is she, not Cupid, who bears "shivered bowe, chaste arrowes, quenched flame" (I.11). Even in her encounter with death (I.72), Laura is (like Cleopatra) given a degree of agency, telling death not to "do to me what you do to all" (*"farai di me quel che degli altri fassi"*) but stressing her own active hospitality: "As others doe, I shall thee entretaine." In such slight deviations from her "original," Sidney's translation seems to attempt to open a small space in Petrarch's *Triumph* itself for the writing woman.

## Divine Poet

Both Petrarch's *Triumph* and the biblical Book of Psalms have been seen as "mastertexts" of the Renaissance on which writers could test their capacity as poets.[38] Sidney's bold choice of such central texts, as well as her choice of both religious and secular material, belies the apparent conservatism of the translator's humble role. Her versification of the Psalms goes well beyond idiomatic translation, unlike the translation of Petrarch, which reveals its craft in its close adherence to the Italian. The Psalms allow her to insert her writing into the gap created by contradictions in contemporary ideas about translation as slavish repetition or original re-creation.[39] Representing the work as "superficiall tire" that clothes a substance "not ours," she develops imagery, situation, and personae from mere hints in a variety of sources which provide ostensible authority for her poetic meditations on the biblical text. Here more than anywhere, her writing deconstructs the conventional dichotomy between translation and "original," a deconstruction implicit in Renaissance views of poetry as an art of imitation (of nature, of authors, of texts). Such imitation, as R. E. Pritchard points out, was at the heart of the Renaissance and its attempts to recover and imaginatively repossess the wisdom and the eloquence of the past.[40]

The Book of Psalms, a central text for Reformation worship, was repeatedly translated into English in the 16th century.[41] Traditionally believed to be a compendium of biblical subject matter, a miniature of the Bible as a whole, the inclusiveness of the Psalms was asserted again and again. Calvin called it an "anatomy of the soul" which described all human emotions. Basil maintained that it was a compendium of knowledge, encompassing such disciplines as history, law, politics, and ethics.

In attempting to classify its contents, commentators increasingly concluded that it was a compendium of rhetorical modes and poetic kinds.[42] Philippe de Mornay's account of the Psalms, instead of contrasting secular and divine poetry, works to assimilate the one to the other, so that the Book of Psalms becomes a compendium that encompasses all kinds of secular lyric: "if we seek there for songs of victory, we have of them, but they concern the God of Hosts; if for bridesongs, they be not wanting, but if they be of God and of them that fear him; if for burning loves, there be songs of the very love itself, howbeit kindled of God himself: if for shepherd's songs, it is full of them, but they concern the Everlasting for the shepherd and Israel for the flock."[43]

Mary Sidney's decision to complete the metrical psalms begun by her brother rather than to publish his work in its incomplete state is a remarkable sign of her self-assertion as a poet, despite her dedicatory insistence on Philip Sidney's "double int'rest" in the finished product.[44] It is possible that Mary Sidney's pointed rejection of epic in her dedication of the Psalms to Elizabeth mediates an anxiety about the nature of the poetic territory which she is traversing. Certainly her brother identified divine poetry, including the Psalms, as the chief kind of poetry, and de Mornay asserted that "the art of them is so excellent that it is an excellence even to translate them."[45] In line with her denial of "art" and her erasure of the reference to an artistic project aiming to better "what the vulgar form'd" in the revised version of "To thee pure sprite," Mary Sidney alludes to the inclusiveness of the Psalms in terms of their various emotions and modes of address: "How well beseeming thee his Triumphs are? / his hope, his zeale, his praier, plaint, and praise" ("Even now that Care," ll. 59–60). On the title page of the presentation copy, the compendium of knowledge remains absent, while the compendium of poetic modes and the artistic project of the Sidneys reappears, distanced from Mary Sidney's voice: "The Psalmes of David translated into divers & sundry kindes of verse, more rare & excellent, for the method & varietie then ever yet hath bene don in English: begun by the noble & learned gent. Sir P: Sidney Kt., & finished by the R. honnorable the Countesse of Pembroke, his Sister, & by her dirrection & appointment" (Rathmell 1963, xxxiii). Protected by the submissive act of translation, by the poetic authority of her brother, and by the attitude of the wise virgin—chastely and devoutly meditating on religious truths in communion with an angelic spirit—Mary Sidney maneuvers herself into the position of a "master" poet.

While Mary Sidney is most often addressed as a generous patron in contemporary tributes, it was her psalms that won her recognition as a writer from such men as John Donne, Samuel Daniel, Sir John Harington, and Joseph Hall. John Donne's poem of praise, "Upon the translation of the Psalmes by Sir Philip Sydney, and the Countesse of Pembroke his Sister," casts the Sidneys as "this Moses and this Miriam," David's successors who in "formes of joy and art doe re-reveale" divine song.[46] Samuel Daniel, sometime servant in the Pembroke household, paid particular tribute to Mary Sidney's Psalms in the dedication to his play *The Tragedie of Cleopatra* (1594):

> Those Hymnes that thou doost consecrate to heaven,
>
> Which Israels Singer to his God did frame:
>
> Unto thy voyce eternitie hath given . . .
>
> By this, (Great Lady,) thou must then be knowne,
>
> When Wilton lyes low levell'd with the ground.[47]

Sir John Harington and Joseph Hall both call attention to the lack of a published edition of the Sidney Psalms. Joseph Hall, writing about his own metaphrases of the Psalms (published in 1607), comments on the difficulty of the task: "Many great wits have undertaken this taske; which yet have either not affected it, or have smothered it in their private desks, and denied it to the common light. Amongst the rest, were those two rare spirits of the *Sidneys;* to whom, Poesie was as naturall, as it is affected of others."[48] Likewise, Sir John Harington's *Treatise on Playe* (c. 1597 and itself not published until 1779) comments on the "imprisonment" of the Sidney Psalms: "meethinke it is pitty they are unpublyshed, but lye still inclosed within those walls [of Wilton] lyke prosoners, though many have made great suyt for theyr liberty."[49] Manuscript circulation becomes invisible in both these critiques, which represent Mary Sidney's writing as fully enclosed and private. The devout "hims that she doth consecrate to Heaven" (as Harington, alluding to Daniel, describes the Psalms) are criminally but also chastely "inclosed within those walls like prosoners" and "smothered . . . in their private desks." Mary Sidney's avoidance of the "common light" and the public circulation of print becomes particularly marked in the context of the early publication of the Garnier and de Mornay translations and her concerted efforts to publish Philip Sidney's works. Clearly she did not perceive her own contribution to the Psalms as negligible, despite the disavowals of the dedicatory poems.

The Sidney Psalms are recognized now as a landmark, because of their innovation in utilizing the conventions of secular poetry to revitalize the

English religious lyric. Recent critics, whether they consider her psalms more or less successful than those of her brother, agree that her achievement is outstanding both in terms of craft and interpretative power. Mary Sidney's psalms themselves are striking refutations of her claim that Philip Sidney's work is "but peec't" by her artless effusions of love. Variants and early versions of her psalms show how she reworked and revised individual poems over a period of several years. While Ringler labels her an "inveterate tinkerer" (1962, 502) for her layers of revision, it may be more appropriate to conclude, as Ringler does of Philip Sidney's extensive revisions (lx), that this process is evidence of "great seriousness" and a desire to bring her work "as near as [she] could to perfection."

Mary Sidney's psalms have been most often praised for their formal variety, the "divers & sundry kindes of verse" that the presentation copy recommends. Maintaining and developing directions established by Philip Sidney in the first 43 psalms, Sidney provides a "School of English Versification" in the sheer range of lyric forms she employs (Smith 1946, 269).[50] Waller identifies 164 distinct stanzaic patterns, of which only one is repeated, and 94 distinct metrical patterns (1977, 37). This formal virtuosity is expanded in the variety of styles, voices, modes of speech, and address which make the diversity of the biblical "original" a springboard for extended poetic exploration and experiment.[51] In stanzas ranging from three to 14 lines, with subtly varied patterns of rhyme, rhythm, and line length, Sidney not only forestalls Hall's complaint (in 1607) of the "negligence of our people; which endure not to take paines for any fit variety" but also attempts to adapt form to content.[52]

Sidney's psalms display their formal art in many ways. Stanzaic patterns of varied line length are frequently matched with resounding songs of praise or with the intense psychological and spiritual struggles of a speaker pleading with God. Psalm 92, for example, adapts its swelling praise to the swelling of the verse form, each tercet of the nine-line stanza expanding from four to six to eight syllables:

O lovly thing
To sing and praises frame
To thee, O Lord, and thy high name. (ll. 1–3)[53]

More regular and weighty stanzaic forms tend to be chosen for narrative sequences. Psalm 78, for example, is rendered in ottava rima, a form praised for its majesty (Rathmell, xviii). The form is a fitting medium for the narrative of origins related to the children of Israel by a speaker who announces an (unbiblical) intention to utter "A grave discourse" (l. 1). The art of Mary Sidney's psalms is also on display in the acrostic poem constructed on the phrase "Prais the Lord," which marks the "essence" of the shortest biblical psalm, the two verses of Psalm 117; in the acrostic built on the alphabet, [e]nglishing the Hebrew acrostic that Calvin identifies in Psalm 111; and in the sequence of 22 poems in Psalm 119, each of which each begins with the appropriate letter of the alphabet, again translating the Hebrew practice. Less visible, but equally skilful, are such effects as the closure of Psalm 58. The psalm begins with a scathing address to the powerful, questioning their justice:

> And call yee this to utter what is just,
>
> You that of justice hold the sov'raign throne?
>
> And call yee this to yeld, O sonnes of dust,
>
> To wronged brethren ev'ry man his own? (ll. 1–4)

The expansion here of the Geneva Bible's "o sonnes of men, judge ye uprightly" may pointedly allude to Christ's rebuke of the chief priests and scribes (Luke 20:25), differentiating between debts to Caesar and to God.[54] The question is echoed in the final line of the poem, where these unjust judges are finally displaced by "a God that carves to each his own" (l. 32; cf. Geneva Bible 1991, 58:11, "a God that judgeth in the earth"). Careful crafting is evident too in poems such as Psalm 114, where the repetitions of the biblical prose are carefully cast into the mirror-like structure of Sidney's 20-line stanza. Just as biblical verses 5–6 repeat the statement of verses 3–4 as a question, the repetition framed by two initial and two concluding verses, Sidney's psalm repeats lines 5–10 in the questioning of lines 11–16, and frames her repetition with two couplets. At the same time, this formal mirroring is extended into the content of the poem; the brief biblical statement, "Jordan was turned backe" (Geneva Bible 1991, 114:3), is amplified to include a parallel return: "Jordan with swift returne / To twinned spring his streames did turne" (ll. 5–6). The "twinning" of the poem's form is reflected in the river's "twinned spring." The art of this poem is evident also in its elaborate sound play and its amplification of the biblical prosopopoeia. Lines 7–8, for example, build on the simple comparison, "the mountains leaped like rams" (Geneva Bible 1991, 114:4): "The mountaines bounded soe, as, fedd in fruitfull ground, / The fleezed Rammes doe frisking bound." Familiar rural life and literary pastoral mingle in this rendering, so that the text transforms what Calvin calls the "rude kind of speech" aimed at "the minds of the illiterate" into a much more courtly poem.[55]

Sidney's Psalm 119S is particularly interesting with respect to the matching of form and content, since it can be read as a comment on the art of the poet-speaker. Two versions of the psalm exist: the early poem of four sixains mingling six- and eight-syllable lines is compressed in the later version to two stanzas of eight iambic trimeter lines. The revision, like the sequence of 22 poems in Psalm 119 as a whole (and like the late revisions of the early quantitative meters of Psalms 120–27), seems to aim for the artful simplicity of the Elizabethan plain lyric. Rather than elaborating and amplifying the biblical text, the revised version is tightly wrought in its brevity. The Geneva Bible's "My zeale hathe even consumed me, because mine enemies have forgoten thy wordes" (119:139) is rendered loosely in the early version: "How neere my heart it goes / And paines me to endure / Thy words, forgotten by thy foes" (Waller 1977, 161, ll. 7–9). Revised, this becomes: "I flame with zeale to see / My foes thy word forgett (ll. 5–6). The new simplicity and compression are heightened by the predominance of monosyllables and the alliterative linking of words. Thomas Sternhold and John Hopkins aim in their explanatory wordiness and their use of common meter at a didactic ritual function. Sidney's plainness here is a far cry from their popular but banal verse:

> With zeale and wrath I am consumde,
> and even pinde away:
> To see my foes thy word forget,
> for ought that I doe may. (ll. 139–42)[56]

The brevity of Sidney's revision, moreover, can be read as a reflection of the psalm's focus on the word of God. Compressing the biblical statement of proven excellence, "Thy worde is proved moste pure" (Geneva Bible, 119:140), into the bare "Pure wordes" (with its ambiguity of reference), the poem emphasizes the speaker's love for God's words: "Pure wordes, whereon by me / A servantes love is sett" (ll. 7–8). God's words and the words of the poem become conflated in the compression. The revision of the following lines continues this adaptation of the biblical text to the voice of the poet. The Geneva Bible's "I am smale and despised: yet do I not forget thy precepts" (119:141) is rendered in the early version with emphasis on the speaker's inward obedience:

> Who though to them most base
> And most despisd I grow,
> Oblivion yet could not deface
> Thy statutes in my breast. (Waller 1977, 161, ll. 13–16)

In the revision, however, the diction allows an implicit comparison of God's shaping "precepts" with the rules of poetry:

> Though bare, and though debast
> I yet thy rules retaine. (ll. 9–10)

The revision, "bare" in its translation of the biblical original, suggests that divine "rules" are nevertheless at work in the simplicity of the poem. In this context, the rather obscure compression of the revision's lines 3–4 may also point to the artistry of the poem. "What rightly bid thou dost, / Is firmly bound by thee" may have its poetic parallel in the linguistic binding of stanza, meter, and aural device. The speaker of the psalm is made analogous to Sidney herself, both divine servant and poet at once, displaying a love of God's words in her attention to her biblical text.

While the technical virtuosity of Sidney's psalms has attracted most critical notice, other aspects of her achievement have been reassessed in recent years. Critics have drawn attention to the idiomatic and at times vigorously colloquial language of her psalms, to their succinct and colorful diction; to their verbal wit; to their effective use of the rhetorical devices of compound epithet, paradox, balance, parallelism, and inversion; and to their concrete and graphic imagery, drawn often from contemporary Elizabethan practices and women's experience. The dramatic quality of Sidney's psalms has also been recognized in their arresting openings, their subtle shifts of tone, and their employment of logical structures of antithesis and argument. The intensification and dramatization of the speaker's inward conflict has been singled out as a mark of Sidney's individuality and success. Metaphor and the use of turbulent syntax provide an illusion of immediacy and spontaneity, and by such means Sidney brings the emotional intensity of the love lyric to religious verse.

Such "sacred parody," as Fisken argues, allows Sidney to explore an emotive range that would be transgressive in the context of secular poetry for a woman writer (1989, 227). Philip Sidney could speak in Neoplatonic terms of David as a "passionate lover" of divine beauty, while the dedication of the Marot-Beza psalter, addressed to the ladies of France, encouraged them to read the Psalms as the highest kind of love lyrics (Waller 1979, 189). Excluded from the literature of love by her gender, Mary Sidney could take advantage of the possibilities such courtly Neoplatonism made available to the woman writer by substituting the feminized position of desiring servant courting God for the (equally feminized) position of male lover courting his disdainful or absent mistress. Indeed, Psalm 73 appears to act as a witty comment on this very process, laying claim to the territory of the secular lyric even as it rejects it for the privileged voice of divine poet. The psalm's allusion to Philip Sidney's sonnet sequence, *Astrophil and Stella*, has often been noted. The first stanza, "It is most true . . . Most true" echoes the repetition of sonnet five, "It is most true . . . True" (Ringler 1962, 167), while the opening question of the final stanza—"O what is he will teach me clyme the skyes?"—echoes the lover's address to the moon in the opening line of sonnet 31, "With how sad steps, o Moone, thou climb'st the skies" (180). Moreover, the 12-line iambic pentameter stanza works like a compressed sonnet in itself.[57]

The poem as a whole narrativizes the spiritual history of the speaker in a form similar to that of 17th-century spiritual autobiography, dramatizing the speaker's crisis in faith as a fall from belief to doubt, with tragedy finally averted through the help of God's guidance. Opening with the speaker's assertion of faith in God's favor to Israel, the speaker recalls a past fall from "this truth" as a consequence of seeing the success of the wicked. The fourth and central stanza operates as a pivot, recalling the speaker's own crisis in faith and sketching the inward struggle against such treacherous thoughts. The three stanzas that follow describe the revelation of God's purpose, the speaker's recognition of God's guidance through this time of folly, and a final stanza that reasserts faith in divine goodness and contrasts the fate of the "faithless" with the speaker's faithful future as the singer of God's works.

The stanzaic movement of the narrative is intensified by such devices as initial negation ("Nay heav'n it self," l. 25; "Nay ev'n within my self," l. 37), interrogation ("Then for what purpose was it?" l. 61), and the suggestion of lapsed time ("Untill at length," l. 49). Such words as "Nay," "Then," and "Untill" help to build logical tension and progression into the juxtapositions of the biblical verses. The poem fills in the "gaps" of the psalm text by developing motivation and explanation. The turning point of the speaker's history, for example, is emphasized by the rendering of verse 15. Sidney intensifies the sense of the speaker's psychological conflict and turns the verse into a startled question and anxious prayer: "And shall I then these thoughts in wordes bewray? / O lett me, Lord, give never such offence / To children thine that rest in thy defence" (ll. 43–45). Expanded into an explicit contrast between thought and word, the biblical manner of speaking takes on greater significance, and the addition of a direct appeal to God helps to rein back the speaker's doubt prior to the internal shift of direction in line 46, "So then I turn'd my thoughts another way." The stanza, with its emphasis on "inward sight" (l. 48) and inner dialogue, draws on conventions of secular love lyrics like *Astrophil and Stella* to dramatize the turbulent emotions of the speaker. Like the Petrarchan poet/lover, the speaker becomes what Waller has called a "radically decentered self" attempting to stabilize an identity through language.[58] The representation of the speaker's conflict as a "chase" (l. 49) in the manner of the Petrarchan sonnet helps to point up the relationship.

While assimilating such conventions, the poem also marks out its difference from the secular love lyric. The opening allusion to Philip Sidney's sonnet five, a sonnet that contrasts the speaker's love for Stella with the recognition that Cupid is a false god and that the soul should be aspiring toward heaven, turns Sidney's psalm into a witty comment on the lover's desire. The psalm's narration of a fall from "right conceit into a crooked mynd" (l. 5) parallels the "fall" that produces the secular lyrics, but, in this case, the speaker's crisis is narrated as a passion of the past from a position of renewed faith. Moreover, Sidney renders verse 27, which asserts that God will destroy "all them that go a whoring from thee" (Geneva Bible), as a form of idolatry, substituting "whoorish idolls" (l. 81) for "whoring," a phrase that recalls the adored "image" of "Cupid's dart" in sonnet five (Ringler 1962, 167).[59] The poem's intertextuality not only pays yet another tribute to Philip Sidney but also wittily acts as a rejection of the call of the flesh and the secular lyric of love, as well as suggesting that Sidney herself, climbing the skies to sing God's works, as does the speaker of Psalm 73, is engaged in a poetic task superior to that of the lover whose voice she simultaneously assimilates and transcends.

The assimilation of the language of love was inevitably attended by anxieties, which occasionally surface in Sidney's translation and revisions. In Psalm 63, for example, which is a vivid evocation of the speaker's desire for God, the revised version works to purify this desire, as it tellingly distances and displaces the body. In the first stanza, the longing for God is intensified in the poem's repeated exclamations and the

urgency of the speaker's gasping, hunting haste. The longing is attributed in the biblical text to both "soule" and "flesh," which in Sidney's
early version is rendered as soul and body: "Within my soul a thirst of
thee does dwell, / Nay my body more doth crave / Thy tast to have"
(Waller 1977, 115, ll. 5–7). The revised poem removes all reference to
bodily desire: "How is for thee my spirit thirsty dry! / How gaspes my
soule for thy refreshing taste!' (ll. 3–4). By contrast, both physical and
spiritual qualities of the landscape are present in "this waterlesse, this
weary waste" (l. 5). In stanza two, the revised version reinterprets the
biblical text, the early version, and Calvin's interpretation of the
psalmist's ability to behold God in desert as well as sanctuary. It distances the satisfaction of the speaker's longing to an envisioned future
when the speaker is "transfer'd" from desert waste to "sacred place."
Intensifying the speaker's longing by the addition of desire for such a
deliverance, the poem returns in stanza three to the present: "And lo,
ev'n heer I mind thee in my bedd" (l. 15). At this point, the body
returns, but safely detached from the soul and divorced from longing:
"And, though my body from thy view be brought, / Yet fixt on thee my
loving soule remaines." (ll. 19–20). There is nothing in the biblical text,
which speaks of the soul cleaving or hanging on to God, to suggest this,
although Calvin comments that the psalmist would follow God with
perseverance: "yea and although God himself should go afar off, yet
would he not be wearied" (Vol. II, 168). The final stanza completes this
divorce of soul and body in the poem. The Geneva Bible's "thei shal be a
portion for foxes" (63:10) becomes, in the early version, "foxes teeth
shall have them in their power" (Waller 1977, 116, l. 36), but this is
characteristically made more concrete in the revised version: "their flesh
to teeth of foxes leave" (l. 25). The word "flesh" reappears here, displaced
from its biblical context in the opening description of desire for God to
the carcasses of the speaker's enemies.

The pervasive influence of gender ideology on women's writing seems
evident in the revision of Psalm 63; it is perhaps even more visible in
Psalm 68, where Sidney's revision not only moves closer to the biblical
text (in all its ambiguity) but also removes the bold claims made for the
woman's voice in her early version. The revision of this poem works
toward stately rhythm and phrasing, a sustained tone of triumph, and an
extended and more integral use of conceit. Thus, for example, the eight-
line stanza of hexameters concluding in an alexandrine, a form that
resembles not only the diffuse and jogging rhythms of popular ballad
but also Sternhold and Hopkins's use of common meter, is revised in

favor of the more flexible pentameter line, concluding with a hexameter. The revision likewise develops image patterns, cuts wordy phrasing, and abandons indecorous imagery. The similitude of God "coachman-like" mounted "on highest Heavens back" (Waller 1977, 123, ll. 101–2), for example (developed from the Geneva Bible's "him that rideth upon the moste high heavens," 68:33), is replaced by the more courtly reference to his raised "throne" (l. 87), while the overtly anachronistic "Perrukes" of God's enemies (Waller 1977, 121, l. 68; translating the biblical "heerie pate"/"hayrie scalpe," 68:21) is abandoned for a less vivid but also less grotesque reference to "proud lookes" (l. 58).

The revised stanza four, however, gives a more conservative reading of the biblical text. The early version (Waller 1977, 119–24) renders the triumph song of a group of women as a celebration of liberty from domesticity as well as a song of victory. Framed by the voice of the authoritative speaker and by divine authorship of the song (the Geneva Bible reads "The Lord gave matter to the women to tel of the great armie," 68:11), both versions of Sidney's psalm render the women as a "virgin army" (l. 26; Waller 1977, 120, l. 31).[60] The heroic action of this army is rendered virtuous in the early version, where it is armed with "chastnes" (Waller 1977, 120, l. 31). Possibly the addition registers unease in the face of Calvin's commentary and the Geneva gloss, both of which distance such singing from contemporary life. The gloss explains that such was "the fashion then" (Geneva Bible 1991), while Calvin talks of the "ancient custom" and then attempts to obscure the practice first by generalizing to the implications for "the faithful" (who are put "in mind of their duty, to publish God's benefits") and then by suggesting that the song "may as well be taken in [David's] own person" (Vol. II, 203). Later, too, in commenting on the biblical reference to "maides playing with timbrels" (68:25), Calvin reiterates this emphatic histori-cizing to ridicule such activity: "it was the custom in those days for women to play upon timbrels, though now-a-days it would be absurd among us" (Vol. II, 213). Sidney's early version, rejecting the Great Bible's "company of the preachers" for the "women" of the Geneva Bible, develops the image of women dividing the spoils of victory, and the poem continues to follow the Geneva text in rendering verse 12, at least in its use of the feminine pronoun "she" rather than the Great Bible's ambiguous "they." However, the biblical "house" or "household" is realized in the early version as a domestic prison for women: "Wee house confined maids with distaffs share the spoyle" (Waller 1977, 120, l. 34). In the hands of this heroic virgin army, the distaff, emblem of female industry, becomes a tool for sharing in the spoils of male glory. The celebration of liberation becomes more explicit in line 36, where the biblical shift of pronoun to "ye" is erased in the continuation of the poem's gendered "we," and the juxtaposition of verse 19, in its referential ambiguity, is turned into an explicit comparison between the newly freed women and doves in flight: "Whose hew though long at home the chimneys glosse did foyle / Since now as late enlarged doves we freer skyes do try" (Waller 1977, 120, ll. 35–36).[61] This interpretation diverges not only from biblical text, Calvin, and the Geneva gloss, who interpret the lines as a general reference to the "Church" and the "faithful," but also from the Marot-Beza psalter, which shifts pronouns from the gendered *celles* to the ungendered *ceux* (107). In the context of the household, the "chimneys" that appear in both versions of Sidney's psalm render the biblical "pots" metonymically.

The revised poem, however, removes both the sense of confinement and the liberation, following Calvin in returning the women to a more passive acceptance of their inferiority: "We . . . that weake in house did ly" (l. 28).[62] At the same time, the revision recreates referential ambiguity in shifting to the second person address of the biblical text: "Though late the Chymney made your beauties loathed, / Now shine you shall, and shine more gracefully" (ll. 29–30). The flight of the singing women that "dasleth gazing eyes" in the early version (Waller 1977, 120, l. 39) is analogous to poetic flight, as it is in Sidney's "Even now that Care," which warns "my muse" to "forbeare this heav'n, where onely Eagles flie" (ll. 79–80). Like the dedicatory poem, however, the revision reins back to a more circumspect and subdued flight, which places emphasis not on the newfound freedom of the virgin army as they "try" the skies but on a generalized movement from "loathed" beauties to graceful shining, a movement in which the now ungendered beauties are carefully positioned as objects rather than as dazzling singing subjects who cannot be "defined" by eyes. The revised poem retracts the early version's bold claims for female freedom.

The ungendered "I" of the Psalms keeps open the possibility of identification of poet/translator with singer/psalmist, an identification encouraged by the rendering of the act of singing as the "framing" of praise (as in Psalms 96 and 145) and by approving references to the singer's "skill" (as in Psalm 111). Sidney's revision of Psalm 68 indicates the difficulty faced by women in attempting to claim the freedom of the literary skies. The strategies of Sidney's writing—her translation of male authors; her emphasis on death and dying; her use of religious material;

MARY SIDNEY, COUNTESS OF PEMBROKE, FROM AN ENGRAVING BY
SIMON VAN DE PASSE (1618). *Reproduced courtesy of the National Portrait Gallery, London.*

her contribution to the myth of Philip Sidney, which allowed her to locate her own work within the context of the family—show her conforming to gender ideology even as she develops the voice of a fine lyric poet. Much of this paradoxically assertive self-effacement is encapsulated in a portrait engraved by Simon Van de Passe, dated 1618 (see figure five).[63] The engraving shows the countess dressed in ermine and pearls, signifiers of her gendered virtue (chastity) as well as her class, and holding an open book of "Davids Psalmes" in her right hand. The frame of the portrait is crowned with a laurel garland and supported by a plaque that identifies her as an aristocratic widow, "wife to the late deceased Henry Herbert Earle of Pembroke." At the same time, she retains her own family name, identifying herself not only as dowager Countess of Pembroke but also as a Sidney, an identity reaffirmed in the crowned heraldic "pheon" of the Sidneys above her head. The engraving represents Sidney in terms of piety and learning, in a familial and social context. The book of Psalms she holds defines her primarily as a pious reader. Yet pious Protestant readers were encouraged to apply the Psalms to their own condition and situation, just as Sidney herself suggests in "Even now that Care," making the Psalms find their perfect fit in Queen Elizabeth: "Theise holy garments each good soule assaies, / some sorting all, all sort to none but thee" (ll. 63–64). The theologian Athanasius emphasizes this identification of reader and psalmist speaker in a statement that was often quoted during the Renaissance: "Whosoever take this booke in his hande, he reputeth and thinketh all the wordes he readeth (except the wordes of prophecy) to be as his very owne wordes spoken in his owne person . . . first by him conceyved and pronounced."[64] Given the wide circulation of manuscript copies of the Sidney Psalms, such views help to conflate this representation of the countess as reader, "booke in . . . hande," with a submerged identification of the countess as writer, crowned with the laurels associated with her family name.[65] Almost obscured at the edges of the frame, angelic wing merges with feather pen and inkwell scroll. The woman writer makes her claims surreptitiously but insistently from the margins.

## Chapter Five

# "This worke of Grace": Elizabeth Middleton, Alice Sutcliffe, Rachel Speght, and Aemilia Lanyer[1]

Mary Sidney's writing negotiated gender ideology skillfully through its deployment of translation, pious subject matter, and familial positioning. Few women writers could hope to construct such an advantageous literary context for their writing, however, or had such privileged access to the coterie circulation of the aristocratic text. In this chapter, I look at the poetry of four women writing in the early 17th century who all, like Sidney, find their voices through religious piety and the subject of death, while framing their work in quite different ways. The "works of grace" of Elizabeth Middleton, Alice Sutcliffe, Rachel Speght, and Aemilia Lanyer span 26 years and the reigns of two monarchs; each writes a long meditation—two on Christ's Passion (Middleton and Lanyer) and two on human mortality (Sutcliffe and Speght). Two of the poems were published with a dense frame of prefatory verse, while one (Middleton's "Passion") remains in manuscript form alone.[2] The works of these four women are particularly suggestive in their modes of self presentation and in the selection and shaping of their pious material.

## "This Womans Godly meaning": Elizabeth Middleton

Elizabeth Middleton's "Death, and Passion of our Lord Jesus Christ" has been preserved fortuitously in a manuscript dated 1637 in the Bodleian Library.[3] Middleton presents her work as a gift to a woman friend in an acrostic verse that prefaces her poem.[4] It is "Sara Edmondes" rather than her own name that is here inscribed in the verse, but rather than effacing Middleton's writing, the acrostic centralizes it, both in terms of its own subject matter and as the "free guifte" she offers.

Suche is the Love I beare thy Honest Hart
As makes me this free guifte to thee Impart
Reade theise Ensuing lynes, and thowe shalt see
A Rare Effect of Divine Charitye.

The gift of the poem itself is doubled with the sacrificial gift of Christ's life, Middleton's love with divine love, so that poem and Savior merge to become "a Soveraigne Salve for Every Sore," a curative offered by one woman to another.

Middleton draws on the authority of religion and, like Anne Dowriche, on the authority of the (male) recorders of the events she describes. Her title suggests her fidelity to her source: her passion is "as it was Acted by the Bloody Jewes, and Registred by the Blessed Evangelistes," and while she does not include marginal scriptural references as Dowriche does in *The French Historie*, she pays close attention to the gospel versions of Christ's death in her narrative and her phrasing. Nevertheless, this is a poem (like Mary Sidney's psalms) that goes far beyond the scriptural passages on which it is based. It is a verse meditation, in which narrative dramatization, interpretative comment, and emotional response are primary. Middleton focuses her "Passion" on Christ's Agony in the Garden (rather than on the Crucifixion), on Judas's betrayal, and, balancing that action, on Peter's denial and repentance. Divine redemption and human frailty are the complementary emphases of the poem; its interest is less in Christ's enemies and their actions than in Christ and his individual followers, with the concomitant articulation of the way to live and die in the Church. In 173 sixains of iambic pentameter rhymed *ababcc*, Middleton writes a sustained and often lyrical narrative poem, which has not as yet received the critical attention it deserves.

The "Passion" opens with a succinct declaration of Christ's intentions on earth and the announcement of the destined moment of death and redemption. In a speech to his disciples, Christ announces his own death "To strength theyr doubtfull thoughts" (st. 7) with a confirmation of scriptural prophecy. The intention of his "playne" foretelling is emphasized in stanza six:

But least the suddayne storme, yf unforetould
Should drowne the Seedes of faythe so lately sowne
Or make newe kyndled love of him growe Could

In weake Conceites not to perfection growne
Hee shewes them Every thing must Come to passe
That of him in the Scripture written was.

Telling, foretelling, and retelling converge here so that Middleton's poem itself participates in the strengthening of the faithful. Her poem reiterates at several points the transformation from types and "shaddowing figures" (st. 9) to "the figur'd thing" (st. 46), "Figures for better Truth Exchaundg'd away" (st. 48). In the process, it claims the truth of its own figures.

The narrative proper opens with the account of the anointing of Christ by an unnamed woman "late from Sinne set free" (st. 10).[5] Middleton's selection of this event makes a significant claim for women as active Christians; the incident begins a prolonged section that treats the value and valuation of Christ, and provides a frame to and contrast with Judas's betrayal. Moreover, as a discrete event, the woman's action can be read as a submerged plea for the woman writer, acting as a figurative deflection of disapproval:

But Envious Malice soone Occasion fyndes

This Womans Godly meaning to Reprove

Some standers by muche murm'ring in theyre mynde

As Discontent to see suche Zealous Love. (st. 13)

Christ rebukes the detractors for what he calls (unscripturally) their "Synne" and "Envy," praising the woman "whose fayth wrought this good worke on mee" (sts. 15–16). The incident related in Matthew and Mark provides a fitting opening to the poem's narrative, as if it speaks both for women's capacity to value Christ rightly and for the works of godly women like Middleton herself.

The issue of the expense of the woman's oil, which is so firmly excused by Christ in this episode, returns later in the poem to cause the castigation of Judas for his base contract with the Jews. Judas is figured as a false merchant and the Jews as chapmen of a commercially inept deal that does not consider the market value of Christ, let alone his use value. The motives of the marketplace are rejected even as Middleton's market-oriented accounting system provides a yardstick for evaluation. In an apostrophe to the Virgin, the speaker identifies a proper evaluation based on love, an evaluation that also signals true ownership:

> Oh blessed virgin, Hadst thowe present bene
> When Thus Thy Sonne by Thievish handes was sould
> To bloody Merchauntes: It had soone bene seene
> Howe deere true Owners well gott pearles doe hould
> Thy Tender Love had pitcht the price soe high
> That Juryes wealth, on[e] hayre should never buy. (st. 24)

Magdalen and Martha expand the list of women who value Christ aright, alongside Lazarus and the Angels. Judas, however, is ridiculed for his inability to match object and value: his grudging of "Three Hundred pennyworth of oyle bestow'd / Whose costly value should Advantadge thee / Yf thy false hand had sould the same abroad" (st. 32) is juxtaposed to his acceptance of "Thirty pence" as wages for selling Christ,[6] and compared to the unnatural sale of Joseph by his brothers "For Twenty pence to Merchaunt Men unknowne" (st. 34). Middleton's accounting renders Judas both foolish and contemptuous by means of these economic comparisons. The sequence concludes with a stanza of celebration in which the Christian soul is praised for transforming such marketplace relations into true possession by faith:

> Exult O Christian Soule, what Judas sould
> Thowe has made thyne by fayth. . . .
>                                   Oh Happy Newes
> That Thowe alone out of this Theyre Commerce
> Synnes fatall doome Deathes sentence shouldst reverse. (st. 41)

The Last Supper, represented as a carefully organized domestic event, provides the occasion for a speech by Christ rejecting worldly concerns, and the poem then moves to the Agony of Gethsemane, marked by a stanza of parallelism that emphasizes the turn:

> The Night is nowe farre spent, The Supper donne
> The Grace is sayd, The Table tooke away
> The guestes are Risen, and the worke begunne
> For which the Sonne of God on Earth did stay
> Judas Is comming with A kisse to greete him
> And with Th'Eleven, Christ goes forth to meet him. (st. 75)

The garden itself is made analogous with a church, as a place of private prayer, and at the same time is contrasted with the Garden of Eden, Christ restoring "What in A Garden Adam [not Eve] lost before" (st. 77). Christ's Agony is elaborated in 36 stanzas that emphasize the Redeemer's isolation and torment. While Christ despairs, the speaker floods his three separate periods of prayer with lament, questioning, explanation, and celebration, and offers an anguished and loyal companionship in the face of the laxity of the disciples:

> Accompany Thy Saviour O my Soule
> In outward Signes of Inward grieving woe
> Breake forth in sighes, and with true teares condole
> The Dreadfull Horror, that torments him soe
> Sith, for thy sake, sorrowe did pierce his Hart
> Good Reason, In his Greife, Thowe beare A Part. (st. 95)

The sequence brings Middleton's meditation to its climax, as the speaker's empathetic concern leads to renewed understanding of divine love and the human debt, and to a "vision" of Christ:

> See Howe that Heavnly face is alter'd quite
> Scarce to be knowne by what it was ev'n nowe
> Dead Pale Usurpes the Seate of Redd, and whight,
> And Care sitts figur'd in his wrynkled browe. (st. 96)

Meditating on the isolation of Christ, "Naked of Helpe, forsaken, All Alone / Sought by his bloody foes, Assayld of Hell / Betray'd, or els neglected of his owne" (st. 119), the speaker's urgency increases, marking a contrast with the sleeping disciples:

> Awake, my Soule, Runne forth with Joye, and Dread
> Into this Garden, where thy Saviour lyes
> There shalt Thowe see the booke of lyfe wyde spread
> With lessons stor'd of Heav'nly Misteryes
> There shalt thowe see thy Truth, thy strength, thy foode
> Thy way, thy Light, thy life, and All thy good. (st. 120)

This "vision" of Christ is amplified in a list of epithets that make up the following two stanzas; the repetitions of the phrase "There shalt thowe see" act like a rhetorical arrow pointing toward a visionary understanding of Christ's meaning. It is the speaker who becomes the pattern of proper faith and love in this sequence, able to "see" the value of Christ with a fully awakened soul. The long passage closes when Judas comes to give his traitor's kiss, concluded by a singular interruption that marks the speaker's return from this impassioned flight of empathy: "But lett me Breathe, before I doe proceede, / Surchardging loades will crave a little Rest" (st. 134). The self-conscious pause leads into a conflation of speaker and writer in the stanza's final couplet, the material process of writing brought to attention (though retaining the authoritative masculine pronoun) after the "vision" it has produced: "And He that wrightes, what does I'th wicked Lurke / Shall breath him Twyse, before He end his worke" (st. 134).

The poem continues with the narrative of Christ's capture and the Crucifixion, but the events related in the four Gospels are now abbreviated. There is no mention of Peter's violence in the garden; the inquisition and sentencing of Christ are treated summarily; Herod, Barabbas, and Simon of Cyrene remain absent. Instead, Peter's denial is explored, allowing him a long speech of repentance, which carries an emotive doctrinal message to all sinners. The speech, as Greer has noted, draws several lines from an earlier poem by Robert Southwell, lines that are seamlessly woven into the fabric of Middleton's poem.[7] The tale of the two thieves is also expanded, providing a further example of repentance, faith, and divine mercy, and allowing for an interpretative aside:

> Tis sayd Gods kingdome suffers violence
> And ofte the violent take it by force
> Which wordes being taken in the Rightfull sence
> Are Here fullfyll'd: This Thieves true Remorse
> Made an Assault uppon Gods Heavnly Throne
> And by His faythe tooke it to be his owne. (st. 165)

The hour of death having come, the poem ends abruptly: "He suddenly Cryes Consummatum est / And yeeldes his spirrit to Eternall Rest" (st. 172). The only comment to follow appears in a truncated stanza, the poem cut off with the death of its subject: "Oh Happy Death, which causes us to live / Blest be the Donnor, That such life doth geve" (st. 173).

## The "vertuous tract" of Alice Sutcliffe

Middleton's "Passion" is well structured and carefully modulated; the assurance of her writing marks the poem as a fine example of the way that religion could offer both "language and role" to women of the Renaissance. Alice Sutcliffe, writing in the same decade as Middleton, takes the model of the godly woman further in the self-publicizing stance she adopts.[8] Her work, unlike that of Middleton, was published. Not only that; it was published with a phalanx of commendatory verses by well-known contemporary writers and courtiers who claim her as an exceptional woman, beyond her sex in virtue and literary skill, a "Celia" who is inspired with divine poesy. Sutcliffe's work is a bold venture, yet it is far more deeply implicated in gender ideology than Middleton's manuscript poem. Public exposure brings with it a heavy burden of defense for Sutcliffe which, while it provides her with a means of displaying her work, also demands a high degree of conformity to the patriarchal evaluation of women and operates at the expense of women in general.

Sutcliffe's "Of our losse by Adam, and our gayne by Christ" is a poem of 88 stanzas written in the same stanzaic form as Middleton's "Passion," except that the pentameter lines are divided typographically on the page into irregular trimeter/dimeter lines, an arrangement that heightens the impression of lyric verse but gives the verse a jogging rhythm.[9] "Of our losse" is appended to a series of prose meditations in Sutcliffe's *Meditations of Man's Mortalitie* (1634).[10] The text loudly promotes the novelty value of this woman's work. In her dedication to the Duchess of Buckingham and the Countess of Denbigh, Sutcliffe craves "a favourable Censure of my proceedings, it beeing, I know not usuall for a Woman to doe such things" (sig. A4v), and cites a scriptural text to justify her work while at the same time associating women with innocence and infancy: "Out of the mouthes of Babes and Sucklings, thou shalt perfect Praise" (sig. A5). Her subject, moreover, is stressed as one that is more profitable than pleasing; one item of the Horatian pair is given additional weight to emphasize the moral seriousness of the text. The two acrostic verses she writes to her female patrons focus on their virtue as women, but her acrostic to Philip Herbert, Earl of Pembroke and Montgomery, like her dedication, maneuvers a limited space for her writing. Initially, she emphasizes the weakness of her writing; her "weake pen," "weake endeavours," and "imbecilitie" are the signs of her "infant Muse" (sigs. a2v–a3). Her humility as a mere woman is underlined:

> Right Noble then, view but the vertuous tract,
>
> Of this small Volume, and if you shall finde,
>
> Ought good expressed, by our Sexes act,
>
> Know honor'd Lord, my starres are very kinde. (sig. a3)

Yet the virtue of her subject leads to a transformation that turns her infant Muse to a "Coelique Muse" mounting to heaven, and she ends by comparing her work with the biblical Deborah's "sweet tuned song" and "sacred Peale" (sigs. a3v–a4).

The commendatory verses that accompany the text are likewise profuse in their attention to Sutcliffe's sex. Ben Jonson's focus is on the subject itself, but his poem concludes with an anagram drawing attention to Sutcliffe's name (and his own wit): "I sayd, who had supp'd so deepe of this sweet Chalice, / Must CELIA bee, the Anagram of ALICE" (sig. a5). Thomas May's advice to the reader incorporates misogyny even as it overtly deflects it: "nor disdaine to take / That knowledge, which a Womans skill can bring. / All are not Syren-notes that women sing" (sig. a6). Sutcliffe's sex is central to the emblematist George Wither's praise: "To be a woman, 'tis enough with me, / To merit praise" (sig. a6v), he states, but his admiration is aroused when piety and the "rare Abilities . . . to which our Sexe aspire" are united in a woman (sig. a7). He asserts his approval of women who can improve their "gift," against those who censure or disbelieve in female literary skills. Yet the terms he uses are heavily gendered and assume male superiority: the ripening of "Female-studies" can only result in "Masculine successe" (sig. a7v).

The verses of Peter Heywood and Francis Lenton mark Sutcliffe as the exceptional rather than the model woman. Heywood, for example, tells her to "Live still a praise, but no example to / Others, to hope, as thou hast done, to doe" (sig. a8v). Heywood's verse commends Sutcliffe for her subject matter and aligns her with "instruments less notable" who are nevertheless inspired to express such divine themes; her work "seemes to me above thy Sex and State" (sigs. a8–a8v), a sign of heavenly illumination. Lenton, the self-styled "Queen's Poet," praises her as the "Rara Avis in our Nation," "the Paragon of these our Times" inspired with "sacred flame" (sigs. a10–a10v). He plays on the gendered assumptions of literary "mastery": matter and form "i'th end hands shooke, / For that they have a Mistresse to theyr Booke" (sig. a9v). Even with his emphasis on piety, Lenton's verse ends with an address to an imaginary audience of "Ladies" who are constructed as envious of his praise; the sexual innuendo suggests the erotic connotations that shadow women's writing: "But thinke not Ladies that I doe contrive, / Numbers to mend ought that is done amisse; . . . / For I ne're knew her, when I framed this" (sigs. a10v–a11).

The prefatory material to *Meditations of Man's Mortalitie* is careful to locate Sutcliffe's position in family and court. The title page itself identifies her as "Mrs. Alice Sutcliffe, wife of John Sutcliffe, Esquire, Groome of his Majesties most Honourable Privie Chamber." The display of patrons and literary supporters that precedes the text proper helps to suggest an elite social circle emanating from her husband and his court office, which can approve her literary aspirations while maintaining her conformity to feminine virtue.

"Of our losse" continues the exploration of death and of godly living and dying that is the subject of the earlier prose meditations. The poem begins with an explanation of death's presence in the world, while gesturing toward Christ's promise, then inveighs at length against specific vices and sins that are seen as Satan's lures to damnation:

Whole Armies of his Furies forth he sends,

In shape transformed, to delude our mindes . . .

He marks, to what men are by nature given,

And unto that, he turnes his Compasse even. (153)

The Bible is the predominant source of examples, incidents, and phrasing, but Sutcliffe draws also on natural history, classical mythology, folklore, and emblematic analogies to amplify her didactic message:

Who on this Panthers skinne doth gazing stand,

Had need beware who lyes in wayte to catch,

Who holdes a Woolfe by th'eares but with one hand,

Must with the other muzzell up his chaps. (171–72)

Calling for repentance, the poem goes on to explore the contrasting responses to death of the godly and the wicked; it concludes with advice on how to live and die well, and with a celebration of death that leads to the possession of heavenly bliss:

Thus each weake Christian may this tyrant foyle,

For by Christ's Death man armed is with strength . . .

And with a courage bold, man now may cry
Death where's thy sting? Grave where's thy victory? (196)

Sutcliffe makes use of her subject matter as well as her condemnation of
Eve in the initial section of the poem, to maintain the position of conformity which allows her to publicize her work:

Wicked woman to cause thy husband dye. . . .
The gaine which thou by that same fruit didst winne,
Thou now dost find to bee but little worth:
Obedience to thy Husband yeeld thou must,
And both must Dye and turned be to Dust. (144–46)

On this foundation she can go on to write of universal human mortality
and frailty, sins like pride made "Hermaphrodite" (161), and every soul
equally confronted by death.

## Coveting Knowledge: Rachel Speght

Rachel Speght is more radical in the strategies she employs to make herself a place in an overwhelmingly masculine literary tradition. In what
Elaine Beilin describes as the "mythmaking" of the "Dream" narrative
prefixed to Speght's *Mortalities Memorandum* (1621), this middle-class
London woman explicitly claims access to what she calls "Eruditions garden."[11] The main poem of *Mortalities Memorandum* is a meditation on
death comparable to that of Alice Sutcliffe. In the stanzaic form later
employed by both Sutcliffe and Middleton (different only in its rhyme
scheme, *abcbdd*), Speght's poem marshals her scriptural and classical
reading to expatiate at length on mortality. More explicitly than
Sutcliffe's poem, the "Memorandum" is both meditation and sermon at
once; nearly half the 126 stanzas are devoted to the motives for and benefits of meditation on death. Like Sutcliffe, Speght opens with a description of death's entry into the world, but where Sutcliffe dwells on the fall
(and Eve's part in it), Speght's exposition is sketched in four stanzas that
emphasize the joint nature of the transgression: "And Sathan thinking
this their good too great, / Suggests the Woman, shee the man, they
eate. / Thus eating both, they both did joyntly sinne" (13). Speght continues not with an extensive description of vices tempting humanity, but
with an analysis of several kinds of death (death by sin, to sin, in sin) and

death's "good effects," comparing the evils of this world with the joys of heaven. The analysis leads into a description of the divergent responses to death of the godly and the wicked (24–27), and then turns to look at the need for meditation on mortality for the remainder of the poem.

Irreproachable in its subject matter, *Mortalities Memorandum* is structured around a series of topics amplified by means of scriptural and classical examples, and by logical subdivisions that are often signaled numerically within the text. Organization, Latinate diction, and range of reference all display Speght's education. Yet it is in the prefixed "Dreame" and Speght's prefatory addresses that we find the most striking claims to learning and to the rights of authorship. Both the "Dreame" and the dedication to "her most respected God-Mother Mrs Marie Moundford" refer back to a tract published by Speght in 1617, a defense of women written in response to Joseph Swetnam's popular attack, *The Arraignment of Lewd, Idle, Froward and Unconstant Woman* (1615).[12] Speght's *A Mouzell for Melastomus* was one of several responses to Swetnam. It is the only text from the controversy literature that is openly acknowledged by its author; others use carnivalesque pseudonyms like Ester Sowernam, which disguise the identity and possibly the sex of the author.[13] Speght's initial justification for the publication of her second work, "divulging of that to publique view, which was devoted to private Contemplation" (sig. A2) is the justification of the pious teacher: "I levell at no other marke, nor ayme at other end, but to have all sorts to marke and provide for their latter end" (sig. A2v).

Hard on this statement comes a contradictory purpose. Claiming that the publication of *Mouzell* was greeted with criticism and the suspicion that it was the work of her father, she springs to assert her "rights" as an author: "having bin toucht with the censures of the other ["criticall Readers"], by occasion of my *mouzeling Melastomus*, I am now, as by a strong motive induced (for my rights sake) to produce and divulge this of spring of my indevour, to prove them further futurely who have formerly deprived me of my due, imposing my abortive upon the father of me, but not of it" (sig. A2v). She makes nothing of her sex in this assertion, assuming the universal nature of proprietorial rights of authorship. Yet the dedication to her godmother and the "Dreame" that concludes with the announcement of her mother's death, which inspires her to write on mortality, both work to construct a literary genealogy that displaces male precedence. The piqued dismissal of the "fathering" of her earlier text is supported by this new "of spring of my indevour," an offspring offered in thanks for godly mothering and represented as a revenge of her mother's death: "But sith that Death this cruell deed hath done, / I'le blaze the nature of this mortall foe, / And shew how it to tyranize begun" (11). The new genealogy that Speght is constructing is made more apparent in the "Dreame" itself. In an allegorical narrative that leads the female dreamer from a state of Ignorance to "Eruditions garden," with the help of Experience, Industry, and Truth, Speght makes a case for Knowledge as the "mother" of virtue:

> True Knowledge is the Window of the soule,
>
> Through which her objects she doth speculate;
>
> It is the mother of faith, hope, and love;
>
> Without it who can vertue estimate? (8)

This mother Knowledge, moreover, is of more value to "Great Alexander" than the biological father he can displace for Aristotle:

> Great Alexander made so great account,
>
> Of Knowledge, that he oftentimes would say,
>
> That he to Aristotle was more bound
>
> For Knowledge, upon which Death could not pray,
>
> Then to his Father Phillip for his life. (8)

It is as if, in dedication and "Dreame," a maternal genealogy is being tortuously reclaimed for women even as fatherhood is limited to biological reproduction.

The "Dreame" includes a more explicit argument for women's access to "Eruditions garden" in Truth's assertion of women's intellectual capacities. The obstacles which the character "Disswasion" puts forward include "dulnesse, and my memories defect; / The difficultie of attaining lore, / My time, and sex, with many others more" (4). All obstacles but that of sex are removed by Industry; but sex is recognized as an ideological issue that must be confronted more carefully. It is, significantly, Truth that is brought in to argue "by reason" for women's access to Knowledge. Grounding her position in scriptural texts on the faculties of "mind, will and power" equally bestowed on men and women, and (like Margaret Tyler) on the proper use of talents given by God, Truth goes on to give classical examples of learned women. The kinds of knowledge they exemplify, moreover, are made quite specific; primarily they are women skilled in poetry, rhetoric, and art, and among them is a woman writer. Cornelia is held up not only for her eloquence but also for her writing: "A Roman matron that Cornelia hight, / An eloquent and learned style did write" (5). Truth goes on to represent the search for knowledge as a task requiring constancy, valor, and maturity, castigating in the process the "vulgar talk" that opposes learning as the product of animal baseness and ignorance: "For dung-hill Cocks at precious stones will spurne, / And swine-like natures prize not cristall streames" (6). As Experience had taught earlier, good knowledge "by labour is attain'd" (4), and Truth reinvests the search for knowledge with the pains that guarantee its virtue:

> If thou didst know the pleasure of the place,
>
> Where Knowledge growes, and where thou mayst it gaine;
>
> Or rather knew the vertue of the plant,
>
> Thou would'st not grudge at any cost, or paine. (6)

The poem repeatedly emphasizes the significance of Industry in its rewriting of Eve's ambitious theft from the forbidden Tree of Knowledge: it is the promptings of Truth, not Satan, that inspire desire for knowledge here, a "Desire" that can claim it is "a lawfull avarice, / To covet Knowledge daily more and more" (8). The morally suspect terms of this claim, however, suggest an attempt to revise a fundamentally transgressive desire.

"Eruditions garden" is represented as a place of pleasure, a place to wander "with Desire":

> Instructions pleasant ayre
> Refresht my senses, which were almost dead,
> And fragrant flowers of sage and fruitfull plants,
> Did send sweete savours up into my head;
> And taste of science appetite did move,
> To augment Theorie of things above.
> There did the harmonie of those sweete birds . . .
> Yeeld such delight as made me to implore,
> That I might reape this pleasure more and more. (7)

The very eroticization of women's speech and writing seems to be appropriated here, relocating the garden of love in a garden of learning.

Speght's "Dreame" seems to be working to provide a context sufficiently powerful to allow reinterpretation of the very figurations of women's writing that conventionally function to keep women in their place. Given the fraught nature of that project, it is perhaps not surprising that the "Dreame" has to come to an abrupt end, the dreamer "called away" from the garden and finally awakened by the vision of her mother's death. Fictional dream and autobiography interact to construct a new myth of the Fall, in which it is merely "some occurrence" that denies the dreamer rights to Erudition's garden. Speght's eviction, however, does not prevent her from finding ways to write. Her "Dreame" overtly asserts the capacity and ability of women to challenge men's position as "sole possessioners of knowledge" (Tyler 1578, sig. A4).

## "For knowledge sake": Aemilia Lanyer

The title page of Aemilia Lanyer's *Salve Deus Rex Judaeorum* ("Hail God, King of the Jews"; see figure 6), published in 1611, locates her in relation to men and male authority much as Sutcliffe is identified in her *Meditations*. *Salve Deus*, we are told, is "Written by Mistris Aemilia Lanyer, Wife to Captaine Alfonso Lanyer, Servant to the Kings Majestie." Yet Lanyer's meditation on the Passion is flanked not by a host of commendatory poems by prominent male writers but by an elaborate sequence of dedications in verse and prose that she addresses to royal and aristocratic women and to her readers. Her verse meditation occupies pride of place in the text, unlike Sutcliffe's appended poem, and is printed not with pious prose meditations but with an original topographical or country-house poem entitled "The Description of Cooke-ham." While piety still provides an enabling context for Lanyer's writing, *Salve Deus*, like Speght's "Dreame," is much more radical in the claims it makes for women in general and for the woman writer in particular than either Sutcliffe's heavily gendered exploration of death or Middleton's empathetic Passion. The earliest of the four texts chronologically, it is also the boldest.

Lanyer has been repeatedly spotlighted in the last two decades for her poetic innovations and her foregrounding of gender.[14] Several critics have pointed to "The Description of Cooke-ham" as the first country-house poem to have been published and perhaps written in English, pre-dating Ben Jonson's "To Penshurst."[15] Lorna Hutson identifies her as the "author of the first original poem by a woman to be published in the 17th century," and Elaine Beilin (1987, 177) calls her the "first woman

# SALVE DEVS
## REX IVDÆORVM.

*Containing,*

1. The Paſsion of Chriſt.
2. Eues Apologie in defence of Women.
3. The Teares of the Daughters of Ieruſalem.
4. The Salutation and Sorrow of the Virgine Marie.

With diuers other things not vnfit to be read.

Written by Miſtris *Æmilia Lanyer*, Wife to Captaine *Alfonſo Lanyer* Seruant to the Kings Majeſtie.

AT LONDON
Printed by *Valentine Simmes* for *Richard Bonian*, and are to be ſold at his Shop in Paules Church-yard. *Anno* 1611.

TITLE PAGE OF AEMILIA LANYER, *Salve Deus Rex Judaeorum* (1611).
*Reproduced by permission of the Huntington Library, San Marino, California.*

seriously and systematically to write epideictic poetry, the poetry of praise, about women."[16] Critics have taken various positions on the "feminist" leanings of her work. Barbara Lewalski, for example, reads *Salve Deus* as a "comprehensive 'Book of Good Women,' fusing religious devotion and feminism so as to assert the essential harmony of those two impulses" (in Hannay 1985, 207), whereas Beilin does not agree that Lanyer was a feminist "because her advocacy for women begins with spiritual power and ends with poetry" (1987, 320, n. 11). Tina Krontiris argues that Lanyer is not "consistent in her feminist voice," but that in defending women against male charges and by addressing herself to women only, she "thrusts out challenging feminist statements" (1992, 118). Lynette McGrath argues for a more radical feminist position for Lanyer: "Appropriating the most powerful Christian ideological icon as authorization, [Lanyer] textually established a supportive female community under whose auspices she urged women to embark on a process of self-definition beyond the power of male construction and outside the range of male desire" (1992, 345).[17] McGrath qualifies this, however, by adding that Lanyer's work lacks an "agenda for political change, an element considered crucial in modern feminisms" (334). Lorna Hutson, in what is perhaps the most fascinating discussion of Lanyer's work to date, reads *Salve Deus* as an "attempt to produce, from a medium so heavily invested in the articulation of masculine virtue, a poem which celebrates woman as an effective reader and agent, rather than offering her as a dark secret to be disclosed" (in Brant 1992, 14); to do this, Hutson argues, she must avoid the comparative rhetoric that makes women the "analogues and occasions of discursive virtue among men" (30).[18] My own discussion of *Salve Deus* is particularly indebted to Hutson's work.

Lanyer's foregrounding of gender is visible from the title page, which lists four specific topics that are "contained" in *Salve Deus* along with "divers other things not unfit to be read"; the Passion of Christ is the first item, but the list then goes on to identify "Eves Apologie in defence of Women," "The Teares of the Daughters of Jerusalem," and "The Salutation and Sorrow of the Virgine Marie" (1). The list suggests that the poem is divided into four parts, but this is not the case. The story of the Passion is narrated in stanzas 42–165 of the 230-stanza poem, while the three woman-focused items are inset into that story in fewer than 30 stanzas. What appears to be a table of contents, then, proves to be a list of "highlights," which accounts for only about half of the poem and which focuses attention on the role of women in Christian history.[19] The dedications to living women that follow reinforce this emphasis.[20]

Addresses to Queen Anne and Princess Elizabeth decorously head the prefatory poems, and draw attention to the sex of the author. Like Sutcliffe, Lanyer asks the Queen to view "that which is seldome seene, / A Womans writing of divinest things" (3), and the Princess to accept the "first fruits of a womans wit" (11). In a conventional disclaimer, Lanyer excuses her "want of knowledge" and "slender skill" (9), and then goes on to locate her writing outside the competitive arena of masculine art:

> Not that I Learning to my selfe assume,
>
> Or that I would compare with any man:
>
> But as they are Scholers, and by Art do write,
>
> So Nature yeelds my Soule a sad delight.
>
> And since all Arts at first from Nature came . . .
>
> Why should not She now grace my barren Muse,
>
> And in a Woman all defects excuse. (9–10)

Exploiting the gendered opposition between art and nature, Lanyer seems to take up an appropriate feminine position; yet that position also provides more direct access to the divine, since Nature is that "Mother of Perfection, / Whom Joves almighty hand at first did frame" (10). At the same time, Lanyer attributes the "eye of Learning" that she lacks to the queen, who is encouraged to judge the contents of the book for herself, feed on the Passover feast it offers, and reinforce its virtue with her knowing interpretation: "though I see the glory of her State, / Its she that must instruct and elevate" (9). The queen's "judiciall view" is called on specifically to judge Lanyer's defence of women:

> Behold, great Queene, faire Eves Apologie,
>
> Which I have writ in honour of your sexe,
>
> And doe referre unto your Majestie,
>
> To judge if it agree not with the Text:
>
> And if it doe, why are poore Women blam'd,
>
> Or by more faultie Men so much defam'd? (6)

In the context of this attempt to exonerate all women from blame, Lanyer introduces one particular woman who "must entertaine you to this Feast" (7). The unnamed "great Lady," we find later, is Margaret

Clifford, Countess of Cumberland and mother of Anne Clifford. The Countess is both patron and subject of *Salve Deus*, the woman whose knowing presence frames and illuminates Lanyer's narrative of the Passion. Lanyer incorporates class hierarchy into her dedication here, not only by speaking of her own "meannesse" and her loss of fortune "Since great Elizaes favour blest my youth" (8), but also by representing herself as the servant who has "attired" the Countess for presentation to the queen and "prepar'd my Paschal Lambe" (7) for the feast to which the Countess, as aristocratic hostess, welcomes the queen. Similarly, the textual "Glasse" she offers to Queen and Ladies in her verses draws on the service of a maid; her glass acts not as an emblem of female vanity but as the "Mirrour of a worthy Mind" (5).[21]

The voice of the servant, however (a voice that is made literal in the verse to the Countess of Kent, whom she calls the "Mistris of my youth," 18), modulates into a more authoritative voice as Lanyer moves on to address "all vertuous Ladies in generall." The attiring of the countess in "all her richest ornaments of honour" looks forward to Lanyer's appropriation of the parable of the 10 virgins, and her confident advice on preparations for the encounter with Christ as Bridegroom:

> Put on your wedding garments every one,
> The Bridegroome stayes to entertaine you all . . .
> And make no stay for feare he should be gone:
> But fill your Lamps with oyle of burning zeale. (12)

The Passover feast announced in the poem to the queen merges with the wedding feast of the parable, as Lanyer invites "vertuous Ladies" in general and in particular to her textual feast. Unlike Sutcliffe, who alludes to the parable in a universalized reminder that "man" should not "waste his precious time" (189), Lanyer's use is gender-specific. By identifying the women with the wise virgins, Lanyer manipulates the common figure of Christ as Bridegroom of the Church to make women the "natural" recipients of Christ's love; heterosexual marriage becomes the implicit ground for suggesting women's privileged access to Christ and his wisdom.

Lanyer's portrait of the Ladies making their way in pageantlike fashion "To be transfigur'd with our loving Lord" (14) mingles biblical and classical imagery in such a way that learning and the "Muses" are made fit companions for female virtue. The women are to be "deckt with Lillies" (12) and crowned with laurel, their wisdom emphasized in an injunction that they must "In wise Minerva's paths be alwaies seene" (13). Lanyer's verse guarantees the Muses as appropriate companions for virtuous women: "And let the Muses your companions be, / Those sacred sisters that on Pallas wait; / Whose Virtues with the purest minds agree" (13). Far from encouraging wantonness, as so many male authors argued, the "godly labours" of the Muses provide liberation from worldly pleasures, violence, and "ill report" (13), and the Muses themselves are heroic, as they displace the nine traditional (male) Worthies. In the dedications that follow—to Lady Arabella Stuart and to the countesses of Kent, Bedford, Suffolk, Pembroke, Cumberland, and Dorset—the association of Pallas and the Muses and the figures of feast and bridegroom recur, linking Lanyer's patrons through the glass that is her "little Booke" (15) in a female community of wise virgins whose knowing gaze is focused on the "dying lover" Christ (33). Lanyer's eclecticism allows her to stake out a claim both for herself as virtuous writer and for her women readers as learned, wise, and godly.

Lanyer's appropriation of the parable is one aspect of a larger project in which she attempts, as Speght does, to claim knowledge for women. Her praise of Margaret, Countess of Cumberland, is central to that task. As Hutson puts it, Lanyer's poem "sets itself out to unfold or prove the interpretative virtue of Margaret Clifford's mind through a dramatizing of the female recognition of Christ in the historical moment of his Passion" (in Brant 1992, 21). Read in this way, the series of encomiums to the countess that frame the narrative of the Passion are not sycophantic digressions. Rather, they are integral to the construction of a knowing female subject, functioning in the same way as "Eves Apologie" and the grief of the Virgin and the daughters of Jerusalem within the narrative of the Passion. Beginning with a vow to "applie / My Pen, to write thy never dying fame" (ll. 9–10), to ensure the immortality of the countess, Lanyer defers the requested description of Cookham, that "delightfull place" (l. 18), and rejects the Petrarchan language of beauty (with its attendant ideology) as her subject matter:

> That outward Beautie which the world commends,
>
> Is not the subject I will write upon. . . .
>
> For greatest perills do attend the faire,
>
> When men do seeke, attempt, plot and devise,
>
> How they may overthrow the chastest Dame,
>
> Whose Beautie is the White whereat they aime. (ll. 185–208)

Helen, Lucrece, Cleopatra, Rosamund, and Matilda mingle company in illustrating the "dangers and disgrace" (l. 196) that attend on beauty; conventional attributions of guilt and innocence are destabilized by the conflation of stories of beautiful victims and seducers of men. Yet, having rejected outward beauty as a subject for her muse, Lanyer begins to write not of the countess's inner beauty but of Christ: "His Death and Passion I desire to write, / And thee to reade, the blessed Soules delight" (ll. 271–72). Only when her narrative of the Passion is complete, 123 stanzas later, does it become apparent that Lanyer may be fulfilling her declared intention to write Margaret Clifford's "never dying fame" in this Christian narrative. Cutting short a blazon of the resurrected Christ as Bridegroom, she begs leave from the countess to "leave / This taske of Beauty which I tooke in hand" (ll. 1321–22), and suggests that Christ's portrait is fully "discovered" in her heart: "Therefore (good Madame) in your heart I leave / His perfect picture, where it still shall stand, / Deepely engraved in that holy shrine" (ll. 1325–26). In that "shrine," the countess may "reade his true and perfect storie" (l. 1331), embrace his body, and pray for grace. Lanyer's narrative, then, becomes the key to the countess's heart, discovering in advance the image that is "engraved" therein. Her story is put into mutually authenticating circulation between author and patron as the text engraved in the countess's heart reflects the text of Lanyer's "little Booke" and vice versa. From this vantage point, the poem can continue to explore Clifford's virtue for a further 60 stanzas, concluding with a description of Christian martyrs prepared to die for the "hony dropping dew of holy love" (l. 1737); their beauties, like Christ's, are fully disclosed only in the Countess's heart:

> Loe Madame, heere you take a view of those,
> Whose worthy steps you doe desire to tread . . .
> But my weake Muse desireth now to rest,
> Folding up all their Beauties in your breast. (ll. 1825–32)

At the "heart" of both poem and countess, then, is the Passion. But it is a Passion very different from that of Middleton. *Salve Deus* works to privilege women and their claim to knowledge and truth. As the narrative of the Passion proceeds, it increasingly contrasts the actions and responses of men and women in relation to Christ (a contrast heralded in the prose dedication to the "Vertuous Reader"). Opening with Gethsemane, which erases the masculine community of the Last Supper described in Middleton's poem,

Lanyer's Passion emphasizes the repeated failures of the disciples. Both Middleton and Lanyer point to the inattention of the disciples, but whereas Middleton's treatment of the sleeping disciples emphasizes Christ's isolation and helps to prepare for the empathetic climax of Christ's Agony, Lanyer is more insistent on blaming the disciples for their failure to watch with Christ: they "shut those Eies that should their Maker see" (l. 420); their "eyes were heavie, and their hearts asleepe" (l. 465). Rather than focusing on Christ's torment, her poem moves on to spotlight the capture of Christ by the "Monsters" who "could not know him, whom their eyes did see" (l. 504). The "accursed crew" (l. 513) are castigated for their lack of understanding: "Yet could their learned Ignorance apprehend / No light of grace, to free themselves from blame" (ll. 546–47). Christ, meanwhile, makes no resistance "To free himselfe from these unlearned men" (l. 553). The high priests and scribes are fully defrocked of their learning in the shift from "learned Ignorance" to "unlearned Men." Similarly, where Middleton details Peter's triple denial and the pathos of his repentant complaint, returning to Caiaphas only at the end of a night of accusations, Lanyer ignores Peter and focuses on the criminality of the "hellhounds" who accuse Christ and (mis)interpret his words in a blindly literal hermeneutics: "They tell his Words, though farre from his intent, / And what his Speeches were, not what he meant" (ll. 655–56). Christ's silence, in Lanyer's reading, is the only way to avoid the false accusations of men who question him "That by his speech, they might advantage take" (l. 692).

It is with Pilate's judgement, however, that Lanyer most clearly sets the gender politics of her poem in motion. Pilate's wife is made the spokesperson for all women, refusing consent to Christ's Crucifixion, while in an extended reinterpretation of the Fall, Eve's offence is made less transgressive than this now gendered (male) offence against Christ:

> If one weake woman simply did offend,
> This sinne of yours, hath no excuse, nor end.
>
> To which (poore soules) we never gave consent,
> Witnesse thy wife (O Pilate) speakes for all. (ll. 831–34)

Knowledge is at stake both here and in later passages on the daughters of Jerusalem and the Virgin. Eve's fault was to err "for knowledge sake" (l. 797), offering the apple to Adam with "too much love" (l. 801) so that "his knowledge might become more cleare" (l. 804); Adam, however, strong in body and possessing the "powre to rule both Sea and Land" (l. 789), is tempted purely by appetite: "The fruit beeing faire perswaded him to fall" (l. 798). Lanyer draws attention to the contradictions of ideology in which woman is condemned for Eve's fault, which lays a "staine / Upon our Sexe" (ll. 811–12) while men take pride in the knowledge that originates in her action: "Yet Men will boast of Knowledge, which he tooke / From Eves faire hand, as from a learned Booke" (ll. 807–8). In Lanyer's accounting, Christ's Crucifixion provides a balance that challenges male dominion:

> Then let us have our Libertie againe,
>
> And challendge to your selves no Sov'raigntie . . .
>
> Your fault beeing greater, why should you disdaine
>
> Our beeing your equals, free from tyranny? (ll. 825–30)

In this poem, it is women's knowledge that is proved to go beyond "learned Ignorance." The words of Pilate's wife, deriving from a dream and sent from a domestic space beyond the public arena, are privileged over the words of Pilate, a "man of knowledge, powre, and might" (l. 931). Her knowledge is supported not only by Eve's apology but also by the daughters of Jerusalem, whose "Eagles eyes did gaze against this Sunne" (l. 991) in their tearful compassion for Christ, and by the Virgin Mary who knows that Christ is "Her Sonne, her Husband, Father, Saviour, King" (l. 1023), while knowing no man and thus "from all men free" (l. 1078). By the end of the apostrophe to the Virgin, the duplicity and corruption associated with "paint" and the decorated body can be displaced from women to Pilate himself: "Now Pilate thou art proov'd a painted wall, / A golden Sepulcher with rotten bones" (ll. 921–22). The description of the Crucifixion that follows delivers the body of Christ to the Countess of Cumberland, secure in its conviction that she, like these women, has the capacity to "judge if ever Lover were so true" (l. 1267).

*Salve Deus*, then, makes use of the Passion of Christ to construct the countess and, by implication, Lanyer herself as exemplary wise virgins. The pious text writes Lanyer into the position of virtuous author, so that she stands like the personification of Virtue in her dedicatory verse to the Countess of Bedford, who holds the "key of Knowledge" to "unlocke the closet of your lovely breast" (32). That knowledge, as the slippery ambiguity of the possessive form suggests, is something that belongs to both observer and observed, simultaneously inside and outside the "breast" of the countess, like Christ in the Bedford verse and in *Salve Deus* itself. "The Description of Cooke-ham" that follows *Salve Deus*, with its elegiac unfolding of the Countess of Cumberland as temporarily and blissfully meditating in the company of women on the Edenic prospect of an estate that welcomes her with courtly entertainment and obeisance, makes the author's "sweet Memorie" (l. 117) an equivalent of the image of Christ engraved within the countess's heart in *Salve Deus*. Just as the countess departs from her estate "Placing their former pleasures in [her] heart; / Giving great charge to noble Memory, / There to preserve their love continually" (ll. 154–56), Lanyer's farewell to Cookham displays and thereby immortalizes the memory of "pleasures past" (l. 13) and the image of the countess "Whose virtues lodge in my unworthy breast" (l. 208): "This last farewell to Cooke-ham here I give, / When I am dead thy name in this may live" (ll. 205–6). At the end of Lanyer's "little Booke," it is as if the complicated structure of textual frames that *Salve Deus* as a whole constructs collapses finally into the originating body of the knowing female subject, Aemilia Lanyer.

## Chapter Six

# "By publike language grac't": Elizabeth Cary, Lady Falkland[1]

In 1612, John Davies of Hereford published a collection of poetry called the *Muses Sacrifice*, which he dedicated "To the Most Noble, and no lesse deservedly renowned Ladies, as well Darlings, as Patronesses, of the Muses; Lucy, Countesse of Bedford; Mary, Countesse Dowager of Pembrooke; and, Elizabeth, Lady Cary, (Wife of Sr. Henry Cary); Glories of Women."[2] The dedicatory poem draws particular attention to the writing of Mary Sidney and Elizabeth Cary and to Davies's personal connections with them. Sidney's writing is represented by her psalms alone: "A Worke of Art and Grace. . . . / So sweet a Descant on so sacred Ground / no Time shall cease to sing to Heav'nly Lyres" (sig. *₊*3, ll. 41–46). Davies connects himself to this pious "Worke of Art and Grace" with a reminder of his preparation of the presentation copy of the manuscript: "My Hand once sought that glorious Worke to grace; / and writ, in Gold, what thou, in Incke, hadst writ" (sig. *₊*3, ll. 53–54). Elizabeth Cary is praised for more secular virtues—for her acquisition of languages and for her dramatic skills, which Davies connects with his own tuition:

> Thou mak'st Melpomen proud, and my Heart great
> of such a Pupill, who, in Buskin fine,
> With Feete of State, dost make thy Muse to mete
> the Scenes of Syracuse and Palestine. (sig. *₊*3v, ll. 69–72)

The focus of Davies's poem, however, is the profusion of second-rate material that pours from the printing press, giving learning, and poetry in particular, a bad name. Ignorance and vanity are blamed for this "Disease of Times, of Mindes, Men, Arts, and Fame" (sig. *₊*4v, l. 117): "vaine Selfe-conceit, how dost thou ply the Presse" (sig. *₊*4v, l. 118). In this context, his statement that the women he addresses "presse the Presse with little you have made" (sig. *A*1, l. 160) is less a polite rebuke (as it has sometimes been interpreted) than a compliment that reinscribes the dangers of public display for the woman writer. As Margaret Ferguson has argued, the terms Davies uses surround publication with "an aura of unseemly sexual importunity," encouraging the women to distance themselves from "a scene of illicit sexual traffic";[3] "pressing the press" becomes an activity that the women, by virtue of their gender and their class, rightly avoid:

> No; you well know the Presse so much is wrong'd,
>
> by abject Rimers that great Hearts doe scorne
>
> To have their Measures with such Nombers throng'd,
>
> as are so basely got, conceiv'd, and borne. (sig. *A*1v, ll. 61–64)

The refusal to publish is explicitly associated with a properly modest and feminine lack of ambition: "And didst thou thirst for Fame (as all Men doe) / thou would'st, by all meanes, let it come to light" (sig. *⁎⁎*3, II. 57–58), he tells Sidney, while assuring her that her psalms shine brightly through these "Clouds" anyway. While several critics have suggested that this tribute may have encouraged Cary to publish her *Tragedie of Mariam the Faire Queene of Jewry* in 1613, Davies's poem seems rather to reinscribe women in the private sphere while maintaining the male poet's role in supervising and displaying female virtue. By addressing the women, Davies can position his own writing in relation to the work of a prestigious literary forebear, Philip Sidney; they are "Three Graces, (whom our Muse would grace, / had she that glory that our Philip had, / That was the Beautie of Arts Soule and Face)" (sig. *A*1, ll. 157–59). Both Sidney and Cary, meanwhile, are represented as women whose writing marks them out in history from other women. Sidney's psalms become a form of exceptional and pious feminine service: "No Time can vaunt that ere it did produce / from femin[in]e Perfections, so sweet Straines / As still shall serve for Men and Angels use" (sig. *⁎⁎*3, ll. 49–51). Cary's writing is a momentary (secular) wonder without past or future:

> Such nervy Limbes of Art, and Straines of Wit
>
> Times past ne'er knew the weaker Sexe to have;
>
> And Times to come, will hardly credit it,
>
> if thus thou give thy Workes both Birth and Grave. (sig. *⁎⁎*3v, ll. 77–80)

Davies's remarks on the fortunes of Elizabeth Cary's writing, if it were left unpublished, proved accurate. Indeed, it is partly owing to his dedication that *The Tragedie of Mariam*, set in Palestine, has been identified as her work. Cary was a prolific writer, but little of her work was published in her own lifetime or later. Her authorship has frequently been a matter of debate, and much of her writing appears to be lost. Known in her own lifetime for her learning and for the scandal of her conversion to Catholicism in 1626, Elizabeth Cary is now best known as the first English woman to write (rather than translate) a play. Her partially versified history of *Edward II* (completed in 1628) likewise guarantees her historical importance, although here again she was not identified as the author of the history until 1935.[4]

## Biographical Constructions

Much of what we know of Elizabeth Cary's life and writing comes from a biography written (c. 1655) after her death by one of her daughters, a Catholic nun in France, which extols her as a conscience-driven and persecuted convert.[5] Cary's life as it is represented in the biography and other surviving documents provides a significant context for her writing, though it cannot be read as a simple explanation of her work. *Mariam* and *Edward II* share many of the concerns and conflicts that are present in the biography. "All her life," Lewalski comments, "Cary seems to have been caught up in conflict between social and ideological pressures to conform and submit and an inner imperative to resist and challenge authority" (1993, 181). Lewalski's dichotomy between external pressures and "inner imperative" may be too simple, but that conflict between conformity and resistance is vividly present in Cary's characterization of the eponymous heroine of *Mariam* and of Queen Isabel in *Edward II*, two women who as wives and queens occupy visibly contradictory subject positions. The biography attests to the volume of Cary's work, but it is neither particularly detailed nor comprehensive in its account of her writing. Neither *Mariam* nor *Edward II*, for example, is mentioned, although there is a reference to an unnamed text "stolen out of that sister-in-law's (her friend's) chamber, and printed, but by her own procurement [it] was called in" (Simpson 1861, 9). This may be a reference not to *Mariam* itself but to the prefatory poem signed E. C. and dedicating the play to "my worthy Sister[-in-law], Mistris Elizabeth [Bland] Carye," a dedication that is not present in most extant copies of the play.[6] In the case of the later history, it is not clear whether the biographer was simply ignorant of the work, or was concerned to emphasize Cary's religious writing in the period after her conversion. The account attributes to this period her translation of the works of the French Catholic Cardinal

*Elizabeth Taunfield wife of S.ʳ Henry Carey ĩˢᵗ Lord Falkland. From an Original picture at Burford Priory.*

ELIZABETH CARY, LADY FALKLAND, FROM A WASH DRAWING BY ATHOW OF A PAINTING BY PAUL VAN SOMER.

*Reproduced courtesy of the Ashmolean Museum, Oxford.*

Perron and adds that "About this time she writ the lives of St. Mary Magdalen, St. Agnes, Martyr, and St. Elizabeth of Portinagall, in verse; and both before and after, many verses to our Blessed Lady . . . and of many other saints" (Simpson 1861, 39).

The texts that have come down to us seem to derive from two periods of writing, a division corroborated by the biography. The first group derives from her youth and the early years of her marriage, when her husband was absent on the Continent; the second, from the period after her conversion, when she was again separated from her husband and living in constrained circumstances. Supplementing *Mariam* in the early period is a youthful translation of a geographical treatise by Abraham Ortelius which she dedicated to her great uncle, the Royal Champion Sir Henry Lee.[7] In the later period, the existence of a Continental edition (dated 1630) of her translation of Cardinal Perron's reply to King James, a work dealing with the rights and duties of English Catholic subjects, corroborates the biographer's account of the controversial publication of this text.[8] Only one other manuscript poem has been identified as her work, a brief epitaph on the death of the Duke of Buckingham in 1628.[9] The biographer adds the "translation of part of Blosius" in her final years, as well as a translation of a defense of Catholicism and of Seneca's epistles in her youth. In the early years of her marriage, Cary's biographer notes that "she writ many things for her private recreation, on several subjects and occasions, all in verse (out of which she scarce ever writ anything that was not translations)" (Simpson 1861, 9). Among these "private" pieces was a verse "Life of Tamberlaine" and, presumably, the play set in Sicily/Syracuse that is mentioned in Davies's dedication and in the dedicatory poem prefaced to *Mariam*.

The only mention in the biography of writing between these two periods appears in a reference to Cary's concern for her children: "Being once like to die, whilst she had but two or three children, and those very little, that her care of them might not die with her, she writ . . . a letter of some sheets of paper . . . full of such moral precepts as she judged most proper for them" (Simpson 1861, 12–13). During the period 1609–25, Cary gave birth to 11 children; both biography and surviving texts suggest that the activities of wife and mother precluded writing, "she being continually after, as long as she lived with [her husband], either with child or giving suck" (14). This statement, erased by the biographer's brother in his revison of what the 19th-century editor called "passages . . . too feminine" (vi), suggests the interrelationship between the material conditions of Cary's life and her writing. Virginia Woolf's need as a writer for a "room of her own" is prefigured in Cary's life. Yet ironically, it is oppressive material conditions that helped to produce her writing. The biographer locates the origin of her poesy, for example, in the harsh treatment of her mother-in-law: Lady Catherine Cary, in the absence of her son, "used her very hardly, so far as at last to confine her to her chamber, which seeing she little cared for, but entertained herself with reading, the mother-in-law took away all her books, with command to have no more brought her. Then she set herself to make verses" (8). Confined to her chamber, or, later in her life, to the isolation of the "little house" outside London where she lived with one servant and no money after her conversion, Cary finds time and space to write.

Cary was born in 1585, the only daughter and heir of Elizabeth Symondes (niece of Sir Henry Lee) and the lawyer and judge Lawrence Tanfield. The biography suggests that her voracious reading originated in her status as a solitary only child: "She, having neither brother nor sister, nor other companion of her age, spent her whole time in reading, to which she gave herself so much that she frequently read all night" (Simpson 1861, 6). It is through her reading that Cary seems to learn to challenge authority. When her mother forbids her servants "to let her have candles" for reading, for example, she bribes them to disobey, although the biography represents this as the failing of servants who "let themselves be hired by her" rather than as a sign of rebellion in Cary (6). It is her reading, too, which gives her access to alternative sources of authority. She is described as self-taught; far from claiming that Cary acquired her learning as a pupil of good masters (as John Davies implies in his dedicatory poem), the biographer specifies that it is not (male) tutors but books that provide her with knowledge. In the biography, reading lays the foundation for her later conversion: "When she was twelve years old her father gave her 'Calvin's Institutions,' and bid her read it; against which she made so many objections, and found in him so many contradictions, and with all of them she still went to her father, that he said, 'This girl hath a spirit averse from Calvin'" (7).

While the narrative is concerned to point to her respect for her father's authority, it also demonstrates that the written word offers itself for independent analysis. The biography implicitly draws attention to Cary's likeness to her father here; her analytical mind assesses the evidence of Calvin's argument as a lawyer assesses a case history. This likeness is made more overt in the story of the old woman who is brought to her father as a witch. While the old woman confesses freely, the 10-year-old Cary observes her fear and prompts her father to ask if the woman had killed one John Symondes (Cary's own uncle, present in the room). When the woman confesses to this "crime" as well, the case collapses and she is acquitted. The story characterizes Cary not only as a precocious wit, but also as a rational thinker with a sound legalistic judgement who can outdo men in authority. That characterization later reappears in her debates with (Protestant) religious authorities such as the Bishop of Durham, the Archbishop of York, and the royal chaplain Dr. Cozens.

The representation of Cary's learning and analytical mind help the biography to affirm the soundness of her conversion, a conversion grounded in wide reading, careful thought, and conscientious debate, and not, as her furious husband interpreted it in a letter to King Charles, a bewitchment or "leprous infection" or a sign of the weakness of the female spirit: "Haply when she shall no more hear the charms of these enchanters, she may recover out of these distractions whereinto they have put her, it being a principal way of theirs first to make apprehensive spirits mad with despair."[10]

Elizabeth Cary was married to Sir Henry Cary in 1602; her fortune promoted her husband's career in the Jacobean court, and her marriage raised her own status in the social hierarchy. Thanks to her jointure, her husband, newly made Viscount Falkland, was able to take up the position of Lord Deputy of Ireland in 1622. The biography renders the mortgaging of her jointure as a sign of her obedience and willed submission as a wife. "[Henry Cary] was very absolute; and though she had a strong will, she had learned to make it obey his. . . . Where his interest was concerned, she seemed not able to have any consideration of her own, which, amongst other things, she showed in this: a considerable part of her jointure . . . she did on his occasions consent to have mortgaged; which act of hers did so displease her own father, that he disinherited her upon it" (Simpson, 14–16). The authorities of husband and father clearly come into conflict here, so that her action can be interpreted both as rebellious folly and as heroic obedience. Cary makes much of this action herself in her later letters of petition to Secretary Coke and to King Charles, where it becomes both a sign of her obedience and a muted critique of her husband's refusal to provide her with financial support after her conversion. In the biography, the mortgage of her jointure comes as the culminating proof of Cary's willed obedience. Her housekeeping, her care in dress, and her horse riding are all marked out as activities pursued only because of her "desire to please [her husband]." Yet even here, there is an implied judgment of Sir Henry's arbitrary will:

the biography tells, for example, of how Cary was no longer expected to ride after she had a dangerous fall from her horse "leaping a hedge and ditch, being with child of her fourth child, when she was taken up for dead" (Simpson 1861, 14).[11] The biographer, then, repeatedly draws attention to Cary's superior intellect and learning on the one hand and, on the other, to her willed obedience to figures of authority: "she seemed to prefer nothing but religion and her duty to God before [her husband's] will" (16). The strict principles she holds, reminiscent of Vives's *Instruction of a Christen Woman*, make conscience itself a fault if not accompanied by a clear reputation: the text inscribed in her daughter's wedding ring, "Be and seem," is interpreted as the conjunction of a conscience "free from fault" and behavior without "the least show or suspicion of uncomeliness or unfitness" (16), a perfect mirroring of inner and outer self in which "seeming" is never duplicitous. Once Cary converts to Catholicism in 1626, however, it is the strict "rules" she professes that allow for resistance and provide justification for her actions, even as her husband and her own mother accuse her of wilfulness. The "rule" that Elizabeth Cary gives her eldest daughter on her marriage to Lord Home encapsulates this potentially resistant submission: "wheresoever conscience and reason would permit her, she should prefer the will of another before her own" (13). Conscience and reason, the attributes Henry Cary denies her in his representation of her "apostasy," are attributes that are heavily emphasized in her biography.

The biography blames the public nature of Cary's conversion on a betrayal by her friend Lady Denbigh, evading the question of how Cary would have been able to maintain her principle to "be and seem" if her conversion had been kept secret. Henry Cary, still in Catholic Ireland and embarrassed politically at a time when the husbands of recusant women were constrained from holding public office, responded furiously. He demanded her confinement, had the children removed from her care, and refused to provide her with means to support herself even after the Privy Council ordered payment to be made. Both the biography and Cary's own letters emphasize her poverty and need over several years; her lack of servants, food, furnishings, and appropriate accommodation reduced her to begging from friends. Yet, throughout this ordeal, she refused to recant or to live with her mother on Sir Henry's orders, arguing that she had "committed no fault" and demanding the legal "freedom of a subject."[12] Sir Henry was recalled from Ireland in 1629, and a formal reconciliation was effected by Charles's Catholic queen in 1631. Cary continued to live separately from her husband, however, and after his accidental death in 1633, the biography focuses on her role in the conversion of several of her children. In yet another provocative act, she arranged the abduction of two of her sons to send them to France for a Catholic education. By the time she died in 1639, four of her daughters had converted and become nuns in France.

## "Fumish words": *The Tragedie of Mariam*

*The Tragedie of Mariam*, published in 1613, was probably written in 1605 and 1606, during the absence of Cary's husband early in her marriage. A Senecan drama strictly adhering to classical models, *Mariam* draws its story from Thomas Lodge's translation of a Jewish history by Josephus.[13] Cary's play is the first of a number of English dramas based on the love of Herod and Mariam, but it is the only play to present the story from Mariam's point of view rather than Herod's.[14] Altering and developing the scant details of her source, Cary turns Mariam into a complex character whose principled stance against her tyrannous and all-too-loving husband results in her death. The play focuses on the role of the wife, its female characters arranged around Mariam in a schematic exploration not of womanhood per se but of wifehood.[15] Working by contrast and comparison, by juxtaposition of character and attitude, the play presents a complex "case history" for judgment. The Chorus says much in criticism of Mariam's behavior, and has sometimes been read as the authoritative voice of the play. Yet, as several critics have pointed out, the play as a whole undermines the conventional and often contradictory judgments that the Chorus makes.[16] It is as if the analytical and legalistic mind emphasized in Cary's biography is again at work here, observing and assessing conflicting positions and expectations, and in the process exposing contradictions in gender ideology.

The dedicatory poem prefaced to *Mariam* and addressed to Cary's sister-in-law and friend bears no suggestion that Cary's play will challenge patriarchal ideology. Locating her work firmly within the context of the family, Cary differentiates husband and sister-in-law by means of a conventional dichotomy of active and passive virtue—a dichotomy that privileges the masculine. She also affirms the proper priority of her husband, to whom she "consecrated" (l. 17) her first play, set in Sicily. The analogies that the poem draws between brother/husband and sun, sister/friend and moon, conform to appropriately hierarchical gender relations. The sister is described as Cary's "next belov'd, my second Friend . . . my second Light" (ll. 9–12); her "fainter beams" (l. 2) are marked for their feminine chastity. Cary's writing is itself almost erased in the poem; the "consecration" of her work represents her offering as an act of worship removed from the material world and from any suggestion of a search for fame.

Yet, while the speaker of the dedicatory poem enacts the role of the properly submissive wife, *Mariam* presents a wife and queen resisting her husband, a king acknowledged as a tyrant and usurper. The argument of the play (sigs. A2–A2v) emphasizes that Herod has supplanted the "rightfull King" Hircanus with Roman support. His marriage to Mariam, Hircanus's granddaughter, is both a political and a personal move, associated with her "high blood" and "singular beautie"; to secure his title to the throne, he murders her grandfather and her brother, reaffirming his kingship "in his Wives right." Mariam, then, is identified as queen of Judea by birth as well as by marriage, and the play uses her royal blood to emphasize the conflict between the subject positions she occupies as wife and queen. Yet her status as wife is further complicated by Cary. Herod does not merely favor Mariam among his many wives, as he does in Josephus; instead, he is turned anachronistically into a husband who has divorced his first wife to marry Mariam. The divorce cannot be justified by impotence (an accepted Renaissance loophole), since we are told "hee reputiated Doris, his former Wife, by whome hee had Children" (sig. A2).[17] Doris, mentioned only briefly in Josephus long after Mariam's death, appears in Cary's play to lament her fortunes, play the good mother in her attempt to reinstate her son as heir, and accuse Mariam of adultery.

The play is structured around a single day, telescoping the chronology of Josephus and conflating separate events of the history. Rumors of Herod's death in Rome prompt a variety of responses in the first half of the play, and his pivotal and unexpected return in Act III leads to a related series of consequences in the final acts. Mariam, already angered by Herod's murder of her kinsmen, is provoked further by the revelation that Herod has ordered that she also be killed, in the event of his own death. Her anger leads to her outspoken rejection of Herod's love and bed, which prompts him to assume sexual transgression on her part, for which he has her beheaded. The play, however, repeatedly emphasizes that Mariam's resistance and her public speech are *not* to be identified with sexual transgression. In her opening soliloquy, she acknowledges that she may have learned to "leave his Love" as a consequence of Herod's jealousy and his "barring me from libertie," but she insists on her chastity: "too chast a Scholler was my hart, / To learne to love another then my

Lord" (ll. 27–31). Unhistorically, she rebukes her mother Alexandra in Act I, scene ii, for attempting to seduce Antony with her portrait: "Not to be Emprise of aspiring Rome, / Would Mariam like to Cleopatra live: / With purest body will I presse my Toome" (ll. 204–6). Josephus, on the other hand, reports that when Herod was being accused by Antony in Laodicea, the "Ladies" (Alexandra and Mariam) "hoped that if Anthony should see Mariamme, she might obtaine all things at his hands whatsoever she desired, assuring [Joseph] that he would restore the kingdome unto her" (15:4, 387). As Gwynne Kennedy argues, the text struggles toward "a definition of wifedom that allows for a woman's voiced dissent within the confines of marital obedience" (1989, 153); but its attempt to dissociate chastity and silence comes up against the force of patriarchal ideology, which offers women no discursive middle ground in which they can convey difference as alternative rather than opposition.[18] Mariam herself capitulates to this ideology when she blames herself for her death:

> Had I but with humilitie bene grac'te,
>
> As well as faire I might have prov'd me wise:
>
> But I did thinke because I knew me chaste,
>
> One vertue for a woman, might suffice. (ll. 1833–36)

It is not in Mariam's own conclusions and death that the play's struggle to make a place for women as speaking subjects can be seen, but rather in the juxtapositions, contrasts, and disjunctions that structure the text.

The play opens with a moral dilemma, which is expressed by Mariam as a conflict of emotions. The dilemma is located in Mariam's conflicted subject positions: as wife and widow, she should mourn the death of the husband who loved her; as sister and granddaughter, she should rejoice at the death of the man who murdered her kinsmen. Comparing herself not with a woman but with a powerful man, the Julius Caesar who both desired Pompey's death and wept at it, she rejects her own public critique of Caesar as "too rash a judgement in a woman" (l. 6). Now she recognizes that internal conflict may produce the same external signs as hypocrisy: "Now doe I finde by selfe Experience taught, / One Object yeelds both griefe and joy" (ll. 11–12). At the same time, she insists that love and freedom are related. Herod, "by barring me from libertie" (l. 27), changed her love to "Rage and Scorne" (l. 21). Now his death frees her once again, and the love she felt "When virgin freedome left me unrestraind" (l. 74) returns to struggle with her anger.

Mariam's dilemma is reinforced in the two following scenes, in which first her mother Alexandra rebukes her for her lack of familial feeling and then Herod's sister Salome accuses her of a lack of wifely feeling. Alexandra and Salome rail at her at length, and yet when Mariam speaks up to defend herself from Salome's slur on her birth, she is immediately condemned by Salome for her "fumish words" (l. 237): "Now stirs the tongue that is so quickly mov'd" (l. 235). Since Salome also accuses her of infidelity and desire for a change of husband, both charges that are disproved in the play, this accusation of rash speech itself becomes suspect, particularly when Salome reveals her own infidelity in the following three scenes of Act I. Salome, left alone, admits that her own reputation is tarnished, shame "written on my tainted brow" (l. 293); she reveals that her love for her husband (like Mariam's love) has turned to hatred, but her change (unlike Mariam's) is not due to her husband's tyrannous actions but rather to her new passion for the Arabian Silleus. Her "will" guides her to transgress the laws and conventions of her society, to become a "custome-breaker" (l. 319) in attempting to divorce her husband. Her adulterous desire leads her to challenge the foundations of patriarchal privilege. Unlike Mariam, she makes no attempt to conform to ideals of moral or feminine behavior, and the play retreats from her radical rebellion when her husband Constabarus accuses her not of custom breaking (with its dangerous exposure of laws as man-made and arbitrary conventions) but of upsetting the laws of nature, with their "natural" gender hierarchy:

Are Hebrew women now transformed to men?

Why do you not as well our battels fight,

And weare our armour? suffer this, and then

Let all the world be topsie turved quite.

Let fishes graze, beastes, swine, and birds descend. (ll. 435–39)

At the end of Act I, Constabarus predicts the future for Mariam in the event of Herod's return: "The sweet fac'd Mariam as free from guilt / As Heaven from spots, yet had her Lord come backe / Her purest blood had been unjustly spilt" (ll. 501–3). The Chorus that follows offers a different verdict. Declaiming against "wavering" minds (l. 513) that "wholy dote upon delight" (l. 508), it sententiously asserts that "To wish varietie is signe of griefe" (l. 526). Juxtaposed against three scenes that have described Salome's infidelity and desire, the Chorus seems to be judging her actions; yet in the fifth stanza, the Chorus surprisingly announces that it is judging Mariam:

> Still Mariam wisht she from her Lord were free,
>
> For expectation of varietie:
>
> Yet now she sees her wishes prosperous bee,
>
> She grieves, because her Lord so soone did die.
>
> Who can those vast imaginations feede,
>
> Where in a propertie, contempt doth breede? (ll. 532–37)

The disjunction between action and judgment, in which the Chorus echoes Salome's falsified accusation that "Mariam hopes to have another King" (l. 214), radically disturbs the apparent authority of the Chorus. Like the Senecan Chorus, it offers a limited perspective, to be assessed and challenged in accordance with the "evidence" of the play's action. The disjunction helps to put in relief the terms that the Chorus uses: Is Mariam simply to be understood as a "propertie" of Herod, despite her royal blood and her right as queen? More importantly, is the "wife" simply a "propertie" of her husband, with no rights of her own? Is she merely a cipher like Graphina, the maidservant bride of Herod's brother Pheroras, who appears in the following scene? Graphina, a character (like Doris) largely invented by Cary, is the exemplary wife of the conduct books—chaste, silent, and obedient. She speaks only when she is asked to do so and says only what she is expected to say:

> You know my wishes ever yours did meete:
>
> If I be silent, tis no more but feare
>
> That I should say too little when I speake:
>
> But since you will my imperfections beare,
>
> In spight of doubt I will my silence breake. (ll. 593–97)

As maidservant turned wife, she is quite literally her husband's humble handmaid. Margaret Ferguson has argued that the name Graphina "plays on the Greek word for writing, *graphesis*," so that the character comes to figure "a mode of 'safe' speech, *private* speech that neither aims at nor produces offense" (in Howe 1991, 47). Her name may also suggest a connotation more rebellious in its implications: Graphina is the woman as written by men, the ideal wife of the conduct books, a blank space to be filled in by (male) ideas of femininity.

The ideal wife is presented most forcefully by the Chorus of Act III. Following hard upon Mariam's announcement to Sohemus that she is resolved on Herod's return to forswear his bed and that she refuses to "inchaine him with a smile" that is hypocritically at odds with her thought (l. 1166), the Chorus concludes that a wife should give both body and mind to her husband. The verses acknowledge her "power" but recommend strict self-restraint in the cause of honor: "But tis thanke-worthy, if she will not take / All lawfull liberties for honours sake" (ll. 1229–30). The "lawfull liberty" that the Chorus is most concerned with is the liberty of speech, for the third and fourth stanzas insist that a wife's honor and glory is wounded ("though most chast," l. 1235) if she speaks "A private word to any second eare" beyond that of her husband (l. 1233). The Chorus asserts that the wife, as "propertie" of her husband, has not even the rights of the humanist subject: "No sure, their thoughts no more can be their owne" (l. 1241). The fifth stanza goes on to elide the distinction between private and public speech, transforming her "private word to any second eare" (l. 1233) into the prostitution of a woman's public speech:

> Then she usurpes upon anothers right,
> That seekes to be by publike language grac't:
> And though her thoughts reflect with purest light,
> Her mind if not peculiar is not chast.
> For in a wife it is no worse to finde,
> A common body, then a common minde. (ll. 1243–48)

For the Chorus, the only form of truly "private" speech for a wife is speech confined to her husband's ears alone—the "safe" speech that Graphina has exemplified. Yet, as Ferguson has pointed out, the Chorus's conclusions are undermined by the action that follows; "it is precisely because Mariam speaks her mind—not only to others but also, and above all, to her husband—that she loses her life. . . . The problem is that she *both* speaks too freely *and* refuses to give her body to Herod— its rightful owner, according to the chorus. She censors the wrong thing: his phallus rather than her tongue" (in Howe 1991, 52).

The disjunction between Chorus and action again suggests that this representation of the ideal wife is not simply authoritative but is available in its very extremism for questioning. It is notable that, like the topical intrusion of the subject of divorce (a subject that was much in debate at the turn of the century), the notion of the husband's legal right to a woman's body and mind was itself being contested in the period.[19] An Elizabethan edict of 1597, for example, denied that a woman was the legal property of a man, thus "render[ing] the female body legally a woman's inalienable property."[20] At moments, too, the very vocabulary that the Chorus uses undermines its conclusions. To be a woman and to be "by publike language grac't" (l. 1244) is, for example, a contradiction in terms which suggests a muted challenge to the Chorus's attitude to female speech. The previous scene, moreover, highlights the unequal distribution of discursive rights when it posits Sohemus's free speech as the sign of the honest unflattering plainness of the good counselor, and at the same time defines Mariam's refusal to affect "gentle words" (l. 1166) as "Unbridled speech" (l. 1187). Sohemus tells Mariam:

> If your command should me to silence drive,
>
> It were not to obey, but to betray.
>
> Reject, and slight my speeches, mocke my faith,
>
> Scorne my observance, call my counsell nought:
>
> Though you regard not what Sohemus saith,
>
> Yet will I ever freely speake my thought. (ll. 1144–49)

His advice is, ironically, to refrain from such free speech, which will "indanger her without desart" (l. 1187). Confronted by the power of Herod's patriarchal "breath," of course, both honest servant and honest wife will be condemned for their free speaking.

Mariam's speech to her husband in Act IV, scene iii, clearly threatens the prerogative of king, husband, and man. "I will not speake", Herod insists, "unles to be beleev'd" (l. 1401). In the face of her refusal to be interpolated into the role of courtly mistress which names her as his "Commandres" and "Soveraigne guide" (l. 1361) without allowing her the effective agency of the autonomous subject, Herod can only name her as unruly woman and whore.[21] Her dissent is branded as "froward humor" (l. 1402), "peevishness" (l. 1411), and finally the falsehood of a "painted Divill" and "white Inchantres" (ll. 1439–40). Yet his immediate association of verbal with sexual transgression is not supported by the play, which shows rather "that Mariam's verbal openness is a sign of sexual closure"; as Ferguson argues, Mariam's behavior "entails a 'property' crime in certain ways more threatening than adultery is to the ideological conception of marriage because it takes to a logical extreme, and deploys against the husband, the concept of female chastity" (in Howe 1991, 53).[22] Mariam's subsequent beheading can be read as a final attempt by Herod to break up the threatening integrity of body and mind that closes off proprietorial control of both. Her death, however, instead of renewing Herod's control, only serves to deny him the last vestiges of access, as he incoherently demands to hear her words and see her alive again in his presence. In addition, the play, as Beilin has noted, transforms her death into an allegory of the Crucifixion: it unhistorically invents the suicide of the Judas-like butler and alludes to the Resurrection, describing Mariam as a phoenix and making her last words a suggestion that Herod would wish her alive again "By three daies hence" (l. 2019). In one more disjunction, the disobedient wife, who in the Chorus's view left the "due" of love for her husband "unpaide" (l. 1934), becomes a martyr prefiguring Christ and foreshadowing "redemption from the old law, typified by Herod's kingdom" (Beilin 1987, 171).

It is in disjunctions such as these that the play's more radical interrogation of Renaissance gender ideology resides. Through the conflicting and often contradictory positions that render no single voice authoritative and demand to be analytically weighed and assessed, Cary's uneasy struggle to find a place for the speaking (and writing) subject who happens also to be a woman and a wife is visible. Mariam's tragedy indicates the difficulty of that task in a society heavily (and tyrannously) patriarchal.

## Revising Infidelity: *Edward II*

The history of *Edward II*, completed early in 1628 (1627 old style) and concerned as it is with a King whose reign was often compared to that of James I, is a text that critiques the abuses of power in both state and family in a potentially dangerous way. The text remained unpublished until 1680, when the Exclusion crisis made it again highly topical in its critique, and two quite distinct editions were then printed. Neither edition explicitly identifies the author as Elizabeth Cary. The title page of the longer (folio) edition, published by Charles Harper, Samuel Crouch, and Thomas Fox as *The History of the Life, Reign and Death of Edward II*, announces that the history was "Written by E. F. in the year 1627, And Printed verbatim from the Original." The title page of the shorter (octavo) edition, published by John Playford as *The History of the most unfortunate Prince King Edward II*, identifies the origins of the text, and makes a tentative claim for its authorship: "Found among the Papers of, and (supposed to be) Writ by the Right Honourable Henry Viscount Faulkland."[23] Since 1935, when Donald Stauffer first suggested that Elizabeth Cary was most likely to be the E. F. (Elizabeth Lady Falkland) identified by the folio edition, the case for her authorship has been augmented by Isobel Grundy and Barbara Lewalski.[24] A variety of external evidence provides support for the identification of Cary and "E. F." Cary's biographer asserts her knowledge of history and poetry; *Mariam* demonstrates her ability to write drama developed from a historical source; another manuscript clearly identified as her own work was also found among Henry Cary's papers; the prefatory remarks of both *Edward II* and the translation of Cardinal Perron's *Reply* claim that the author had completed the texts in only a month; and the circumstances of her own life in 1627–28 agree with the author's prefatory remarks in the folio edition (dated 20 February 1627/28) on her "melancholy Pen" and its attempt to "out-run those weary hours of a deep and sad Passion."[25] The nature of the text itself, its protodramatic form, its concerns with the limits of patriarchal power, and its unusual emphasis on the plight and actions of a troubled wife and queen add internal support to Cary's claim.

The folio *Life*—"Printed verbatim," its publisher asserts, along with its "obsolete words" and "Masculine . . . Stile"—is a hybrid of prose and blank verse, despite its typographical presentation as prose. The text includes more than 20 speeches at key moments in the history, all written in blank verse, and many of the more dramatic passages of narrative and philosophical commentary fall into verse, although in the printed text they merge indistinguishably with the surrounding prose text. The octavo *History*, on the other hand, is much shorter; it includes few of the speeches, and is written entirely in prose. The edition, which appears to be an abridgment made in 1680, concentrates mainly on producing a bare narrative in plain style with little of the folio's rhetorical ornament or its political, moral, and philosophical commentary, and with even less concern for the dramatic development of psychological motivation and emotional depth. Thus, for example, the octavo's brief rendering of a comment early in the text on the promising looks of the youthful Edward replaces the metaphorical elaboration of the folio. The folio amplifies its point: "But the judgment, not the eye, must have the preheminence in point of Calculation and Censure. The smoothest waters are for the most part most deep and dangerous; and the goodliest Blossoms nipt by an unkindly Frost, wither, or produce their fruit sowre or unwholsome: which may properly imply, That the visible Calendar is not the true Character of inward perfection; evidently proved in the Life, Raign, and Death of this unfortunate Monarch" (*Life*, 1–2). The octavo retains the main point while cutting the amplification and clarifying the context: "But the judgment, not the eye, must have preheminence in the Censure of human Passages. The visible Calendar is not the true Character of inward perfection; evidently proved in the Life, Raign, and untimely Death of this unfortunate Monarch" (*History*, 1). In the instances in which the octavo edition retains the folio's speeches, they are rendered as prose. In Queen Isabel's speech to her brother the King of France, for example (the first of such speeches to appear in both texts), the italicized prose of the folio falls into blank verse:

> My burthen is grown greater than my patience:
>
> Yet 'tis not I alone unjustly suffer;
>
> My tears speak those of a distressed Kingdom,
>
> Which, long time glorious, now is almost ruin'd. (*Life*, 96; my lineation)

The octavo version makes the style consistent with the whole: "my Burthen is grown too heavy for my long abused Patience. Yet 'tis not I alone, but a whole Kingdom, heretofore truly glorious, that are [sic] thus unjustly wronged" (*History*, 41).

The folio text, with its emergent verse and its dramatic speeches, has much in common with Anne Dowriche's verse history, with its invented orations "fully & amply expressed" and "lively set downe" to illustrate the narrative. Cary, like Dowriche, lays claim to the authority of her sources while drawing attention to her own lively writing when she points out in the preface to the *Life* that "I have not herein followed the dull Character of our Historians, nor amplified more than they infer, by Circumstance. I strive to please the Truth, not Time." Her "truth" is closer to the "truthfulness" of Philip Sidney's poet, who is superior to the historian in paying attention to the "universal consideration" rather than to the "particular": "the historian, bound to tell things as things were, cannot be liberal (without he be poetical) of a perfect pattern. . . . Many times he must tell events whereof he can yield no cause; or, if he do, it must be poetically" (*Defence*, 36). Cary's history of *Edward II* is the product of a poetical historian. It also participates in the fashion for "politic history" modeled on Tacitus, which was popular in the early 17th century, a genre whose fashion, as F. J. Levy has argued, was prepared for by poets and playwrights. Levy, who includes *Edward II* in his account of politic history, defines the genre by its laconic and epigrammatic style, its focused subject matter, and its inclusion of fictitious explanatory speeches that construct human causes for otherwise inexplicable events.[26] He also suggests the risky nature of such historiography: with its practical politics, its didactic purpose, and its association with Machiavellianism, it offered a potentially challenging analysis of the processes of power (Levy 1967, 250–52). *Edward II* is no exception: strongly critical of the king's judgments and actions, particularly in relation to his unaristocratic and homosexual favorites, who abuse the privileges and power that his patronage (and desire) bestows, it repeatedly asserts the rights of the subject to reform the state, although it draws back from supporting a rebellion that intends to replace the monarch.

Much of the early part of the history, when the king is enamoured with Gaveston, debates the nature of kingship and, as *Mariam* does, the limits of obedience. The king himself and his flattering courtiers are, for example, given speeches that assert the royal prerogative and absolute power. "Are you a King (Great Sir)," asks an invented Page, "and yet a Subject? . . . Who dares oppose, if you command Obedience?" Yet the aristocratic barons remind the king that where the "Royal Ear is so guided" by "Parasitical Minions," the result can be only the "Subversion of all Law and Goodness" (*Life*, 9–10), and it is their duty "to guard the King's Life and Honour," even by taking up arms to reform the state. Like Cary's advice to her daughter, in which obedience and self-erasure are qualified by the potential opposition of "reason and conscience," the Earl of Lincoln tells the barons in a deathbed speech that Edward is "your Sovereign, you must so obey him, unless the Cause be just enforc'd your moving. . . . The Kingdom's good must give your Arms their warrant" (*Life*, 34). In an echo of parliamentary debates about Stuart absolutism that culminated in a scandal over forced loans in 1627 and in the 1628 *Petition of Right*,[27] the narrator asserts the proper limitations on the king's power and the mutual obligations of king and subject: "The power Majestick is or should be bounded; and there is a reciprocal correspondence, which gives the King the obedience, the subject equal right and perfect justice, by which they claim a property in his actions" (*Life*, 68). Like Mariam, who refuses to act in accordance with the Chorus's absolutist assumptions that a wife is the "propertie" of her husband, the narrator rejects the notion that a subject is merely the "propertie" of the King.

The second half of *Edward II*, making use of a variety of historical and literary sources from Grafton's chronicle history to Marlowe's tragedy, develops the character of Edward's queen.[28] The text makes Isabel central to the action associated with the king's second favorite, Hugh Spencer, with the rebellion, and with the subsequent deposition of Edward. As Gwynne Kennedy has asserted, it is the striking representation of Queen Isabel that distinguishes Cary's history from male-authored historiography, in which Isabel appears as "a marginalized figure whose actions are recorded only when they impinge on patriarchal concerns" (1989; 33). Cary, Kennedy argues, "places the Queen back into history, but her presence in the text finally forces Cary to banish her 'to the margent.' There, Isabel becomes a commentary on Cary's history and on women's position in masculine historiography" (33–34). The octavo version, moreover, regularly compresses or cuts the commentary and action associated with Isabel. Thus, for example, where the folio version makes Edward's virtuous father "confident that *Wedlock*, or the sad weight of a Crown," would transform his son to "thoughts more innocent and noble" (*Life*, 3), the octavo text has him imagining *"Age*, and the sad burthen of a Kingdom" would work the transformation (*History*, 3; emphasis mine). Similarly, it cuts Spencer's political courtship of the queen in order to secure his position at court (*Life*, 52), cuts the later description of the dramatic antagonism between Spencer and Isabel (*Life*, 86), and cuts the narrator's commentary on "the female wit that went beyond" Spencer's craft (*Life*, 91–92). At the same time, the octavo text retains and emphasizes the gendered critique of the queen's behavior present in the folio. Both texts describe Spencer's undermining of Isabel's embassy to the king of France, in which he argues that "a woman's passion was to weak a motive to levie Arms" (*Life*, 100). Her cruel punishment of Spencer, which the folio calls "a kinde of insulting Tyranny, far short of the belief of her former *Vertue and Goodness*" (*Life*, 128), is criticized in more specifically gendered terms in the octavo text as "far unworthy the Nobility of her *Sex and Virtue*" (*History*, 59; emphasis mine). Such changes in the octavo *History* suggest its return to the traditions of masculine historiography.

The folio's critique of Isabel's cruelty to Spencer is characteristic of the text's refusal to mark a separation of feminine and masculine spheres of activity by aligning them with the private domestic realm of the family and the public realm of politics and the state. Isabel is criticized here for her cruelty in terms of Christian piety and generalized virtue; elsewhere she is described as a cunning politician and a courageous leader without recourse to statements implying that she is an "exceptional" woman beyond her sex. The narrator makes much of her "female wit" outwitting Spencer, but while this is marked as unusual ("Thus Womens Wit sometimes can cozen Statesmen," *Life*, 109), it is causally related not to any characteristics of heroic womanhood in Isabel but rather to her circumstances, "not rightly valued" by her husband and king, and displaced from her roles in family and kingdom by a Machiavellian manipulator. As long as Isabel's actions remain aimed at reform of Edward and not dominion, the text supports her as it supports the barons. Her agency is made quite explicit: she challenges Edward's actions not as Mortimer's mistress or dependent but as his rightful partner and as the queen of England, who speaks not only for herself but for her "distressed Kingdom" and claims the "Justice of my Cause" (*Life*, 97). The text refuses to associate what it represents as the justifiable "Infidelity" of wife and queen with sexual infidelity, just as *Mariam* refuses to associate verbal with sexual transgression. The exchange of amorous letters between Isabel and Mortimer is noted while he is in prison, but the text leaves the reports of their adulterous liaisons open to question and maintains Mortimer's absence from the text until the concluding scenes after Edward has been overthrown. At this point the narrator's attitude to Isabel's action changes; as reform is replaced by overt rebellion, Isabel is increasingly associated with the giddy multitude and their irrational cruelty, and for the first time she is represented as ambitious. When the king is seized, the queen "having thus attained to the full her desire, resolves to use it to the best advantage," but this "advantage" is no longer a matter of the public good: "Ambition seis'd her strongly, yet resigneth to her incensed Passion the precedence" (*Life*, 127–28). Even here, neither the queen's desire nor her ambitious actions are associated with an adulterous liaison with Mortimer. It is only sometime after the narrator concludes that the king lost his kingdom "partly by his own Disorder and Improvidence, but principally by the treacherous Infidelity of his Wife, Servants, and Subjects" (*Life*, 137) that the queen and Mortimer are mentioned as joint regents during the minority of the prince. "Infidelity," in the context, is shorn of its sexual connotations. Wife, servants, and subjects share the same political crime.[29] The text never includes any moral commentary that makes adultery a microcosm of or incitement to political crime. Instead, it concludes that Isabel was "guilty but in circumstance, and but an accessory to the Intention, not the Fact" of Edward's murder (*Life*, 155). As elsewhere in the text, "Intention"—the human motivation and cause that historical narratives so often lack—is made the guide for interpretation and judgment. Cary's *Edward II*, through its "poetical" rendering of history, develops Isabel's

"Intention" as wife, queen, and subject in a way that challenges both the masculine tradition of historiography and the relegation of women to the private domain.

In these two extant literary texts, one a dramatic history, the other a historical drama, the concerns of Cary's own life, as dramatized in the biography, are repeated. Conflicts between conformity and challenge to authority, between submission to the role of the good wife and subject on the one hand and justifiable self-assertion on the other, mark all three texts. That her "owne rich inventions" (referred to by the anonymous writer of a commendatory verse in Cary's translation of Perron's *Reply*) remained either in manuscript (now largely lost) or publicly unacknowledged (as *Mariam* was) testifies to the difficulty of a woman writer's attempt to be "by publike language grac't."

## Chapter Seven

# "To beg their fees": The Emergence of the Professional Woman Writer[1]

The ambivalence of John Davies's address to Elizabeth Cary, Mary Sidney, and Lucy Russell when he rebukes them for "press[ing] the Presse with little you have made" is a reminder of the stigma of print, which operated as a constraint on the publication of women's writing. Both Elizabeth Cary and Mary Sidney were prolific writers, but much of their work clearly remained in manuscript, circulating among family, friends, or a select coterie in a context that promoted literary exchange as a form of aristocratic display and denigrated the commodification of the published text. For male writers of lesser rank, publication offered an avenue for social advancement and financial gain. Humanist claims for learning and eloquence as necessary attributes of the statesman and ruling classes proffered education as a means to social advancement. Social mobility depended on the display of learning, and publication, despite the stigma of print, offered a wider audience to the aspiring male writer.[2]

Women, however, could make no such claims to the public sphere through a display of learning. If writing for a public audience could be interpreted as unchaste, then writing for financial gain could be read as a form of prostitution. The class-conscious stigma of print was complicated further by gender. In this context, it is not surprising that there are no women writers in the Renaissance who openly claim to be writing for money, as Thomas Nashe did.[3] Nevertheless, a small number of women do seem to be working toward a sense of themselves as "professional" writers addressing a particularized (and paying) readership. In this chapter, I look at the work of two women of the lesser gentry, Isabella Whitney and Mary Fage, along with the calligraphy of Esther Inglis, to explore the emergence of the professional woman writer in Renaissance England.[4]

What does it mean to be a professional writer, or, more specifically, a professional poet, in the Renaissance? Richard Helgerson has argued that a new configuration of "author-functions" was emerging in the late 16th century, a system of authorial roles that provided a paradigm for self-definition.[5] The poet ambitious to acquire "laureate" status, he suggests, had to construct an authorial identity by negotiating a position within and against two other available roles, the amateur and the professional. The literary system that Helgerson outlines is essentially a system of male authorial roles. There is no place for the woman writer, for example, in his Elizabethan paradigm of prodigal sons and humble professionals. The amateur as prodigal son, a rebellious youth temporarily escaping his public duties, cannot be translated into prodigal daughter: the woman writer has no future of humanist public engagement to avoid. Similarly, the anonymity of the Elizabethan professional, a man who makes it his humble profession to entertain a paying audience, cannot serve to define the professional woman writer, since self-effacement and humility are characteristically "feminine" traits. How, then, was a woman to negotiate a role as a professional writer? It seems to me that Whitney and Fage, like Helgerson's "laureates," are actively engaged in negotiating positions for themselves as professionals—positions marked by distinctive combinations of self-effacement and self-aggrandizement.

## The "matchles Mistresse of the golden Pen": Esther Inglis

I want to frame my discussion of the work of Whitney and Fage by first describing the work of a third writer, a calligrapher called Esther Inglis. Inglis was both expert and prolific: to date, 55 manuscripts written between 1586 and 1624 have been identified as her work.[6] Her calligraphy has recently been discussed by Jonathan Goldberg in his book *Writing Matter*. He points out that while humanists claimed that the extension of literacy would maintain social hierarchy and support the status quo, they simultaneously displayed anxiety that such an extension would "put power in anyone's hand," an anxiety expressed most clearly in relation to women (1990, 145–46). Goldberg argues that Inglis and her woman's hand exemplify the possibilities and register the contradictions in that humanist discourse of writing. I would suggest further that her work illustrates the strategies of the woman who writes for money.

Inglis's manuscripts are primarily copies and translations of biblical and moral texts; she adheres to the pious reading material recommended for women by educationalists.[7] By means of such conformity, she can subordinate her writing to her material and justify her activity in terms of the usefulness of her copytext. Her choice of copytext imitates the strategy of women translators and helps to define her own appropriately feminine identity. It also enables her to represent her manuscripts as the matter for private meditation rather than public circulation; in her dedications, she repeatedly suggests that her work belongs to the enclosed and solitary space. In her dedication to Prince Charles in 1624, for example, she wishes "that her handiwork might find 'sum retired place' in your Highnesse Cabinet.'"[8]

The volume of her work, however, and the extensive list of royal and aristocratic patrons to whom she addresses her dedications bespeak a less retiring position. Inglis's early dedications seem to operate in a traditional patronage system, supporting her husband's activities as Clerk of all Passports and seeking or confirming bonds with individuals who can offer him social advancement.[9] Increasingly, though, her manuscripts are presented in her own name, without the addition of verses by her father or her husband, and are dedicated to individuals who are acknowledged as strangers. Gifts to such dignitaries as Christian Friis, Chancellor of Denmark, who was reknowned for his generosity, indicate an opportunism that expects and depends on financial reward. It seems that in some cases at least she was rewarded handsomely for her work: Prince Henry's accounts record two payments made to her, the first of £5 in 1609 ("for geving a booke of armes to his highnes") and the second of £22 made to her in 1612 (Scott-Elliott and Yeo 1990, 14, 68). Inglis's ability as a calligrapher, combined with her work as a scribe for her husband, appears to have provided her with a sense of writing as marketable work.[10]

In her dedications, Inglis shows a remarkable mixture of self-effacement and self-aggrandizement. As Goldberg suggests, she "insist[s] on the impropriety of the circulation of the woman's hand" (1990, 147). Repeatedly she excuses her boldness, a "hardiesse plus que feminine," by asserting her proper humility, modesty, and piety.[11] At the same time, her boldness becomes the signifier of exemplary and exceptional virtue. In a 1599 dedication, she lays claim to the spirit of an Amazon queen; near the end of her life, in 1624, she represents herself simultaneously as biblical widow (like Anne Prowse), offering her mite to Prince Charles, and as Amazon Lady (Goldberg 1990, 149; Scott-Elliott and Yeo 1990, 81). While she abandons the verses of her husband and father, she continues to reinscribe their commendatory verses that praise her as the "glorie of thy sexe," the "matchles Mistresse of the golden Pen." There is a similar Janus-like doubleness in Inglis's inclusion of self-portraits in a number of her manuscripts. She makes herself visible, and visible specifically as a writer, in portraits that depict her at work, with pen in hand and the tools of her trade before her (see figure eight). Yet, in many of these portraits, the words she is shown writing are self-effacing, a version of the lines inscribed in the self-portrait of 1624: *"De l'Eternel le bien, De moy le mal ou rien"* ("From the Eternal, good; From me, bad or nothing"). She defines herself as a vehicle for God's word, with no active role.

ESTHER INGLIS, SELF-PORTRAIT INSERTED IN HER 1624 MANUSCRIPT
BOOK OF GEORGETTE DE MONTENAY'S EMBLEMES CHRESTIENS.
*Reproduced by permission of the British Library, London, from Royal Ms. 17 D XVI, folio 7.*

Perhaps more significant in relation to an emerging sense of professionalism is the way Inglis casts her work as the work of the industrious
nonaristocratic woman, the good housewife of the conduct books. She
emphasizes the labor and industry involved in producing her manuscripts, and in a 1605 dedication to Lady Herbert, she makes a remarkably confident assertion of her ability: "The Bee draweth noght . . . huny
from the fragrant herbes of the garding for hir self: no more have I
payned myself many yearis to burie the talent God has geven me in
oblivion—And therefore albeit I be a stranger and no way knowen to
your Ladyship yitt have I tane the boldnes to present you with thir few
floures that I have collected of Dame Floras blossomes: Trusting your
Ladyship will accept heirof . . . and the rather becaus it is the work of a
woman" (Scott-Elliott and Yeo 1990, 26). She compares herself to the
industrious bee that works selflessly for the well-being of the hive; she
alludes to the parable of the talents to legitimate not only the practice of
her calligraphy but also the circulation of her manuscripts; she casts her
copying as analogous to the feminine activity of flower gathering; and
she emphasizes the painstaking labor involved in the development of her
hand.[12] She represents her manuscript, in other words, both as the work
of a woman and as woman's work.

Inglis's manuscripts are also constructed in such a way that they
emphasize appropriately feminine industry. In the early stages of her
career, she displays her skill in a multiplicity of styles. The writing book
she presents to Lady Herbert, for example, includes 40 different styles.
After 1608, she abandons this kind of versatility and instead concentrates on producing miniscule script and manuscript miniatures. Her
work demonstrates simultaneously both self-effacement and virtuosity;
the miniatures in particular are little books that declare themselves to be
the work of a woman's hand: *"cette petite oeuvre escrit et illuminé d'une main
feminine"* ("this little book written and illuminated by a feminine hand";
Scott-Elliott and Yeo 1990, 54). They are also books that draw attention
to themselves by their diminutive proportions. Throughout her career,
too, Inglis regularly surrounds the lines of text with brightly painted
foliage, flowers, and fruit. Her calligraphy, with its variety, decorative
initials, and borders, displays itself as ornamental. The work of her hand
comes to approximate tapestry, the pen made the equivalent of the needle.[13] Her skill with the needle is in fact mentioned in commendatory
verses she attaches. Robert Rollock, for example, claims that her virtue
(though unrewarded) prevails over both needle and pen, and Inglis may
have embroidered her own bindings, which are often elaborate works of

art in themselves. In her dedication to Baron Wotton in 1606, she tells him she has "adorned this little book with a party coloured cote for yrself" (Scott-Elliott and Yeo 1990, 21, 56).

Inglis's self-portraits confirm her work as the product of feminine industry. Goldberg, in his discussion of a portrait based on the one shown in figure eight, suggests that Inglis is "sporting the masculine attire (hat and ruff) that became popular early in the seventeenth century," and asserts that it displays the "humble Amazon" (1990, 150–53). I would argue, however, that this self-portrait represents Inglis primarily as the industrious bourgeoise, sober and pious, a woman marked off from the fashionable adornment of aristocratic display. Her bodice buttons to the neck, her sleeves are narrow and unadorned with elaborate cuffs, she wears no jewelry, her head is piously covered as St. Paul recommended in 1 Corinthians 11. Moreover, the portrait Goldberg discusses does not derive from 1600, as he thinks; it is a later portrait (explicitly dated 1624) which has been inserted into an old manuscript.[14] Given this later date, a significant comparison can be made with the emblematic illustration on the title page of *The Needles Excellency* (1631; see figure one). Inglis's self-portrait bears a striking resemblance to the emblematic picture of Industry; her pen, then, is analogous to Industry's needle.

The portrait represents Inglis as a model of pious industry. In the book of emblems dedicated to Prince Charles from which this portrait is derived, Inglis takes measures, as the good housewife, to preserve her book unspoiled. In an address to the "Gentle Reader" that clearly envisages the circulation of her manuscript, she says she has provided an index "least you should soyl this booke in searching out the names in particular of any of the fiftie nobles therin conteined. You have a Table in the last leafe therof that shall direct you to them" (Scott-Elliott and Yeo 1990, 82). The rhetorical fiction of the industrious housewife so dear to Renaissance conduct books provides Inglis with room to maneuver. In her presentation and representation of her work, she extends industry to encompass writing itself, a writing that not only saves and preserves the pious texts she copies but also ventures into the marketplace.

It is in Esther Inglis's productive combination of self-effacement and self-aggrandizement that I suggest we find an emerging sense of professionalism, a legitimation of writing for money. Isabella Whitney and Mary Fage are neither so prolific as Inglis nor associated with the craft of the scribe. Nevertheless, there are some suggestive similarities between the three writers.

## The "good wyll" of Isabella Whitney

Isabella Whitney published two collections of verse, *The Copy of a letter . . . to her unconstant Lover* in 1567, and *A sweet Nosgay* in 1573; both were printed by Richard Jones, who dealt largely in popular ballads and practical treatises.[15] Ann Rosalind Jones has drawn attention to the way that Whitney "link[s] learned and popular languages into a set of permissions to write" (1990, 8), strategically mixing genres to characterize herself as an unfortunate but virtuous woman writer. Jones's assertion (1990, 36) that Whitney made a living by her pen may be overly emphatic, but Whitney's work does indicate that she is negotiating a position as a professional woman writer. She invokes domestic labor to explain her writing, as Jones argues; more than this, she transforms her writing into a mode of housekeeping. Like Esther Inglis, she makes use of the model of the good housewife to legitimate her writing. She also acknowledges her writing as commercial transaction even as she represents that transaction as a more traditional form of neighborliness.

Whitney's work, then, is self-consciously popular, capitalizing on contemporary fashions and highlighting its own novelty. Her first publication, *The Copy of a letter* (1567), includes a verse epistle supposedly from the author to her "unconstant Lover" and a verse "Admonition" to single women to beware of men. A "Loveletter sent by a Bacheler . . . to an unconstant and faithles Mayden" is printed alongside these two addresses in the pamphlet. The printer advertises the novelty of the text both on the title page and in a prefatory verse to the reader: it is a letter "lately written" and "Newly joyned to a Loveletter"; if his readers lack "some trifle that is trew," then this pamphlet will "serve your turne / the which is also new" (sig. A[1]v). Her second collection, *A sweet Nosgay* (1573), is a more varied miscellany of moral verse and verse epistles. Both collections capitalize on contemporary fashions. *The Copy of a letter* draws on the success of Ovid's *Heroides*, with its famous lovers and its series of addresses by forsaken heroines, and it is likely that Whitney made use of George Turbervile's verse translation of the text published in the same year.[16] *A sweet Nosgay* draws on the success of commonplace moral wisdom, and Whitney's aphorisms versify prose sentences selected from a compendium published the previous year by Sir Hugh Plat.[17] Both works also capitalize on the growing popularity of collections of letters: Erasmus had recommended the *Heroides* as a model for letter writing, and the Horatian moral epistle was inspiring Continental and English publications of familiar letters.[18] On the Continent, letters were already being incorporated into the narrative structure of novella and romance, and Whitney's "Familiar and friendly Epistles" similarly help to construct a narrative structure for her miscellanies.[19] The organization of the *Nosgay*, in particular, makes it a collection as strikingly innovative as George Gascoigne's *A Hundreth Sundry Flowers*, published in the same year.[20]

It is Whitney's use of the epistle in both of her collections that marks her most telling maneuver. The verse epistle, as Claudio Guillén has said, presents itself as writing rather than as lyrical poetry, and as writing structured on absence. Like the letter in general, it involves the writer in a "silent, creative process of self-distancing and self-modeling" (in Lewalski 1986, 78). Whitney's letters to faithless lover, and to family and friends, present themselves as intimate and private correspondence, offering the illusion of access to private thoughts. Unlike Inglis, whose participation in a system of patronage involves her in hierarchical forms of address, Whitney manipulates the letter to establish horizontal relations of address. She draws around herself a network of family, friends, and ultimately readers who are effectively her equals rather than her superiors or inferiors. Her letters are grounded in the occasion, ostensibly private communications dealing with the mundane concerns of a group of people who are forced by distance to perform their exchanges in writing. By means of the letter, Whitney constructs a position for herself from which she can write, and write for money, without apology.

*The Copy of a letter* suggests an initial development of strategies that become more fully realized in *A sweet Nosgay*. The pamphlet is made marketable by the illusion of privacy it constructs, and Whitney maintains anonymity in this first work. She is described as a young gentlewoman on the title page and identified by her initials alone. The title itself claims to print not a letter, but a copy of a letter; it gestures toward an original that guarantees the "truth" of the matter. The printer's address to the reader stands in for an authorial preface that might damage the pamphlet's claim to offer access to private intimacy; the combination of "true" matter and "fained tales" is held out as lure to a valid commercial transaction with male buyers:

What lack you Maister mine?
    some trifle that is trew? . . .
Therfore, bye this same Booke,
    of him that haere doth dwell:
And you (I know) wyll say you have
    bestowed your mony well. (ll. 1–2, 17–20; sig. A[1]v)

But these buyers are excluded from the audience specified in Whitney's verse. The "unconstant lover" is addressed in an ostensibly private letter prior to the Admonition "to all yong Gentilwomen: And to al other Maids being in Love" (sig. A[5]v); private communication modulates into a collective address that nevertheless maintains the distinction between public and private spheres by particularizing an audience of female equals who, like the speaker, are entangled in private relations of love. The audience of male voyeurs that the printer calls on serves to highlight the propriety of the author's ostensible audience, while placing the pamphlet firmly within the marketplace.

Whitney seems, initially at least, to corroborate the ostensible privacy of *The Copy of a letter*, effacing her participation in the act of publication. The letter "to her unconstant lover" constructs a critical turning point in a love affair, a moment when the writer has "yet now" (l. 3, sig. A[2]) heard rumors that her lover is about to marry another woman. She writes in the context of an absence produced by her lover's faithlessness, sketching in their past intimacy and mutual promises, demanding that he "Now chuse whether ye wyll be true, / or be of SINONS trade" (ll. 27–28, sig. A[2]v), and finally wishing him well whatever his choice. Yet the conclusion to this letter points in another direction. In the penultimate stanza, she continues the fiction of the letter and its actuality:

> And when you shall this letter have
>> let it be kept in store?
> For she that sent the same, hath sworn
>> as yet to send no more. (ll. 133–36, sig. A[5])

Whitney appears to conclude the correspondence, signing off with a vow of silence and a reference to the sending and keeping of the material object; but the verse continues with a final stanza:

> And now farewel, for why at large
>> my mind is here exprest?
> The which you may perceive, if that
>> you do peruse the rest? (ll. 137–40, sig. A[5]v)

The stanza provides a bridge between the letter and the Admonition, which is directed at an audience of young women. The farewell opens out ambiguously to include an address to the reader of the pamphlet.

The phrase "at large" encompasses both the supposed original and the printed letter; the Admonition provides an explanation not for the letter to the lover, which is motivated by its own occasion, but for the expression of her mind "at large" in print, a medium that allows for the collective general address.

The Admonition itself, while it is constructed as an address to young women, has an eye for its double audience. Two stanzas suddenly and without transitional markers shift away from advice for women in love and into a direct rhetorical questioning of male lovers, men who are set up in opposition to a collective female "us," "us simple soules" (l. 28, sig. A[6]). Nevertheless, Whitney's strategy here is to take up the position of a friendly adviser who speaks not as a superior but as an equal, an equal who happens to have experience of male deception and can therefore offer good counsel to other young women like herself:

> To you I speake: for you be they,
> > that good advice do lacke:
> Oh, if I could good counsell geve
> > my tongue should not be slacke?

> But such as I can geve, I wyll
> > here in few wordes expresse:
> Which if you do observe, it will
> > some of your care redresse. (ll. 5–12, sig. A[5]v)

She offers to help as best she may, defining her tongue as a properly restrained instrument of cure, unlike the "flattering tongues" of men:

> Beware of fayre and painted talke,
> > beware of flattering tonges:
> The Mermaides do pretend no good
> > for all their pleasant Songs. (ll. 13–16, sig. A[6])

Jones and Krontiris have pointed to the unsettling imagery of this stanza: Whitney demonstrates that the language available to her is "saturated with suspicion of *women*" by figuring male deceit in negative feminine terms (Jones 1990, 49). Yet she also manipulates the narratives of a male literary tradition to support her position as friendly adviser: in citing examples of classical heroines who placed too much trust in men, she claims that good counsel would have prevented their tragic fates. If Scylla, for example, "had had good advice / Nisus had lived long" (ll. 45–46, sig. A[6]v); "Or if Demophoons deceite, / to Phillis had ben tolde: / She had not ben transformed so" (ll. 69–71, sig. A[7]).

Whitney elaborates on the position of friendly adviser in *A sweet Nosgay* to construct a horizontal set of relations that offers a more explicit legitimation of professional writing. By moving away from the dangerous literary territory of love and toward moral philosophy, with its concern for individual behavior, she can explore social relations less circumscribed and regulated by gender and heterosexuality. In this text, through her letters and prefatory addresses, she shapes a self betrayed not by love but by Fortune, a role that she can share with men as well as women. She maintains the self-effacing anonymity of initials, but at the same time this collection includes a commendatory verse by Thomas Berrie that names her openly:

> my great good wyll must never slake
> From WHITNEY: loe, herein some partie take
>   For in her worke is plainly to be seene,
>     why Ladies place in Garlands Laurell greene. (sig. B1)

Berrie acts as arbiter of her work, authorizing the Ladies he addresses to adorn her head with their laurel garlands. He places her specifically as a woman writer in his verse; he defines his love for her as "good wyll," an ungendered delight in her worth, but he can only do so by first dismissing the claims of heterosexual love. Similarly, he suggests that Whitney has maintained gender decorum in rejecting the serious (masculine) genres of epic and tragedy, "sithe Maides with loftie stile may not agree" (sig. B1v) but he goes on to identify Whitney as a writer with a past and future career.[21] The *Nosgay*, he says, is her "seconde worke," and in the future, "when her busie care from head shall lurke, / She practize will, and promise longer worke" (sig. B1v).

Whitney herself, in her dedication to George Mainwaring, gestures toward the continuation of her writing as a practice when she tells him that if he appreciates her collection she will "endevour my selfe to make a further viage for a more dayntier thing (then Flowers are) to present you withall" (sig. A5). That practice is represented conventionally as a form of gift giving, a return for favors and benefits conferred. Yet the collection as a whole places such exchanges not in a vertical system of patronage but in a horizontal system of neighborly relations, a system that allows for fluctuations of relative position, according to the whims of Fortune.

In the *Nosgay*, Whitney constructs the persona of an unemployed domestic servant in London, an unfortunate urban gentlewoman. In her address to the reader, she provides a narrative frame for her versification of Plat's moral sentences, representing her writing as the product of forced leisure when unemployment and sickness plunge her into isolation:

> This Harvest tyme, I Harvestlesse,
>     and servicelesse also:
> And subject unto sicknesse, that
>     abrode I could not go.
> Had leasure good, (though learning lackt)
>     some study to apply. (sig. A5v)

This frame is complemented by the letters that follow the versified aphorisms, letters that insistently draw attention to her poverty and misfortune, and reiterate her loss of service to a "vertuous Ladye" (sig. C6v). She writes from the margins of society, from an isolated urban space in which she is "all sole alone" (sig. A6), but from this position she can construct a network for the exchange of friendly advice and support. As in *The Copy of a letter*, her verse epistles draw around her a group of individuals whom she can address with relative equality: brothers who are constrained to travel by their employment and service, "two of her yonger Sisters servinge in London" (sig. C7v), a married sister kept busy with house and children, young men and cousins as yet unmarried, and male friends who are suffering similar misfortune. The network Whitney constructs is marked by significant absences: there is no letter to her parents, for example, although in the letter to brother G. W., she places him "next our Parentes deare" (sig. C6v) as her chief support. Nor is there any address to her past mistress, the "vertuous Ladye" to whom she refers in the same letter. The men she corresponds with bear none of the marks of full patriarchal authority: they are young, they are in service or they lack wives. Not one is addressed as the head of a household. Even in the dedication to George Mainwaring, which notes his more elevated status as an "Esquier," she links herself to him geographically and chronologically in a joint country childhood. She addresses him as a "yong Gentylman," a "dere frind" and countryman, from whom she has received benefits "even from our Childhood hetherto" (sig. A4).

How, then, does this horizontal set of relations operate to authorize the woman writing for money? Neighborliness in the 16th century was a concept that recognized reciprocal obligations of a practical kind, exchanges between neighbors as effective if not actual equals.[22] In *A sweet Nosgay*, Whitney makes London her neighborhood, and draws both her readers and her printer into a set of neighborly relations which allow for mutual exchanges of advice and economic assistance. In her versification of Plat's sentences, she revises some of his precepts to sketch out the terms of neighborly exchange. Flower 97, for example, revises Plat to emphasize the mutuality of that exchange. Plat's "Aske nothing that thou wouldest deny, and deny nothing that thou wouldest aske thy selfe" becomes:

> Ask nothing of *thy neighbour*, that
>     thou woldst not let him have:
> Nor say him nay, of that *which thou*
>     *woldst get*, if thou didst crave. (sig. C3v; emphasis added)

Whitney calls for such exchanges most explicitly in her letters to family and friends. To her brother, G. W., for example, she acknowledges that since Fortune does not provide for her, she must depend on the support of friends. "No yeldyng yeare she me allowes, / nor goodes hath me assind. / But styll to friends I must appeale." She offers her "Nosgay" to him as a "simple token" after identifying him as the "chiefest staffe / that I shal stay on heare" (sigs. C6–C6v). In her letter "To her Sister Misteris A. B.," she offers her "simple lynes" in exchange for favors already received (sig. D1v). She draws attention to the economic transaction that her writing is facilitating: her sister will think she "vainely had bestowed expence" (sig. D1v) if she is not included in Whitney's correspondence. While the nature of the exchange is quickly revised in favor of the natural bonds of blood, the letter nevertheless acknowledges the economic exchange that underlies this "gift."

The advice that flows back and forth in Whitney's letters helps to confirm the equality of the neighborly relations she establishes. She does not only seek counsel, she also gives it, and the inclusion of replies to her letters helps to confirm the mutuality of the exchange. "Good wyll," the friendly feeling that Berrie differentiates from heterosexual love, is identified as the driving force of such exchanges, rather than any concern for reward. Yet this goodwill is expanded to authorize not only Whitney's personal letter writing, but also her published writing. Whitney draws her readers themselves into this neighborly set of relations as she gives them Plat's flowers "for good wyll," and she offers her nosegay to her patron "to express the good wyll that should rest in Countrie folke" (sig. A4v). In her dedication to Mainwaring, she acknowledges the disparity of their positions when she draws on a classical story of the Persian King Artaxerxes; she compares herself with "the pore man which having no goods, came with his hands full of water to meett the Persian Prince withal, who respecting the good wyll of the man: did not disdayne his simple Guift." Yet she focuses attention not on their difference in rank but on her own poverty, a poverty that also explains her versification of Plat: "not havyng of mine owne to discharg that I go about (like to that poore Fellow which wente into an others ground for his water) did step into an others garden for these Flowers."[23] For all her declared poverty, however, the gift to her countryman is validated by her industry and her neighborly goodwill: "yet considering they be of my owne gathering and makeing up: respect my labour and regard my good wil" (sig. A4v).

It is quite literally Whitney's goodwill that concludes *A sweet Nosgay*, as she adds her "Wyll and Testament" to London. It is here that the neighborly exchanges expressing goodwill are made to encompass market relations between printer, author, and reader.[24] Initially, Whitney berates London for its very lack of neighborly support:

> Thou never yet, woldst credit geve
> > to boord me for a yeare:
> Nor with Apparell me releve
> > except thou payed weare. (ll. 32–35)

She links her fictional death to a money-oriented economy that has no place for friendly credit and charity, an economy that she rejects as cruel. Her will ranges humorously over the various markets that sell the goods and services required by city dwellers and the institutions that lap up the poverty-stricken unfortunates with whom she sympathizes. Her introduction of the book trade, however, appears not in relation to other forms of market activity in the first half of the will, but sandwiched between a reminder of her own weak credit following a legacy to Ludgate, the debtor's prison, and a sequence dealing with the redistribution of wealth through marriage, where she leaves rich husbands for poor maids:

> For Maydens poore, I Widdoers ritch,
>> do leave, that oft shall dote:
> And by that meanes shal mary them,
>> to set the Girles aflote. (ll. 251–54)

The organization of her will at this point appears to mirror her letter to A. B., which asserts that "til some houshold cares mee tye, / My bookes and Pen I wyll apply" (sig. D2). Writing and publication quite literally mediate between female poverty and marriage.

Whitney acknowledges the market relations of the book trade while drawing her printer into the neighborly relations that provide the context for her writing:

> To all the Bookebinders by Paulles
>> because I lyke their Arte:
> They evry weeke shal mony have,
>> when they from Bookes departe.
> Amongst them all, my Printer must,
>> have somewhat to his share:
> I wyll my friends these Bookes to bye
>> of him, with other ware. (ll. 243–50)

Book buying (and, implicitly, the buying of *her* books, "these Bookes") is transformed into a neighborly exchange in a three-way relationship between printer, author, and a buyer who is also reader and friend. Her goodwill to her printer, in the context of the framework of neighborly relations established in *A sweet Nosgay*, shows Whitney acknowledging her writing as commercial transaction even as she represents that transaction as a more traditional form of neighborliness.

When Whitney links her writing with her lack of a husband and house in her letter to sister A. B., she draws attention to her unconventional activity as a woman writer, her difference from "other women." Whitney brings her letter to its conclusion with a comparison of the activities of housewife and writer:

I know you huswyfery intend,
    though I to writing fall:
Wherfore no lenger shal you stay,
From businesse, that profit may. (sig. D2)

Yet Whitney transforms her writing into a mode of housekeeping, a "businesse" with its own profits (moral and economic). This is most evident in her letter of advice to her two younger sisters, in which she outlines rules of behavior for a domestic servant. She suggests that both her lines and her own behavior have an exemplary function: "Hencefoorth my lyfe as wel as Pen / shall your examples frame" (sig. D1). Her letter represents her as a woman whose experience as a domestic servant has given her the authority to speak as a good housewife, appropriating the masculine voice of guides to housewifery in the same way that she appropriates the voice of the marriage manuals to describe the ideal wife in *The Copy of a letter*.[25] The industry of the good housewife is evident elsewhere in the collection too. In "The Auctor to the Reader," Whitney elaborates on the image of Plat's title, *The Floures of Philosophie,* to describe the production of her own flowers as a form of housewifely physic.[26] She represents Plat's text as a garden of "fragrant Flowers" located in the middle of London's "stynking streetes," a garden that can combat the "noysome smell and savours yll" of the infected urban air (sig. A6–A6v). In this context, she figures her versification of Plat's precepts, like Inglis, as a flower gathering that demonstrates her "good skyll" (sig. A8). She insists too that the flowers act as preservative rather than cure. Like the good housewife, she provides for the health of her readers without laying claim to the professional knowledge of the male physician:

yf thy mind infected be,
    then these wyll not prevayle:
Sir *Medicus* with stronger Earbes,
    thy maliadye must quayle. (sig. A7–A7v)

Her qualification shows her following recommended practice; Thomas Tusser, for example, in his popular guide to housewifery, reminds his housewife to "Ask Medicus councel ere medicine ye make."[27] Yet Tusser also advises "Good huswives [to] provide ere an sicknes doth come, / of Sundry good thinges in her house to have some" (f. 36v), and the "soveraigne receypt" (sig. C5) with which Whitney concludes her selection of aphorisms helps to reaffirm her writing as the housewifely provision of necessaries:

> The Juce of all these Flowers take,
>     and make thee a conserve:
> And use it firste and laste: and it
>     wyll safely thee preserve.

Like Esther Inglis, who provides an index to avoid spoiling her book of emblems, Whitney figures her concern for the reception of her book as housewifely preservation of goods: "I must request you spoyle them not, / nor doo in peeces teare them" (sig. C5v). Yet, also like Inglis, she uses this housewifely preservation as the means to facilitate the circulation of her text. She tells her readers that if they do not appreciate her verses, they should pass them on to another:

> Refer them to some friend of thine,
>     till thou their vertue see. . . .
> A number may such pleasure finde,
>     to beare it in their brest. (sig. A7v)

Whitney suggests that her writing will be enclosed in some retired place, not in a private cabinet but "kept in store" in the individual breast. The representation of her writing as the housewifely provision and preservation of goods allows her to envisage the circulation of her text "in place where it shal goe" (sig. C6), in a public world beyond the boundaries of the household.

In the "Wyll and Testament," Whitney converts London itself into an estate, an ungainly household that must be carefully and prudently provided for at her death. The first half of the poem pays attention to the basic household necessaries with which the good housewife was concerned: food, clothing, household furnishings, and medicine are provided, with a proper consideration paid to the different requirements of sex and rank. The second half focuses primarily on charitable provision for the needy and marginal. The fiction of her death provides the context in the "Wyll and Testament" for a virtuoso performance of writing as good housekeeping. "Paper, Pen and Standish" (l. 371) become witnesses to Whitney's model housewifery.

## "Bounded with the Letters": The Acrostics of Mary Fage

I would argue, then, that in Whitney's two collections she is negotiating a position for herself as a professional woman writer, proclaiming her virtuous industry and the usefulness of her neighborly advice while at the same time self-effacingly couching her activity in the privacy of the letter and in her borrowing from Plat. Like Inglis, she draws a self-portrait of an industrious working woman, to which she adds not the role of the humble handmaid but that of the neighborly and unfortunate adviser. Mary Fage, on the other hand, addresses her patrons as superiors and emphasizes her position as handmaid, as Inglis does. She claims to prostrate herself before her patrons even as she draws attention to the heroic task she has set herself. *Fames Roule,* published in 1637, is her only work in print, but it is an extraordinary exploitation of the system of patronage; in a literary tour de force, she individually dedicates over 400 acrostic verses to the secular and religious aristocracy of Great Britain.[28] Fage's choice of acrostic verse is as significant a strategy as Whitney's choice of the verse epistle. It allows her to address a courtly audience with both self-effacing humility and aggrandizing display of her virtuosity. She makes use of a popular amateur genre, a genre associated with courtly games of wit, and turns it into an elaborate ordering exercise, a kind of civil housekeeping that constructs the kingdom and its nobility as a model community; in the process, she calls on her patrons to observe their reciprocal obligations, be it in terms of bounty to the poor or bounty to the industrious handmaid whose poetry serves to order their names aright.[29]

The acrostic visibly displays its own restrained confinement. The narrow scope of the genre is emphasized in two small collections of acrostics by Francis Lenton, printed in 1634 and 1638.[30] Lenton compares the acrostic with translation:

> Translators, and your Anagrammatists,
>
> (All know) are both confin'd to narrow Lists;
>
> Nor can a Rapture, or fantasticke Flame,
>
> Fly in it's full carreire upon a Name,
>
> 'Cause bounded with the Letters. (1638, sig. B1)

The bounded confines of the acrostic, which in Lenton's case are represented in terms of a masculine and chivalric challenge, are registered by

Mary Fage as proper (feminine) obedience and decorum. In choosing not only to versify each name as an acrostic, but also to build her verses around a thematic center "discovered" in an anagram of the name, Fage is able to suggest that she is merely reproducing (in verse) an essential identity already present in the name. Her writing becomes an activity similar to biblical exegesis or humanist classical scholarship, in which she can represent herself merely as the innocent decoder of the "true sense" immanent but obscured in the fallen word.[31]

Such an activity also capitalizes on the Caroline court's revival of Neoplatonism, exploiting notions of the transcendent ideality of Neoplatonic forms.[32] In her prefatory dedication to the nobility as a whole, she speaks of having "adventured to present each of you with a glimps of his owne glory naturally innated in your Names," and in her verse to Lord Maynard, she reminds him that "Many affirme, that Anagrams declare / A hidden nature of the mans whose they're" (114). Her poetry appears to be subordinated not to an original text that she copies, translates, or versifies, but to the essential signified she discovers in the signifier: "I cannot say more," her verse declares to Lord Zester, "than your Anagram . . . sets forth in your mind" (173). Similarly, she describes her activity to Lord Tenham with a pun that again links anagram and mind: "Choisely pourtraid, in Noblenes I find / Heroick Trops, or trophies of the mind" (98). Often, too, it is the anagrams themselves that seem to legitimate her requests for reward; meekness or mildness discovered in a name, for example, is regularly interpreted as a sign of bounty toward the poor and towards the poet. The acrostic dedicated to the Earl of Pembroke, whose name and title become the tortuous anagram "O Prim Meek Peer Mount On, I Lodg By Hap," calls on him to express his meekness in accepting her book:

> Prime Peere, then daigne to gerdon my weake pen,
> Expressing of your vertues unto men:
> Meekenesse in you hath boldnesse bred in me,
> Boldly enough this to present to thee;
> Right noble then like a true noble man,
> O daigne not my infirmity to scan:
> On my sex cast your Eye with free faire looke,
> Keeping your ancient meekenesse, take the Booke
> Expressing so you are a Prime meeke Peere. (274)

The verse suggests that Fage sent at least one copy of her "Booke," her collection as a whole, to an individual noble; significantly, Philip Herbert, Earl of Pembroke (and son of Mary Sidney), was noted for his patronage of literature.[33]

The double confinement of acrostic and anagram also allows Fage to claim that she is merely the handmaid of the Muses, commanded by them to reveal the significance of each name. Addressing Lord Johnstoun, whose name becomes the anagram "Unto Lords on Hy," she asserts this dutiful position:

Loe, by the Muses nine charged am I,
O noble Peere *unto* the *Lords on hy,*
Respecting each according to his place:
Declare must I how them the Muses grace. (194)

Lord Johnstoun is a Scottish noble whose full name Fage does not (or cannot) provide, and she acknowledges in this verse that her characters are based on the letter and not on her knowledge of the individuals concerned:

I know them not, 'tis true; but yet the Muses
Have skill enough, and Learnings Art infuses
On rather into those who have a will
Nobly their workes with Heroes acts to fill.
So, since I am commanded thus to wright,
These letters will not blush, if they not right
On: as their Letters teach, so I doe frame
*Unto by Lords* each severall Anagramme.[34] (194)

In this representation of her writing, she provides only "a will," while she is "taught" by the letters of each name and "infused" with a skill and learning that appear to exist outside herself. The Muses provide her with an externalized voice that can greet, warn, and advise the nobles she addresses while she maintains a pose of modest obedience, displaying decorum and propriety in her attention to "place."

*Fames Roule* orders its verses into a hierarchical sequence, separating secular and religious nobility, and making careful distinctions of place in relation to both rank and geopolitical borders. Thematically, also, Fage pays attention to place: the sons and heirs of earls, for example, are often addressed in terms of their lineage, and court officials in terms pertaining to their function. In her verse to William Juxon, identified as Lord Bishop of London, Lord High Treasurer of England and a member of the Privy Council, Fage carefully enmeshes the lord's triple roles as well as her anagram, "Ne, you vail my lux," into the frame of the acrostic:

> Why should a woman, who is fraile and weak,
> Into the praises of your vertues break,
> Londons great Prelate, whom true vertues lore
> Lively proclaims, thee rich within, not poore;
> Insuing which true riches, Charles our King
> A meet Bird thinks thee in his Church to sing;
> Marking the just accounts 'twixt God and thee,
>
> Intrusteth thee with his high Treasury:
> Very well maist thou counsell good be giving;
> Xenophon like, Philosopher-like living;
> O! I confesse, the Muses lend a light,
> (Ne, you vail my lux tho: to do you right,)
> Ever to those who in their laws delight.[35] (74–75)

Appropriately, Fage acknowledges her own place on the title page, where she is identified as "Mistress Mary Fage, wife of Robert Fage the younger, Gentleman."[36] She concludes her joint dedication to the nobility with an assertion of the confined and private space from which she writes, signing herself as "The honourer of your vertues in my Cell."[37]

Fage's self-confinement as handmaid to the Muses and innocent decoder of the "true sense" present in the name is nevertheless accompanied by an insistent emphasis on her virtuosity. Like Inglis's manuscripts, with their minuscule script and variety of hands, Fage's collection emphatically displays her ingenuity in the confined space of the acrostic. A commendatory verse written, significantly, by Thomas Heywood (an archprofessional who wrote for court, city, and public stage alike) emphasizes Fage's sex, to proclaim not only her modest virtue but also her virtuosity and the heroic daring of her task:

> Shee's (as all women should be) modest, claimes
> But what becomes her Sex, yet to our shames

And just taxation, hath late undergone

A difficult attempt, which hereto none

Of us durst enterprise.

Fage herself, in a prefatory poem called "Certaine Rules for the true discovery of perfect Anagrammes," asserts her right—even as a woman—to write in this mode, as she defends her writing from malicious critics:

*Momus,* I know, at this my worke will wonder,

And blaming me, will belching envy thunder. . . .

Tush say they, what! a Woman this worke frame?

Her wit will not attaine an Anagramme;

There many may be false within her Booke.

Yet Monsier *Critick,* notwithstanding looke

I pray thee on these following Roules, and than

Anagrammes here according to them scan.

In her prefatory dedication to the nobility as a whole, she represents her project as both heroic and deserving, even as she asks them to excuse her for "disadvantages, either of sexe or want of learning": "Great assayes," she says, "neede great patronage. . . . I shall not need apologise for my selfe; your names of honour pleads my pardon." Protected by the honorable names inscribed in her acrostics, Fage can draw attention to her "great assaye." Her eulogies of an elite community also allow her to conflate the role of humble handmaid with a representation of herself not as Amazon but as a female Virgil whose poetry has the power to immortalize her patrons. In her address to Lord Gray, for example, she compares him to both Maecenas and the Augustan Consul Pollio, praised by Virgil in Eclogue IV: "A my Maecenas great, regard but me, / You very rightly shall my Pollio be, / Eternize shall my Muse your memory" (172). In the acrostic to Lord Maynard, she combines the roles of handmaid and modern Virgil to make a more explicit bid for reward. The anagram of Maynard's name, "Urania Myld, Vail Me," provides the context:

If true in you, then you affect to be

Nam'd in their Roules who loved poetrie;

Amongst great *Pollio, Gallus, Varus,* e'rst

Rewarding Poets, yet themselves well verst:

Daigne then, if that *Urania myld vail* you,

Ev'n *me,* her handmaid, but your favour due. (114)

By associating her own patrons with such eminent patrons of Virgil as Pollio, Gallus, and Varus, Fage lays claim to what she calls the "favour due" to her "great assaye" while maintaining the modest humility of the handmaid.

Like Inglis and Whitney, Fage markets her writing with a combination of self-effacement and self-aggrandizement that suggests an emerging sense of herself as a professional woman writer; manipulating the system of patronage, she exploits the acrostic to give her access to the bounty of the entire aristocracy of Great Britain, while maintaining a position of humble obedience and industrious service. In her initial dedication to King Charles and his family, she, like Whitney, draws an analogy between her poetry and the handful of water presented to Artaxerxes.[38] The two versions of the story differ significantly in their emphases, however. Whitney, addressing George Mainwaring as a young gentleman who is also her country neighbor, uses the story to emphasize her poverty and her debt to Plat. Fage, addressing the monarch and his "Royall posterity" from the margins of gentility, uses the story to mark her obedience, her art, and her hope for reward:

> It was a law amongst the *Persians,* that whensoever any man met his Monarch, he should forthwith present him with somewhat as a testimony of that duty alwaies owing unto Majesty. One meeting the *Persian* King on a time, by the suddennesse mooved, and having no better for the present, tooke up one handfull of water, and prostrating himselfe presented the same to the King; which the magnanimous Monarch gratefully accepted, and liberally rewarded him for the same. Take this most magnificent Princes, as a bowle of water from the fount of Helicon. (sigs. A3–A3v)

Whitney's "poore Fellow" becomes simply "One," a subject marked not by status or wealth but by duty and obedience. The gift in Fage's dedication is not so much the sign of the man's poverty, his "having no goods," but rather the sign of "suddennesse," a gift offered to meet the demands of an unexpected occasion; he has "no better for the present," with its suggestion of more valuable future offerings. Fage, like Whitney, seems to be figuring her writing here as an ongoing activity, as do certain of her acrostics that speak of her "Poet's pen" or ask for encouragement of her "poore Minerva."[39] Similarly, the water that Whitney's poor man takes from "an others ground" becomes, in Fage's dedication, "water from the fount of Helicon." The simplicity of her dutiful gift is overlaid with a claim to the valued poetic territory of classical Greece. Like Whitney, Fage presents her poetry as a gift, but through her rendition of the story she makes an overt bid for recompense: her own hope of gain is signaled in the "liberal reward" of the magnanimous Persian monarch.

Like Inglis and Whitney, Mary Fage seems to be working toward a sense of herself as a professional writer addressing a particularized and paying readership. All three women imitate the strategy of women translators in appearing to subordinate their writing to the material they work with, be it Inglis's copying, Whitney's versification of Plat, or Fage's use of the acrostic. Each woman chooses to write didactic moral verse in which she can display her feminine virtue, and each claims that her work belongs to an enclosed and solitary private space: the cabinet, the individual breast, the cell. Despite such apparent self-effacement, the narrow confines within which these women work become the context for self-aggrandizement. Inglis's minuscule script, Fage's acrostics, and even Whitney's misfortune provide the bases for displays of virtuosity—displays that draw attention to their writing as industrious work. Similarly, their opportunism—Inglis's gift to Christian Friis, Whitney's exploitation of popular genres, and Fage's amazing deployment of the rhetoric of praise—suggests a real sense of their writing as marketable work. The three women, all members of the lesser gentry, extend the rhetorical fiction of the industrious bourgeoise to encompass writing, and writing for money.

## Chapter Eight

# "This strang labourinth": Lady Mary Wroth[1]

Isabella Whitney's miscellanies and Mary Fage's acrostics manipulate genre so that it can accommodate the work of these industrious women. The writing of Lady Mary Wroth, niece of the Countess of Pembroke, provides us with a rather different but perhaps even more bold manipulation of genre.[2] Wroth is particularly significant because she chose to write in courtly genres that were traditionally the preserve of male writers—romance (*The Countesse of Mountgomeries Urania*), sonnet sequence (*Pamphilia to Amphilanthus*), and pastoral tragicomedy (*Love's Victorie*).[3] The publication of her romance and sonnet sequence in 1621 violated the aristocratic codes of manuscript circulation with sensational results. The literary quarrel that ensued focused attention on Wroth's sex as well as her class, and it provides a vivid example of the ways in which the discourses of gender difference could be called on in an attempt to silence a woman writer. Wroth's writing is itself marked by the struggle to open up a space for woman both as desiring subject and as writer. In this chapter, I focus primarily on the *Urania* to explore Wroth's labyrinthine engagements with gender ideology.[4]

The "crowne of Sonetts dedicated to Love" that is embedded in Wroth's sonnet sequence, *Pamphilia to Amphilanthus,* opens and closes with the image of a "strang labourinth." The labyrinth (and in particular, the labyrinth of love) was popular with English sonnet writers, but it takes on new significance in a text written by a woman and spoken in a female voice.[5] The mythological labyrinth provided a context for male heroism when Theseus slew the Minotaur that haunted its depths. This story, however, as Nancy Miller argues, "might be said to figure the production of the female artist," as "female desire becomes the enabling fiction of a male need for mastery."[6] It is Ariadne who gives Theseus the thread that enables him to perform his heroic self; "She is that which allows the male adventurer . . . to penetrate the space of the great artist like Daedalus (or Ovid himself)" (285). How, then, is the image of the labyrinth to be used by a woman writer? Surely Wroth's (and Pamphilia's) use of this image is a dangerous reinscription of gendered discourses of love and letters? How can Ariadne's thread come to represent a woman's guide to both the labyrinth of heterosexual relations and the labyrinth of a literary tradition dominated by men? Wroth's writing, I would argue, recognizes and manipulates the double bind of that Ariadnean position to produce and yet claim for herself the thread to the labyrinth.

## The Writing Subject

One of the most obvious strategies that Mary Wroth makes use of to authorize her production of a literary "thread" is the self-conscious locating of her writing in a family tradition. In particular, Wroth represents her appropriation as an imitation of the work of her uncle, Philip Sidney. Each of the three genres in which she writes was a genre for which Sidney was famed. All three were genres, however, that had seen their heyday in the late 16th century, when the discourses of courtship and courtiership overlapped in the vicinity of a female monarch.[7] In imitating Sidney, Wroth represents her radical appropriation of courtly genres as an orthodox inheritance along patriarchal lines. The thread she produces is defined as a thread derived from a male forebear. The very titles of her romance and sonnet sequence announce that genealogical positioning. *Pamphilia to Amphilanthus* echoes Sidney's *Astrophil and Stella*. The strategy operates in two directions here: on the one hand, the title announces its genealogical right to speak; on the other, it renounces any claim to speak with a male voice. The change from conjunction to preposition avoids the suggestion that Wroth is appropriating a male voice, speaking for the lover Amphilanthus. *The Countesse of Mountgomeries Urania* also points back to Sidney and *The Countess of Pembroke's Arcadia*, with its lost shepherdess Urania. Other familial literary connections were available to Wroth: at times she echoes her father's sonnet sequence in her poetry, and the literary Queen of Naples in the *Urania* can be read as a fictional representation of the Countess of Pembroke.[8] Within the narrative of Wroth's *Urania,* however, the heroine Pamphilia notably inherits her kingdom from her uncle, not her father; and it is Sir Philip Sidney whose status provides Wroth with the literary genealogy that gives her access to a privileged territory.

This familial locating of her writing echoes the strategy of her aunt, Mary Sidney. On the surface, at least, it does no more than is intimated by the praise of writers such as George Chapman and Joshua Sylvester, who represent Wroth as "The Happy Starre, Discovered in our Sydneian

Asterisme,"[9] "In whom, Her Uncle's noble Veine renewes."[10] This literary genealogy, once inscribed in her own writing, provides an effective authorizing strategy for her work. It has also, however, given some critics fuel for their dismissive commentary. Graham Parry, for example, wrote in 1975 that the *Urania* "is written in a style that is almost indistinguishable from Sidney's. . . . It is fairly evident that Urania has lost the philosophic garb of the *Arcadia* and has become the central figure in an infinitely convoluted history that lacks the intellectual strength of Sidney's work."[11] Betty Travitsky, likewise, calls the romance derivative, adding "nothing original to her uncle's contribution" (1980, 136).

Such attribution of influence has led to analyses that represent her work as an eclectic compendium imitating an assortment of Renaissance male poets. May Paulissen, for example, concludes: "In verse form and Petrarchan imitation, Mary Wroth's verse resembles Sidney; in utilisation of classical modes it resembles Jonson; in the new way of writing and reaching beyond Petrarch and in the realisation of a paradoxical world, it is like Donne's; in the conceptualisation of her poetry and the revelation of her philosophy of love, like Shakespeare's."[12] Paulissen also argues that Wroth, addressed by Ben Jonson in two epigrams and a sonnet, was Jonson's protégée (1982, 38–39). Though Paulissen is clearly wanting to valorize Wroth's work by arguing for a close personal connection between Wroth and Jonson and by including her in a canonized group of Renaissance (male) poets, her comparisons are problematic in that they evaluate Wroth's writing in relation to a privileged male norm, a positive standard from which it can only fall short. Her speculation about the close "bond" between Wroth and Jonson, moreover, sexualizes the contact in much the same way as Renaissance writers sexualized women's writing. It is a gendered critique that mirrors the eroticization at work in Jonson's own representation of Wroth as writer. His sonnet to Wroth reaches its climax when he attributes the power of Venus's Ceston to "every line you make." Wroth's writing becomes seductive, able to arouse passion in the beholder, able to make Jonson a "better lover" as well as a better poet.[13] Jonson may offer Wroth, the Ceston, the girdle of Venus, but in doing so he also positions himself as arbiter. In his masque *Hymenaei,* the power of the Ceston is made subject to the power of Reason; in the sonnet to Wroth, it is Jonson as speaker who is implicitly cast in that governing role. Paulissen's argument repeats the tropes of this gendered discourse of women's writing.

Wroth's work has recently received a great deal of serious critical attention, and her literary imitation has been the subject of more productive discussion.[14] In an article on *Love's Victorie,* for example, Margaret Anne McLaren argues that Wroth's "choice of Venus as the presiding genius in her play can be construed as a delicate compliment to the part played by [Queen] Elizabeth" in Philip Sidney's pastoral entertainment, *The Lady of May,* while Naomi J. Miller has discussed *Pamphilia to Amphilanthus* as a rewriting of the "ancient fictions" of both Philip and Robert Sidney: Wroth's sequence "writes against tradition in restructuring certain conventions of the genre to assert a feminine perspective on love."[15] Maureen Quilligan has explored the *Urania*'s use of scenes from the *Arcadia* and from Edmund Spenser's *Faerie Queene,* arguing that such scenes are "short-circuited" and rewritten in a way that marks the gendered nature of family relations and reformulates female desire.[16] What such critics draw attention to is a productive intertextuality in Wroth's writing that serves to authorize her writing while also rendering its difference visible, not in terms of a shortfall from a male norm but in terms of its inscription of gender.

Wroth's writing explicitly acknowledges the authority of the male writer while at the same time negotiating a space for the writing woman, marking out boundaries, and self-reflexively laying claim to its own territory. *The Countess of Mountgomeries Urania* includes a number of its own women writers, who are variously condemned and celebrated for their practice. In such narrative representations of writing women, we may discover what Nancy Miller calls "the marks of the grossly material, the sometimes brutal traces of the culture of gender; the inscriptions of its political structures" (1986, 275). In the manuscript continuation of *Urania,* for example, the character Antissia goes mad and is possessed by what she herself later calls a "poetticall furie." Mary Ellen Lamb suggests that the commentary of characters responding to Antissia indicates the cultural pressures against female authorship (1990, 161). Prince Antissius, for example, nephew of Antissia, defines Antissia's poetry as self-display that aims to make her "more admired" than Ovid. He concludes that it is a "dangerous thing att any time for a weake woeman to studdy higher matters then their cappasitie can reach to" (Ms. Book 1, f. 13). Antissius generalizes from the particular in the shift from "a weake woeman" to "their cappasitie"; the specific criticism of Antissia widens out to include all women as he draws on gender ideology to interpret her actions. Antissia, as Lamb points out, becomes a negative model as both woman author and lover, defining by contrast the "heroics of constancy" practiced by other women, and "embodying the negative cultural attitudes towards women's writing that must be suppressed" for women to write (1990, 168).

Pamphilia, the heroine of the romance, provides a more positive model. Scattered through the romance narrative are a number of poems that she composes, and the sonnet sequence that follows in the printed text as *Pamphilia to Amphilanthus* is given her voice. Her writing makes visible some of the strategies that Wroth uses to negotiate a space for the woman writer. Pamphilia writes in private, in seclusion—either alone in her closet or bedchamber or alone in the woods—and is consistently concerned with secrecy. Her verse makes no direct address to her beloved; it is not an overt act of courtship. As in Wroth's own practice, Pamphilia always has the literary tradition and the theory of imitation to fall back on to maintain at least a veneer of secrecy.[17] Elsewhere in the romance, women writers do make their poetry available, but, like the modest women of so many Renaissance prefaces, they have to be persuaded at length before they agree (out of pure courtesy) to speak or show their verse. In the *Urania,* the ability to write well is associated with the ability to control passion. Bellamira, for example, talks of how she put her "thoughts in some kind of measure, which else were measurelesse; this was Poetry" (333), even though she disclaims her own ability at the same time by telling Amphilanthus that she was taught this exercise by her lover. Amphilanthus goes on to act as literary arbiter when he reads Bellamira's verse and praises her "rare . . . gift" (337), since it is, he says, a "quality rare in women" (336). These, then, are the broad boundaries that *Urania* establishes for the woman writer. She must at all cost refrain from engaging in writing as public display, since that will gain her a reputation for pride, madness, and immodesty. To articulate herself as desiring subject, she cannot simply invert Petrarchan roles, since speaking as a Petrarchan lover would be transgressive. Lamb argues that the creation of the female self as author in *Urania* is bound up with the creation of the self as lover: authorship is entangled with the heroics of constancy in love (1993, 166). I would like to suggest further that the very silence enjoined on women by the gendered discourse of love becomes in *Urania* a validating condition for female authorship. Pamphilia writes because she must not speak. Her poetry is intimately bound up with her virtuous bashfulness, because it is represented as what Prince Antissius calls a "rare, and covert way" of expressing love (Ms. Book 1, f. 13); it acts as a coded articulation of desire that allows the release of suppressed passion in the most controlled and concealed way. Writing, then, becomes a practice supremely suited to women, rather than a transgressive act that trespasses on male territory. It is a thread that paradoxically both articulates and withholds desire and meaning.

## "In her owne shape": The Materiality of *Urania*

Wroth's self-conscious imitation of Philip Sidney did not save her from an attack by Sir Edward Denny after the publication of the first part of *Urania*. Denny's often-quoted attack on Wroth accused her of slander, and certainly the romance appears to include elements of roman à clef, as do other romances including the *Arcadia* itself.[18] Denny identifies himself as the "father-in-law of Seralius" in a verse satire addressed to "Pamphilia," and many of the details of the Sirelius story in the *Urania* have been corroborated by external evidence.[19] The marriage of Denny's daughter Honora to Lord Hay in 1607, her subsequent death and Hay's remarriage to Lucy Percy against the wishes of her family parallel the account of Sirelius told to Queen Selerina by his brother Procatus early in Book 4 (438–39). Inserted in the narrative is a description of the "strange" behavior of a father whose furious attempt to kill his daughter for suspected adultery is only prevented by the intervention of her husband. Lord Denny, in one of his two extant letters to Wroth, attacks her for making him "the onely chosen foole for a May-game, before all the World and especially before a Wise King and prince, with all the nobility."[20] Wroth repeatedly denies any intentional parallel in letters to the Duke of Buckingham, the Earl of Denbigh, and Denny himself. She never "meant" him, she says; "I never thought on you in my writing, nor meant you." What she calls (in a letter to the Duke of Buckingham) the "strang constructions . . . as farr from my meaning as is possible for truth to bee from conjecture" nevertheless led her to withdraw the book from sale, and several stories have been identified as fictional versions of events in Wroth's own life.[21]

It is Wroth's female authorship that provides the focus for Denny's attack in his satirical verse. Wroth, like other women writers of the period, does not escape a gendered discourse that represents female authorship as a sexual act, and an act that transgresses gender boundaries. The verse opens with a representation of Wroth as androgynous "monster":

> Hermophradite in show, in deed a monster
>
> As by thy words and works all men may conster
>
> Thy wrathful spite conceived an Idell book
>
> Brought forth a foole which like the damme doth look. (ll. 1–4; Roberts, 32)

Denny defines Wroth's writing, then, as an unnatural birth, unlike the writing of those male authors who appropriate childbirth to represent their work as legitimate offspring.[22] The verse concludes as it began, with another attack on female authorship:

> Work o th' Workes leave idle bookes alone
> For wise and worthyer women have writte none. (ll. 25–26; Roberts, 33)

It is specifically her sex that disqualifies her from "bookes," while the phrase "o th[er] Workes" suggests more socially acceptable activities— the good works of religious charity, perhaps, or domestic activities such as needlework and spinning. Denny's satire attempts to foreclose Wroth's narrative "thread" as a product of idleness, irrational feeling, and excess desire. The "Thrid" he calls up is a "Thrid but of thine owne," (l. 20; Roberts 1989, 33), bereft of the literary genealogy Wroth has devised for her work. In Denny's verse, the thread is represented not as the guiding thread of Ariadne, but as a tissue of lies "which thou hast spunn" (l. 20), the thread of Arachne's artful weave condemned by Pallas for its ambitious pride.[23] One of Denny's letters, however, is prepared to offer a carefully restricted territory to Wroth as writer, when he advises her to "follow the rare, and pious example of your vertuous and learned Aunt," the Countess of Pembroke. Romance (the genre of "lascivious tales and amorous toyes," as Denny calls the *Urania*) is to be replaced with "a volume of heavenly lays and holy love," in imitation of Mary Sidney's versification of the Psalms.[24] Denny takes up Wroth's own authorizing strategy and makes it gender-specific: he suppresses Philip Sidney as literary forebear and replaces him with Mary Sidney, despite the fact that the Sidney Psalms were the product of joint authorship.

Denny's advice attempts to make Wroth turn her attention from earthly to heavenly love, from the body to the soul. It is an attempt that has been repeated by those of Wroth's critics who argue with Elaine Beilin that her sonnet sequence "redirects her love and constancy to the divine" (1987, 233). I would argue that, on the contrary, Wroth refuses this orthodox effacement of the body and female desire. *Urania*'s emphasis on the material existence of women is one avenue that this resistance takes. It is an emphasis that counters the discourse of Petrarchan love poetry and Neoplatonism, which effaced women's material existence so as to idealize woman. In the romance narrative, the characterization of Urania herself illustrates this process. Maureen Quilligan has argued that the absence of the lost shepherdess Urania in the *Arcadia* is an absence that produces humanist self-awareness in Sidney's shepherds; her presence in Wroth's romance, on the other hand, acts as an insertion of gender difference in the text.

Urania opens Book 1 with a lament for her lost origins, a lament that in Quilligan's words speaks "a complete lack of self-presence." Instead of achieving humanist self-awareness, she "discovers a knowledge that knows it does not know itself" (in Logan and Teskey 1989, 260–61). Wroth's text literalizes her position through the common romance device of the lost child; at the same time, it demystifies and materializes Urania. "Why was I not stil continued in the beleefe I was, as I appeare, a shepherdes, and Daughter to a Shepherd?" (1) she asks herself. She may be more than she appears, but the hidden identity has no emblematic or allegorical significance as it does in the *Arcadia*. Rather, it is a matter of class, of her "estate or birth" (1). Her first encounters are marked by an insistence on her materiality. When she comes upon Perissus, he quickly revises his initial assumption that she is a supernatural being, and in so doing marks out her inferior status as a woman: "what divelish spirit art thou, that thus dost come to torture me? But now I see you are a woman, and therefore not much to be marked, and lesse resisted" (4). Selarinus and Steriamus likewise address her as "Divine creature," but she redefines herself as "the most miserable of women" (17). Prince Parselius, in his love-struck meeting with her, is unsure whether she is "an incomparable Shepherdesse" or "a heavenly person." She responds by defining herself again in terms of her misery, a misery owing to her lack of identity: "Alas Sir . . . so far am I from a heavenly creature, as I esteeme myselfe the most miserable on earth" (18).

Urania repeatedly rejects the idealizing addresses of the men and insists on her material existence as a woman, and a woman who is in search of herself. This materializing process takes some amusing turns in these early scenes. In the *Arcadia*, the best known emblematic representation of Urania occurs in Book 1, chapter 16, where she appears as a young shepherdess pulling a thorn out of a lamb's foot. In Wroth's text, Urania's search for a lost lamb provides the context for a fortuitous meeting with Steriamus and Selarinus. The lamb, once that meeting has been brought about, is quickly disposed of in the most material way: "Goe to your father," Urania tells the two men, "I will accompanie you; this Lamb shall feede him, at this time sent of purpose without doubt" (17). In Wroth's pointed rewriting of the scene, the sacrificial lamb is travestied rather than inscribed with allegorical significance.

It is not only Urania, however, whose bodily existence is made emphatic in Wroth's romance. The story of Ollorandus and Melisinda, for example, repeats this process in its reworking of the dream vision common to medieval romance. Ollorandus, at first known only as the "forest knight," tells Amphilanthus his own love story as a declaration of friendship. Echoing Edmund Spenser's Arthur in *The Faerie Queene* (I.ix.13), he falls asleep in a wood one night after riding too far in a hunt. A woman appears to him. She is dressed in green, with a garland of pansies and woodbines, and she comes to ask him for help. Her request, though, far from presenting him with a spiritual quest, is politically and geographically specific: she wants him to rescue her from rebels in Hungary. The dream vision is located firmly in the world; unlike Arthur's vision, it cannot be read as "the soul's new-kindled raptures at its first meeting with a transcendental or at least incorporeal object of love."[25] Its allegorical possibilities are firmly closed off: Ollorandus wakes, gets himself knighted at the Emperor's court, and travels to Hungary. There he finds Melisinda, the rightful heir to the throne, besieged by the illegitimate son of her uncle, the dead king. The best he can do, despite the mutual love that develops between them, is to arrange a peace treaty that hinges on the marriage of Melisinda and the illegitimate prince. Ollorandus is forced to leave Hungary when he falls out of favor at court, and it is only after Melisinda is widowed that the couple are united. Ollorandus's story works to demystify the dream vision, in the same way that the delayed naming of Ollorandus himself demystifies the "forest knight," who is at first known only by the device on his armor.

Margaret Witten-Hannah has pointed to the influence of spectacular theatre, and in particular, the masque, on Wroth's romance. She suggests that in reworking common romance motifs in terms of spectacular theatre, Wroth draws attention to the gap between ideal and practice (1978, 170–71). This reworking, I would argue, can be read in relation to Wroth's engagements with gender ideology. It is one further aspect of the insistence on materiality that occurs throughout the *Urania*. The mechanics of masque pageantry—its scenery, costumes, and lighting effects—as Ben Jonson recognized, had the power to overwhelm the "soul" of the masque: its allegorical narrative and the ideals espoused in the poetry. Wroth's emphasis on such "mechanics," even in her most elaborately emblematic scenes, resists an idealism bound up with with philosophical discourses that produce "man" by displacing "woman."

Even in its central emblematic enchantments, the *Urania* draws attention to the physical and material properties that constitute the "charm": architecture, costume, setting, and machinery. The description of the theatre in Book 3, for example, describes in detail the building and its furnishings; as Witten-Hannah points out (1978, 187), the descriptions resemble a series of settings in a masque, from distant view to interior and magical disappearance. The enchantment has two stages. Initially, the women are trapped in their fantasies of love: "To say these brave princes were in paine, I should say amisse, for all the comfort their owne hearts could imagine to them selves, they felt there, seeing before them, (as they thought) their loves smiling, and joying in them" (322). Once Amphilanthus ends the first part of the enchantment, they regain consciousness, "receiving their best senses, like their owne cloaths about them" (377). Pamphilia now has to endure the "sad spectacle" (377) of Amphilanthus and his affection for Musalina; her previous posture, "leaning her cheeke on her hand, her eyes lifted upwards as asking helpe" (361), is interrupted when she is sharply confronted with the evidence of Amphilanthus's inconstancy. Spectacular enchantment, with all its artifice on display, shifts to spectacular disenchantment. In Book 4, the "hell of deceit" in the enchantment of the Crown of Stones (494) moves in a similar fashion from emblematic representation to demystification. Pamphilia's vision of Amphilanthus's torture, where Musalina and Lucenia attempt to cut the heart inscribed with Pamphilia's name out of the hero's body, is superseded by an account of his discovery on Tenedos, "enchanted" by his two female companions.

A more explicit subverting of idealism is to be found in a scene in which Nereana, the proud and distracted princess of Lemnos, encounters Allanus (or Allanius), a shepherd maddened by the loss of Liana. Nereana's fury when he embraces her makes Allanus believe she is a goddess in disguise. He ties her to a tree and strips her to her petticoat, to discover her "in her owne shape." The narrative gives a detailed account of Allanus's attempt to dress Nereana in accordance with his belief: "her greene silke stockings he turn'd, or row'ld a little downe, making them serve for buskins; garlands hee put on her head, and armes, tucking up her smock-sleeves to the elbowes, her necke bare, and a wreath of fine flowers he hung crosse from one shoulder under the other arme, like a belt" (166). Such masquelike costuming only draws attention to the disjunction between Allanus's Ovidian vision and the angry woman who suffers his ludicrous attentions. Nereana is explicitly being constructed as a goddess; as a result, she comes to seem both more and less than a woman. When she asks a passing knight, Prince Polarchos, to help her, he refuses his service; yet in his very next encounter, he asserts that "his greatest happinesse (and that whereto he onely did aspire) was to serve Ladies, to defend them from injuries, and to bring them to their best content" (169). Nereana, dressed as Allanus's goddess, is dismissed as mad. The narrative juxtapositions here suggest the double displacement at work in the idealizing construction of woman as goddess, even as Nereana is overtly condemned and punished for pursuing the man she loves. There is no place for woman as desiring subject in either Allanus's idealizing imagination or Polarchos's demonising "chivalry." In this context, there is something subversive about Nereana's ignorance of Ovidian rhetoric, she "never having heard of any such thing as a Metamorphosis, her wit lying another way" (168). She does not recognise herself in the transformations of the Ovidian discourse of love.

The elaborate detail present in the account of Allanus's stripping and costuming of Nereana draws attention not only to the constructed nature of woman as goddess, but also to the physical force by which Allanus overpowers Nereana. At times, such detail takes on an almost pornographic quality in the romance, disturbing emblematic scenes with the material traces of power relations between the sexes. The account of Limena's torture by her husband Philargus is a good example of such disturbance. Parselius, entering Naples, comes upon a scene of violence. He watches as a beautiful woman is led by a cruel man to a pillar on the sand, tied by her hair, stripped till she is naked from the girdle up, and whipped. Parselius interrupts the whipping, and strikes the man down. At this point another knight arrives and, without showing "courtesy" to Parselius, sets the woman free. A conversation ensues between the three men, as the dying husband asks forgiveness of the second knight, Perissus.

The scene till this point makes Limena the object of the gaze and of male violence. It is her body that is stripped half naked as Parselius watches, her body that provides the object of exchange (verbal and proprietorial) between men. This is not effaced through emblematic aestheticization. Philargus is reminded by Perissus that he should ask forgiveness of Limena, and Limena then tells her own story. Her first-person account details other tortures to which she has been subjected, and she underlines the impact on her body by relating more precise conditions of the daily whipping. Philargus "whipt me, after washing the stripes and blisters with salt water" (72). She hints too at "many more so terrible, as for your sake (seeing your griefe, my deerest Lord) I wil omit, declaring only this I must speak of, belonging to my story" (72). It is her story that allows her to insist on her corporality, to resist aestheticization.

It is only in her conclusion that she suppresses her corporality to moralize on the events: "Thus my Lords have you heard the afflicted life of poore Limena, in whom these tortures wrought no otherwise, then to strengthen her love, and faith to withstand them" (72). Significantly, the conclusion shifts from first- to third-person narration, as if the interpolation of the woman into a gendered discourse of love entails a simultaneous disavowal of the body and fragmentation of the self into subject and object.

That disavowal of the body, however, is undermined by Urania in her discussion of Beauty in Book 4. Urania's counsel undermines the Neoplatonic discourse that makes Woman the first step on a ladder that leads the lover toward the divine.[26] Like the Neoplatonics, she acknowledges the "attractive power" of Beauty, but this is a beauty singularly corporal and explicitly not equated with goodness. She advises the grief-stricken Pamphilia to "seeke to preserve your excellent beauty, and let not so uncertaine a qualitie hurt you: beautie is besides a vertue counted among men of that excellent worth, as it wil draw their hearts as Adamants doe Iron: yet in this the comparison is not so proper, their hearts too tender to resist an easier invitement, but I say beauty will sooner compasse ones desires in love, then any other vertue, since that is the attractive power, though worth is often made the glosse of their change, which they are in many places forced to take such paines to find, & found is scarce enough to be called so" (398–99). The "vertue" of Beauty here lies in its value to men; it is the magnet that can best "compasse ones desires in love," a powerful asset that a woman must preserve if she is to find any satisfaction for her own desires. Urania reduces male praise of "worth" in women to a "glosse of their change." Her cynical and anti-Platonic analysis is supported in the romance as the material decay of female beauty becomes the mark of the forsaken woman. The frustration of female desire is inscribed on the bodies of Pamphilia, Bellamira, Emilina, and the sad lady of Brittany. Unlike the wasting of the Petrarchan lover, however, this inscription is less a proof of love than one more nail in the coffin of their love.

The elements of roman à clef in Wroth's writing can be related to this insistence on materiality in *Urania*. While the mingling of fact and fiction was not new in romance, the narrative of the *Urania* draws attention to its own technique. Commentary on storytelling within the text, the use of anagrams (like "Bersindor") coding the names of Wroth's family into the text, the inclusion of a poem attributed to William Herbert and ascribed to Amphilanthus in the manuscript continuation, and the excessive and extraneous detail that surrounds certain tales, all hint at a text that points beyond itself to an external referent. As Lamb suggests, such "(pseudo-) autobiographical connections" are significant not as access to Wroth's "real" life but as they are connected with issues of gender and authorship (1990, 143). The roman à clef elements mark out what Nancy Miller calls the "spinner's attachment to her web," in a way that once again resists the appropriation and displacement of "woman" in the service of producing "man" (in Miller 1986, 285). Instead of functioning like the masque, which works toward an idealization of the court through the participation of courtiers in the performance, Wroth's romance works toward demystification by gesturing toward the material existence of the knights and ladies who inhabit its world. The *Urania* refrains from imitating Sidney's literary golden world and turns away from idealism with its patriarchal investments. It is a strategy that points to the literary and social contexts from which the text is produced, and in so doing asserts the art of the writer who has the skill to transform her materials.

The implications of this mode of writing are implicit in the storytelling of Silvarina in Book 3. Steriamus comes upon Silvarina when he passes by a rock at sea, and "casting up his eyes, he saw, as he imagined, Urania sitting upon the top, in a Pastours habite; . . . hee found an excellent fine woman, her staffe and bagge lying by her side, and shee combing her hayre, her thoughts busied so as she tended nothing but themselves, and as she comb'd her hayre, she sung this Song" (355). The description of Silvarina combines elements of the pastoral shepherdess as idealized object of desire with a curious hint of the mermaid, whose seductive song enticed sailors to their destruction. Silvarina turns out to be a forsaken lady, and tells her story unwillingly and in disconnected fragments. Steriamus, we are told, "got knowledge of [her story] by peeces from her who would not complaine, nor tell the story her selfe for feare of misconstruction of the hearers, least the relation so rare should have beene taken for an Allegory, and not a story wherein her vertue should be painted, and not found" (360). The risk of storytelling, for Silvarina, is bound up with allegorical interpretation, an interpretation that will efface her material self and her virtue—or, alternatively, read it as an artificial, "painted" virtue; it is a risk that is illustrated by the contradictory signifiers of her initial description. She consequently attempts to exclude allegory by fragmenting and delaying her story. The narrative itself tells her story in the third person, representing it as a reconstruction from such fragmented "peeces."

Silvarina's story is not only suggestive in relation to the *Urania*'s insistence on materiality. It can also be read in relation to the multiple versions of Wroth's own life that are scattered through the romance. Wroth weaves her self in(to) the narrative, constructing fictionalized versions of her self as writer and as desiring subject. At least three, and probably more, of the stories in the *Urania* can be read as fictionalized versions of her life, as a number of critics have argued.[27] The stories of Bellamira, Lindamira, and Pamphilia all tell of a woman's love for an inconstant lover, in three different contexts: marriage, the court, and the extended family. Wroth's mythmaking, though, does not function simply as idealization; instead, it has a more complex double movement. The multiple selves that Wroth fictionalizes in her writing take up accepted and acceptable representations of ideal womanhood and at the same time lay claim to such positions in a way that excludes idealism. Wroth writes herself into existence through this double movement; she appropriates idealized versions of womanhood and makes it provide space for a female subject. She is, and is not, the ideal.

## The Desiring Subject

At the Temple of Love, the first major enchantment of the *Urania* (see figure nine), Pamphilia and Amphilanthus jointly bring the charm to an end and free love's prisoners when they reach the Tower of Constancy. "Constancy stood holding the keyes, which Pamphilia tooke; at which instant Constancy vanished, as metamorphosing her self into her breast: then did the excellent Queene deliver them to Amphilanthus, who joyfully receiving them, opened the Gate" (141). This masquelike disappearance, as several critics have suggested, seems to transform Pamphilia herself into the emblematic figure of Constancy with her keys. Lamb has argued persuasively that the enchantment reveals "a consciousness of the heroics of constancy as a mechanism of emotional confinement, enclosing its women subjects through its operations upon their own desires" (1990, 169); but the narrator produces a startling reversal, turning the throne of love from prison to seat within the heart. Women, as Lamb suggests, become the houses in which the throne of love is lodged rather than prisoners in Love's Temple. Like Aemilia Lanyer's inscription of Christ in the heart of the Countess of Cumberland, such a reversal acts as an authorization that lays claim to agency for women.

It is specifically Pamphilia in this scene, and not her lover Amphilanthus, who is able to bring about the desired liberation. The pair do not

**TITLE PAGE OF LADY MARY WROTH,** *The Countesse of Mountgomeries Urania*
(1621).

*Reproduced by permission of the Alexander Turnbull Library, Wellington, New Zealand.*

enter the Temple as the most constant couple, but as the "valiantest
Knight, with the loyallest Lady" (40). Amphilanthus has in fact demon-
strated his inconstancy in the tournament immediately beforehand; and
Pamphilia has sardonically drawn attention to his change of favors.
Pamphilia's constancy in this scene is not explicitly directed at
Amphilanthus, nor is it a specular reflection of Amphilanthus's desire.
As she tells herself after Melissea's prophetic warnings, "Joy then
Pamphilia, if but in thy choice, and though henceforth thy love but
slighted be, joy that at this time he esteemeth me" (161). Pamphilia's
"choice" here is analogous to the "choice" of another liberating woman in
Wroth's pastoral tragicomedy, *Love's Victorie*. In the final act of the play,
a pair of lovers enter Venus's Temple of Love to seek liberation from
paternal authority. Musella, constant to her love for Philisses, herself proposes the visit in the hope of escaping a contract to marry the wealthy
farmer Rustick—a contract enforced by her father's will. Recognizing
that her mother is attempting to seal this contract for "bace gaine" (V.4)
to enact "my father's will which bears / Sway in her brest" (V.13–14),
Musella tells Philisses to "Goe with mee to the Temple, and ther wee /
Will bind our lives, or els our lives make free" (V.87–88). But in *Love's
Victorie,* however, where the lovers are mutually constant, it is not
Musella who brings about the desired liberation but Silvesta, a shepherdess whose unrequited love for Philisses has led her to choose a life
devoted to chastity as a nymph of Diana: "Now my loving time is gone.
/ Chastity my pleasure is. . . . / In your shadowes I repose / You then love
I rather chose" (III.6–12). This unlikely savior, who has already stage-
managed Philisses's declaration of love to Musella, offers to sacrifice her
life to prevent the forced marriage of her friend. "I / Will rescue her, or
for her sake will dy" (V.176–77), she declares, taking on the role of the
chivalric hero. To this end, she offers a "sweet potion" to the lovers, supposedly to enable a quiet suicide (V.248). In the miraculous reversal of
the tragicomic denouement, the lovers are revived in the temple while
Venus names Silvesta as "my instrument ordain'd / To kill, and save her
freinds" (V.491–92). Like Pamphilia, Silvesta becomes both "freind and
priest" (V.252) in her hieratic function. Having liberated herself from the
"Slavery, and bondage" of love (V.159) by means of her choice of chastity,
a choice that makes her "freely . . . mine owne" (I.158), she is empow-
ered to liberate others from love's prison. In a play that is, as Margaret
McLaren says, "more commonly marked by a reiteration of the significance of the ideal of heterosexual love," Silvesta provides an "oppositional voice" that disturbs that ideal in its structural prominence.[28]

Silvesta's choice of chastity, as Musella points out, has its origins in love:

Chastitie, you thus commend,
Doth proceed butt from love's end.
And if Love the fountaine was
            Of your fire,
Love must chastitie surpass
            In desire.
Love lost bred your chastest thought,
Chastitie by love is wrought. (III.17–24)

Pamphilia's choice of constancy is similarly rooted in love, but she disassociates her love from a merely reactive passion when she rejects Urania's argument against absolute constancy (391); constant to her "choice," whether that choice is silent or voiced, successful or unsuccessful, she is guaranteed some degree of agency in a world dominated by men and their desires. Constancy, as Elaine Beilin notes (1987, 208), traditionally included piety, obedience, and chastity; but Wroth's *Urania*, like Elizabeth Cary's *Mariam,* marks off constancy from chastity in a way that resists the legal and cultural discourses that transform the woman into "a mediating instrument of the production and passage of property."[29] The *Urania* does not radically dismiss chastity any more than does *Love's Victorie* in its promotion of Silvesta. Lycencia, for example, is thrown off a cliff in punishment for her lascivious excesses; and in *Pamphilia to Amphilanthus,* the Crown of Sonnets at least asserts that lust is a "vice" and "ought like monster borne / Bee from the court of Love, and reason torne" (Roberts 1983, 132). Chastity, however, is a muted presence in the romance, and is not necessarily bound to constancy. The story of Alena, for example, describes how Lincus, after three years of courtship, finds her "unprovided for refusall." After he forsakes her, she laments her state: "I am a shame to my house, a staine to my sex" (189, mispaginated 199). Nevertheless, Limena represents Alena as a "loiall lover" patiently suffering the willful inconstancy common to men (191). Moreover, this tale follows Allarina's story (which bears some resemblance to that of Silvesta in *Love's Victorie*), in which constancy to a faithless lover is rejected for a life of chastity devoted to Diana. In the stories of both Alena and Allarina, constancy and chastity are treated as separate qualities.

The story of Polarchos (344 ff.) provides an example of the way in which chastity is a locus of equivocation in the romance. In an attempt to free Prince Parselius from imprisonment in the house of an unnamed lady, Polarchos carries out a fake courtship of the lady. He and his companions first find the woman "dressed as an inviter to those pleasures useth to bee, her necke all bare as low as her brests could give her leave for too much immodestie to shew, her sleeves loose, and as she stird her armes they would rise up and discover their nakedesse, and surely white, otherwise she shewed too much for an ill skinne, although never so much delicasie, wanting chastity will make men distract, for how ill soever men be in their discourse, or living, yet they love modesty best, and most prize it in their breasts, though their tongues say other" (346).

What is the "distraction" that the lack of female chastity produces in men? Is it madness of attraction or contemptuous distancing, as the subsequent assertion of the value of modesty to men suggests? The assertion draws attention to the disjunction between exterior action and interior value system. Whatever men say or do, the narrator protests (too much?), they "prize" modesty "in their breasts." The statement turns the modest, chaste woman into an object of desire even as it represents the desire aroused by the immodest lady. Polarchos, however, shows little sign of prizing modesty after his enforced enjoyment: "love will bee undone, for it will turne that way, more delight lodging by halfe in this sort then in twenty marriages." His view is mocked, but the narrator waxes equivocal again in describing the lady's "allurements, her sweetnesses, lovingnesses, delicasies, and pleasures, as shee was fit for any servant, and yet such her changing she deserv'd none that had worth in him" (348). It is not her unchastity here that is condemned, but her "changing." Constancy replaces chastity, then, as the primary virtue fitting a woman "for any servant."

Constancy, unlike chastity, is a virtue that is not primarily concerned with the enclosure of the female body—and constancy in the *Urania* is clearly not equated with marital love. Pamphilia herself marries the king of Tartaria in the manuscript continuation, despite her constant love for Amphilanthus, and constant women may or may not be married, may or may not be in love with their husbands. Limena, Melasinda, and Bellamira, for example, are all constant to extramarital lovers. Such constancy does not necessarily damage codes of inheritance and legitimation, but these codes are represented as secondary and often in conflict with virtuous love. In line with the orthodox approval of heroic feminine martyrdom, constancy may be read as passive endurance, as are the grief-stricken deaths of Antissius's wife, Pollidorus's wife, and the lady of Cephalonia. Pamphilia's active "choice" of love, and the repeated emphasis in the romance on the superiority of love that is maintained against all that the world and inconstant lovers can do to alter it, suggests that the *Urania* provides a space within an apparently orthodox virtue for woman as a desiring subject.

As the preeminent virtue of Pamphilia, Beilin argues, constancy becomes the "heroic virtue capable of transforming a lovelorn woman into a great queen, a poet, and finally, a transcendent image of divine love" (1987, 208). She suggests that in the Crown of Sonnets embedded in *Pamphilia to Amphilanthus* Pamphilia becomes divine poet, directing constancy "beyond Amphilanthus to the divine" (1987, 233). Beilin, then, stresses Wroth's attempt to "restore spirituality" to women. I would argue, however, that just as the *Urania* insists on materiality, Wroth resists this spiritualizing of woman at crucial moments in her texts.[30] The Crown of Sonnets announces that the speaker may "take the thread of love / Which line straite leads unto the soules content" (Roberts 1983, 128). As Beilin notes, the Crown is explicitly dedicated to Love, not to Amphilanthus; but Pamphilia is little more present than Amphilanthus in these sonnets. When she takes up the thread of love, the subject position she speaks from disappears. Her voice merges with the constant lovers, now undifferentiated by gender, that she variously speaks for ("we" and "us") or addresses (as "you"). For the duration of her celebration of love, she loses her self. The moment she speaks again as an individualized "I," the enemies of this love reenter, and with them a gendered position reenters. Beilin argues that Wroth "needs . . . a language less trammeled by considerations of gender," and finds it in the "language of harmony and joy" of the Crown, with its climactic "transition from love poet to divine poet" (1987, 238). Yet this "spiritual" reading of the sonnet sequence reinscribes the dichotomy of body and soul, and repeats the idealizing process of Neoplatonic and Petrarchan discourse that the *Urania* so strenuously resists.

Beilin, like Sir Edward Denny, tries to impose a pious model on Wroth. As the Crown's ungendered and undifferentiated voice suggests, such idealizing entails a loss of subjectivity: a language "less trammeled" with gender, in the world of *Urania* and the sonnet sequence, is a language that effaces self. In addition, while the Crown of Sonnets talks of "divine love," it is a love still grounded in the material world of human relationships. The sixth sonnet of the Crown, for example, speaks of joining "two harts as in one frame to move; / Two bodies, butt one soule to rule the minde" (Roberts 1983, 130). Constancy is enjoined on the lover in the face of the mutable material world; in the fourth sonnet, the lover is told "Never to slack till earth noe stars can see . . . / And secound Chaose once againe doe free / Us, and the world from all devisions spite" (129). Love, no matter how constant, still participates in the labyrinth of a divided and divisive world, although the lover may be able to construct an idealized image of the beloved:

> Love will a painter make you, such, as you
> Shall able bee to drawe your only deere
> More lively, parfett, lasting, and more true
> Then rarest woorkman, and to you more neere.
>
>      (sonnet 7; Roberts 1983, 131)

The Crown itself is not the conclusion of Wroth's sonnet sequence; at the end of the Crown's "flight" dedicated to love, the speaker recalls the enemies to the Great King of Love:

> Yett other mischiefs faile nott to attend,
> As enimies to you, my foes must bee;
> Curst jealousie doth all her forces bend
> To my undoing; thus my harmes I see.
> Soe though in Love I fervently doe burne,
> In this strange labourinth how shall I turne? (Roberts 1983, 134)

The "thread of love" has not in the end carried the speaker out of the labyrinth, but only confirmed her conflicted subject position. Significantly, the sequence does not end with a mystical effacement of the self but instead returns to the material world in which the self is always already gendered. The circularity of the Crown, in its labyrinthine enclosure, formally mirrors the speaker's desire.

The poems that follow do not offer an escape into divine love any more than departure from the imprisoning Temple of Love in the *Urania* represents liberation from love itself. Their dislocations of speaking position and mood and the aporetic ambiguity of reference that complicates phrases such as "deere love" ("Yett would I nott (deere love) thou shouldst depart"; Roberts 1983, 141) combine to deconstruct the opposition of body and soul, secular and divine, rather than to transform the speaker into the "image of divine love." In the final sonnet of the sequence the speaker silences her muse:

> Write you noe more, butt lett thes phant'sies move
> Some other harts, wake nott to new unrest . . .
> Leave the discource of Venus, and her sunn
> To young beeginers. (ll. 3–4, 9–10; Roberts 1983, 142)

The "discource of Venus" is put aside, and is replaced by what might seem to be more pious concerns: "Butt if you study, bee those thoughts adrest / To truth, which shall eternall goodnes prove" (ll. 5–6). Even so, Pamphilia is silenced not because of a simple substitution of divine love for secular, but because her love is proved by "what's past"; her "faithfull love" is written indelibly on her heart (and in her book), and any future "study of truth" is grounded in that love. Desire is silenced, but not erased.

> And thus leave off, what's past showes you can love,
> Now lett your constancy your honor prove. (ll. 13–14).

# Chapter Nine

# "The lasting lampe"[1]

In her now classic *A Room of One's Own,* Virginia Woolf concluded that any woman in the 16th century who was a poet or playwright would have faced a "nervous stress and dilemma which might well have killed her. Had she survived, whatever she had written would have been twisted and deformed, issuing from a strained and morbid imagination."[2] Her famous anecdote of the fictional Judith Shakespeare is an imaginative attempt to answer the question "why no woman wrote a word of that extraordinary literature when every other man, it seemed, was capable of song or sonnet" (Woolf 1977, 41). Woolf has her would-be woman writer failing to acquire an education, protesting like Shakespeare's Juliet at an arranged marriage, escaping to London and the playhouse only to face the "pity" of an actor-manager and subsequent pregnancy, and becoming a Lucrece-like suicide victim in the heart of an uncaring city (46–47). Her focus on the "absence" of women writers produced by social, educational, ideological, and economic conditions in the period helps to support her argument that financial independence from men and "a room of one's own" are basic necessities of female authorship. The turning point in literary history, in her view, comes in the late 17th century, when Aphra Behn "made, by working very hard, enough to live on . . . here begins the freedom of the mind." She sets up a dichotomy between "lonely" aristocratic women like the Duchess of Newcastle and Lady Winchilsea, "solitary great ladies" "shut up in their parks among their folios," and "women generally," middle-class urban women like Behn who "rub shoulders with ordinary people in the streets." Woolf's female author is middle-class, not an aristocrat; a professional writing for money, not a bookish amateur writing for "pleasure"; her author addresses a mass audience in print, rather than writing "without audience or criticism for her own delight alone" (61).

While Woolf's assessment of conditions in the 16th and early 17th centuries has in many respects been endorsed by revisionist historiography since the publication of *Room,* her notions of authorship and the literary history she constructs clearly do not accommodate the diverse if relatively small body of writing by early modern women in England. Woolf's notion of the author derives from a concept developed only in

191

the 18th century, along with copyright laws; before this, as Wendy Wall argues, authorial identity involved "a set of provisional and sometimes contradictory roles that had not yet fully melded into our modern definition" (1977, 21). Margaret Ezell has pointed to the anachronistic assumptions that underlie feminist literary histories based on Woolf's model—assumptions that marginalize manuscript writing by women in particular and that render coterie authorship and nontraditional literary forms invisible.[3] Woolf, in an essay on John Donne published in 1932, shows some awareness of the existence of women writers before the mid-17th century: "if they wrote themselves, and it is said that both Lady Pembroke and Lady Bedford were poets of merit, they did not dare to put their names to what they wrote, and it has vanished."[4] For Woolf, however, these traces she discerned do not disturb the silence she perceived, the absence of women's words in the "extraordinary literature" of the Renaissance. In 1928, Woolf points to the invisibility of women in history and literary history: "What I find deplorable . . . is that nothing is known about women before the eighteenth century" (45); and she encourages a new generation of women students to "rewrite history."

It is a mark of the vitality of feminist scholarship in the last few decades that questioning Woolf's conclusions has become possible. The writing that was invisible to Woolf is being made more accessible through the publication of bibliographies of surviving works by women, along with new editions and anthologies of the works themselves. Complementing this scholarship is a fast-increasing body of literary criticism and revisionist historiography. While it is difficult and perhaps theoretically suspect to label the discontinuous and diverse body of women's writing in this period as a "tradition," it is important to resist a genealogical narrative that begins with Aphra Behn. The very existence of earlier women writers, as Travitsky argues, "altered the contours of both the possible and the forbidden for women."[5]

Women had to write their way through limits on their speech, education, and access to masculine literary traditions, but a surprising number did find ways to manipulate the material and ideological conditions of the day without meeting Woolf's imagined end. These writers may internalize and reproduce cultural constraints; they may also resist and transform these constraints in some way, inserting themselves into the gaps opened by contradictions in and between discourses of sexual difference. The central contradiction of humanism, for example, the disjunction between the freedom of man and the subjection of women to men, offered a significant point of resistance, as did the humanist privileging of eloquence and learning.[6] Elizabeth Cary's *Mariam* attempts to mark out a space for untainted female speech, while Cary herself claims both the rights of the subject in her letters to the king and the authority of her learning in religious debates. Aemilia Lanyer and Rachel Speght both attempt to claim knowledge for women, Lanyer perhaps most radically by locating herself outside subjection in her construction of a female community of readers and in her revisionary narrative of the Fall.

Humanist comparisons of the glories of the past with the follies of the present frequently cited models of classical women writers and provided a space for virtuous learning, particularly among women of rank; de Guevara, for example, called on "princesses and great Ladies" to imitate the example of learned women of the past: "they ought not to excuse them selves, saying that for to lerne women are unmete. For a woman hath more ability to learne sciences in the scooles: then the parate hath to speake wordes in the cage. . . . What shal I say more in this matter but that they in times past strived who shuld write better, and compile the best bookes: and these at this present do not strive, but who shal have the richest and most sumptuous apparel" (f. 129v). Mary Sidney could thus be called a "second Minerva" and compared to the "Lesbian Sappho with her lirick Harpe."[7] Class distinctions allowed women to represent their writing as exemplary demonstrations of their status, as in the case of Queen Elizabeth herself, or of the status of their families. Anne Clifford's diary makes its claims most obviously to a family inheritance, while Mary Sidney and Mary Wroth in their different ways call on a literary genealogy to authorize their writing. Lower down the social hierarchy, Alice Sutcliffe frames her meditations with prefatory matter that emphasizes her "marginal" relation to the court through her husband, his office and friends, and her patrons. Mary Fage makes use of class distinctions even more overtly when she grounds her writing in the status of the entire nobility of Great Britain.

Male writers who distinguished between appropriate behavior for aristocratic women and for women of the lesser gentry or the middle classes provided a space for learning even as they spoke against it: "In stead of Song and Musicke, let them learne Cookery and Laundrie. And in stead of reading Sir Philip Sidneys Arcadia, let them read the grounds of good huswifery. I like not a female Poetresse at any hand."[8] In such critiques, the leisure to read and write becomes a marker of gentility. Manuscript circulation could in this context be interpreted as a signifier of class for women such as Mary Sidney and Lady Anne Southwell. Moreover, as active engagement came to be privileged over the contemplative life, women could make use of the Aristotelian alignment of femininity with passivity to conflate contemplation with private study. Prayers conducted privately in the closet paved the way for religious poetry like Aemilia Lanyer's and Elizabeth Middleton's Passion poems and Sidney's versification of the Psalms, while Mary Wroth inserts her sonnets into the romance narrative of *Urania* as private outpourings of a passive but loving Pamphilia.

The flourishing of Neoplatonism in certain circles, influenced by Castiglione's *Book of the Courtier* in the 16th century and by Henrietta Maria's encouragement of French preciosity in the 1630s, offered an alternative model to women. Neoplatonism represented women as creatures with superior spiritual gifts, less weighed down by earthly matter than men (Maclean 1980, 24). Despite women's primary function as stepping-stones for men in their movement toward God, this version of women came into productive conflict with scholastic notions of women's sensuality and worldliness. Lanyer's representation of women in *Salve Deus* is particularly striking in its claims for their spiritual superiority.

The repeated promotion of industry to combat the perils of idleness likewise offered room for maneuver. "Taske your selves then privately, lest privacy become your enemy," said Brathwait; "Let not a minute bee mis-spended, lest security become your attendant. Be it in the exercise of your Needle, or any other manuall employment: attemper that labour with some sweet meditation tending to Gods honour" (49). Such advice could be expansively interpreted as permission to write. The figure of the model housewife could, for example, be appropriated to make space for women in the sexualized discourse of Renaissance poetics: Constantia Mundi, in a dedicatory verse prefaced to her contribution to the *querelle des femmes,* turns the "perpetual labour" of her mother in childbirth into the written "work" that marks her own perpetual debt and proper daughterly duty, while Isabella Whitney develops a miscellany built around housewifely industry.[9]

Protestant thought, also, allowed a small but significant space for independent thought and action in acknowledging the potential for conflict between God's word and the word of the husband and father. Cleaver's marriage guide, for example, despite its strictures against "monstrous" disobedience in a wife, can add a brief qualification: "Yet must not this obedience so farre extend, as that the husband should command any thing contrary to her honour, credite, and salvation, but as it is comely in the Lord."[10] Women could lay claim to this space of conflict to write of their own religious beliefs. Lanyer's Passion poem, for example, focuses on the distance between male and female responses to Christ, validating women and their knowledge, while Anne Prowse and Anne Dowriche write their poetry in the name of their Reformation cause.

Even medicine offered potential support for women writers, as seen in the unusually encouraging argument of Du Bosque: "to say that all the impediment rests in their wit, which is not strong enough for it; methinks, is to judge but ill of their complexion, which according to Physitians, as being more delicate then ours, is also better disposed for study of the Arts and Sciences. . . . See we not in History, how the ancient Gaules . . . left to men as proper to them the exercises of the body, and to women those of the Spirit, and mannage of affaires" (1639; 28, sig. Dd2v). Mary Wroth's romance seems to demonstrate Du Bosque's thesis, its heroes actively engaged in the chivalric exercises of the body, traveling restlessly across sea and land, while Pamphilia in particular concerns herself with managing affairs at home (in household, estate, and kingdom) and with reading and writing.

Such ideological conflicts, then, prevented the blanket victimization that Woolf figured in the life of Judith Shakespeare. Women poets and playwrights did exist, as well as translators, diarists, and letter writers, though in small numbers relative to their male counterparts, and they took up a variety of positions in relation to both text and reader. Their work does not constitute an equivalent to what Fisher and Halley (1989, 4) call "male 'homotextual' activity" in which male-authored texts refer and respond to other men and their writing. Most of the women writers in the period write in an acknowledged vacuum, with no knowledge of predecessors, no consciousness of a female literary tradition. Indeed, women were repeatedly cautioned against the immodest desire to imitate or model themselves on female literary examples. Richard Mulcaster's nationalistic praise of the capacities of English women does not extend to encouragement of their own writing; Italian women, he says, "who dare write themselves, and deserve fame for so doing . . . be rather wonders to gaze at, then presidentes to follow" (168). Salter is more severe still, celebrating female virtue at the expense of learning and writing: he cites examples of famous women who had no learning yet "leaft behinde them more matter to wright on touchyng their vertue, then ever either Erinua, Sappho, or Corinna, did write them selves of excellent and famous men. And who is it that will denie that it is not more praies and honnour too doe noble deedes, then to write of them" (sig. C1).

Of all the writers discussed in this book, only Mary Sidney seems to have figured as a lamp lighting the way for others. Male writers like

Samuel Daniel, Nicholas Breton, Abraham Fraunce, Michael Drayton, Thomas Churchyard, and Thomas Nashe praised her writing and referred to the way she "sets to schoole, our Poets everywhere."[11] More specifically, John Donne, in his verse "Upon the translation of the Psalmes by Sir Philip Sydney, and the Countesse of Pembroke his Sister," interprets the Sidney Psalms as a literary model for religious verse: "They tell us why, and teach us how to sing / . . . may / These their sweet learned labours, all the way / Be as our tuning."[12] Donne's view has been endorsed by Barbara Lewalski, who argues that the Sidney Psalms provide a "secure bridge to the magnificent original 17th-century religious lyric" and links them to the poetry of both John Donne and George Herbert (1979, 241). Sidney's powerful voice could act as enabling and restraining model at once for her niece Mary Wroth. Held up as pious female exemplar by Lord Denny in his castigation of the "hermaphroditic" text of Wroth's *Urania*, Mary Sidney is figured in the same text as both mother of Amphilanthus and Queen of Naples, a queen "as perfect in Poetry, and all other Princely vertues as any woman that ever liv'd" (320). Her maternal approval of Pamphilia's love for Amphilanthus is intertwined in the narrative with her encouragement for Pamphilia's storytelling and verse (*Urania*, 316–20).

For Aemilia Lanyer, the precedent that Sidney provides is made more prominent and more compelling. The longest dedicatory poem in Lanyer's *Salve Deus* is addressed to the countess, who is represented as the poet of the Psalms.[13] In "The Author's Dreame," Lanyer describes a dream encounter with Sidney in the "Edalyan Groves" (l. 1); she is "set in Honors chaire" (l. 8) by Minerva, tied to the Graces, attended by the nine Muses, and honored by Bellona, Diana, Aurora, and Flora, who all agree to sing "Those holy Sonnets . . . With this most lovely Lady" (ll. 121–22). Sidney is made the honorary member of yet another female community, and in this context it is not Philip Sidney who authorizes her position in the seat of honor, but her own "worthier workes" (l. 215). She is named as "Sister to valiant Sidney" (l. 138), but "farre before him is to be esteemd / For virtue, wisdome, learning, dignity" (ll. 151–52). As she does for the women of *Salve Deus*, Lanyer makes a claim for Sidney's superior knowledge. While her brother gives "light to all that tread true paths of Fame" (l. 139), Sidney herself remains an earthly goddess, "Directing all by her immortall light" (l. 157), her work filling eyes, hearts, tongues, and ears of "after-comming ages, which shall reade / Her love, her zeale, her faith, and pietie" (ll. 161–62). Sidney's Psalms and Lanyer's "Dreame" are conflated as the vehicle for "true fames memorie" (l. 128), to be read by future generations. In presenting her text to Sidney, Lanyer doubly "mirrors" the virtues of the woman writer who has "in a higher style her Trophie fram'd" (l. 202), affirming the value of the "many Books she writes" (l. 195) while authorizing her own "unlearned lines" (l. 203) by positioning them in relation to this virtuous literary forebear; the "faire impression" (l. 163) that Sidney's work makes on Lanyer's own text marks out the "cleare reason" (l. 207) of the dream's author, whose waking knowledge proves to be the "selfe same sight" (l. 191) as her sleeping vision. The "worthinesse" of Sidney, like that of Christ within the text, "will grace each line you reade" (l. 220); her "worthier workes" confer value on Lanyer's text. In this way Lanyer claims Sidney as precedent for her own writing and lamp for future generations.

Despite such acknowledgement, Sidney's writing, like that of other women writers in the period, has been largely absent from literary history until the last two decades. The "phenomenon of the transcience of female literary fame" which Germaine Greer identifies with women writers since the Interregnum is perhaps even more visible in the previous hundred years; even women writers like Sidney who did achieve recognition in their lives almost vanish from the "records of posterity."[14] The lack of continuity in early modern women's writing, then, is reenacted and reinforced by the near-silence of later centuries. As Ann Rosalind Jones has asserted, "Fame is never the simple result of independent merit or aesthetic autonomy. The solitary poet goes unread; the famous poet is socially constituted, invented through the gaze, the commentary, the assessment of others" (in Miller 1986, 92). While Jones's "solitary poet" seems to echo Woolf's "solitary great ladies," her rejection of essentialist notions of universal value is important if we are not to accept absence as the mark of insignificance.

By the 18th century, the writings of early modern women had already become dusty collector's items. The antiquarian George Ballard's *Memoirs of Several Ladies of Great Britain, who have been celebrated for their writings or skill in the learned languages, arts and sciences* (1752) is, as Ezell asserts, the "most developed and subsequently influential presentation of early women writers" in the 18th century (1993, 78). Ballard's biographical studies have provided material for later biographical dictionaries and anthologies, which repeatedly draw from the *Memoirs* with and without citation. The *Memoirs of Several Ladies* positions itself as a nationalist monument preserving the memory of "ingenious women of this nation." Unknown to the masses and "passed by in silence by our greatest biographers," Ballard says, these women have suffered a neglect surprising "when it is considered how much has been done on this subject by several learned foreigners . . . more especially as it is pretty certain, that England hath produced more women famous for literary accomplishments, than any other nation in Europe" (vi). Such a position clearly helps Ballard to valorize his work in a hostile climate. Ezell cites letters to Ballard that point to the general "exclamation against Learned Women" and warn him that, at Oxford, male scholars "deny that a thing was or could be written by a woman" (1993, 82–83).

Ballard's *Memoirs* include a number of entries devoted to early modern women; of these entries, Queen Elizabeth, Elizabeth Cooke Russell, Mary Sidney, and Esther Inglis are the only representatives of the women writers discussed in this book. Ezell points to Ballard's careful selection of celebrated and virtuous women, a selection "fundamentally based on the moral character of the subject rather than literary, scientific, or artistic merit" (1993, 86). The *Memoirs,* she suggests, differed from earlier critics and commentators on women's writing in defining women "by their differences from men" and not as potential rivals who could compete with male writers if they chose to write in the approved "masculine" manner (1993, 72–78, 88). The biographical material and small selections of writing that make up the entries tend to characterize the women as virtuous daughters, sisters, mothers, and wives of men; in so doing they help to corroborate the virtue of British men. Anne Bacon, for example is indebted to her "worthy father" for her education, and her learning makes her a fit mother of two "great men" (188–89).

In the same way, the anonymous *Biographium Faemineum* or *Female Worthies* (1766), highly dependent on Ballard's *Memoirs,* insists that the learning of its illustrious ladies made them "excellent wives" who "understood the oeconomy of a family much better than our modern fine ladies are supposed to do."[15] The collection, recalling de Guevara, promotes itself as a model of past virtue for "modern times of luxury and dissipation," offering up its memoirs of women of rank who "found the most agreeable amusements in their closets" rather than in the social pursuits of dressing, dancing, and courtship (v). Like Ballard's *Memoirs,* the text aims to produce a mother who will furnish her sons with acquisitions that "will make a man shine at the bar, in the pulpit, in the senate, and in the cabinet" (vi).

These isolated 18th-century attempts to monumentalize British women were followed in the 19th century by renewed efforts to exhume learned women, in a more "scientific" spirit of observation and acquisition of (male) knowledge. Enlightenment, progress, and the advance of humankind are a common theme in these 19th-century texts. As women achieved increasing popular and commercial success in their writing of novels and didactic literature, critics began to construct a genealogy that could frame their writing in a teleological narrative of human progress. Alexander Dyce, for example, entitles his 1827 anthology *Specimens of British Poetesses* and announces his aim to "exhibit the growth and progress of the genius of our country-women in the department of Poetry" to support the rapid advance that he sees being made by "the human mind, and, above all, the female mind" (iii–v). The American clergyman George Bethune, in his anthology of 1848, entitled *British Female Poets,* makes a similar claim: "The manifestation of female talent is a striking characteristic of our age, and a very interesting proof of its moral advancement" (iii); he offers "specimens" of their verse, with this evolutionary narrative in mind.[16]

Dyce's authorial observation depends upon a firm gender dichotomy in which it is men who have the "grander inspirations of the Muse" and "tremendous thoughts" and women who display sensibility, tenderness, and grace. Ballard's 18th-century *Memoirs* have paved the way for the essentialist assumptions of these 19th-century texts. In G. L. Craik's *Pursuit of Knowledge Under Difficulties* (1847), learned women of the past become specimens illustrating Craik's argument that "an ardent love of improvement will surmount or force its way through almost any barriers."[17] Men, with their more complex reasoning and stronger imagination, have inevitably produced the "classics of ancient and modern literature"; women, with their true instinct, quick but inexact understanding, and grace have produced little of value: "no literary work of the first class has ever yet been produced by a woman" (26). Bethune likewise emphasizes gender differences in his assessment of female talent: women, he concludes, write well on "love, childhood, the softer beauties of creation, the joys or sorrows of the heart, domestic life, mercy, religion, and the instincts of justice" (1848, iii), but they "write from impulse and rapidly as they think . . . without the slow process of reasoning through which men have to pass," and they are "averse to critical restraint" (vi).

For Frederic Rowton, gender differences support his claim in *The Female Poets of Great Britain* (1848) that the "mental efforts of woman have as good a claim as man's to be recorded," the mind of woman acting as a harmonizing and calming influence on the gross and sensual passions of men.[18] "Man rules the mind of the world; woman its heart. . . . He thinks, she feels" (xxii, xxiv). Women's verse, Rowton argues, may be "less exciting than man's, and less 'interesting' to the mass of readers," but it has its own "gentler glow," like "soft starlight" in comparison with the "fiercer fires" of men (xvii). His anthology, like those of Dyce and Bethune, has a clear didactic aim: "Man's Poetry teaches us Politics; Woman's, Morality" (xxvi). He concludes with a plea to let women be partners, not rivals, in the task of enlightenment (xxvii).

Rowton is again concerned to draw attention to the neglect of the "Poetesses of Britain": "this is almost the first book expressly devoted to the poetical productions of the British Female mind" (1848, xvii). Despite this concern, his anthology, like those of Dyce and Bethune, includes few selections of writing by Renaissance women. The "dwindling space given to Renaissance and 17th-century women writers" that Ezell illustrates from these anthologies (1993, 120–21) is more severely marked in the case of Englishwomen writing in the period 1560–1640. Dyce devotes 53 pages (about one-eighth) of his *Specimens* to selections from nine women: Queen Elizabeth, Princess Elizabeth, Mary Sidney, Elizabeth Cary, Mary Wroth, Anne Howard, Anne de Vere, Diana Primrose, and Mary Fage. Rowton includes all but Anne de Vere in *The Female Poets,* but devotes to them only 26 pages of his 500-page text. Bethune includes a mere six pages of selections from Queen Elizabeth, Mary Sidney, Anne Howard, and Mary Wroth, adding one further page on Lady Aburgavenny. Nor is it only such dwindling space that affects the record of women's writing in the Renaissance. As Ezell has shown, the writing chosen for inclusion in these anthologies is of a piece: "early women's writings are presented as uniformly edifying, domestic, and generally melancholy. . . . Sentiment is more in evidence in their selections than wit" (1993, 124–25). These 19th-century anthologies, then, even as they attempt to preserve women's writing, help to marginalize the work of Renaissance women.

Throughout the Victorian period, women's moral superiority to men and their civilizing influence are made the reason for collecting past examples of "richly cultivated minds." Sarah Hale's *Biography of Distinguished Women* (1854) sets out to be "both an aid and incentive to such progress."[19] Women have a civilizing mission, and when this mission "becomes an acknowledged and sustained mode of moral progress, it will be easy for the sex to make advances in every branch of literature and science connected with human improvement" (x).

Jane Williams seems to continue this mission in quoting from Craik and arguing that the "welfare of society must be promoted by an extended knowledge of the lives, principles, and sentiments of the most eminent and excellent English authoresses."[20] Men, she says, "stand, as it were, upon a promontory," while women "sit like Genii of secluded caves, receiving echoes, and communicating mere reverberations from the outer world, but not without their own pure springs and rills, tinkling soft music fraught with peculiar efficacy" (1861, 2–3). Williams's *Literary Women of England* (1861) is perhaps the first overt attempt to construct a female literary "tradition" in Britain. She retains the didactic goals and the essentialist assumptions of other 19th-century writers, yet her text is represented not as a scientific exhibition of specimens making illustrious women accessible to the (male) observer but as a scholarly survey addressed in particular to English women who are "deprived of the benefit and satisfaction of forming a real acquaintance with their lives and characters" (6). After giving a careful account of the anthologies and collections of memoirs already published, Williams concludes that "A uniform reprint of the best works of our English authoresses" would be "useful not only in marking the educational progress of the people . . . but also in exhibiting a concentrated view of what has already been achieved," thus offering incentives to women to further their progress in literary endeavors and social behavior at once (12). What constitutes such "progress" may have changed considerably since 1861, but the incentive Williams envisages seems to underlie much of the recent critical and editorial work on early women writers.

In the 20th century, as women have gained increasing access to university studies and, later, to university careers, Williams's early attempt to locate women writers in "all sorts of improbable corners" (6) has been expanded. The (unpublished) research on Renaissance women writers by women like Charlotte Kohler and Ruth Hughey in the 1930s, for example, took up Woolf's challenge to rewrite history.[21] It is in the last two decades, however, as feminist theory and criticism have had a powerful impact on literary studies, that the writing of early modern women in England and elsewhere has finally become visible to a wider audience. This book is part of a much broader effort to reinsert women writers into the literary history of the early modern period. The task of recovering women's writing and making it accessible, of critiquing that writing and exploring its implications, is still in its early stages.[22] The lamps of women in Renaissance England—however stuttering, however sparse— are once again in the process of being relit, in an attempt to reverse what Du Bosque called the "tyranny of custome [which] hath hindered many of them, to publish their works and to leave their writings to posterity" (1639; 29, sig. Dd3).

# Notes and References

*Chapter One*

1.   The analogy of learned women and the five wise virgins of Matthew 26 is a common one in the early modern period. See, for example, the link made by Aemilia Lanyer (discussed below) in the prefatory poem dedicated "To all vertuous Ladies in generall" (*Salve Deus Rex Judaeorum,* 1611):

> Put on your wedding garments every one,
>
> The Bridegroome stayes to entertaine you all . . .
>
> But fill your Lamps with oyle of burning zeale,
>
> That to your Faith he may his truth reveale.

2.   See Elaine Beilin, *Redeeming Eve: Women Writers of the English Renaissance* (Princeton, N. J.: Princeton University Press, 1987), 65; hereafter cited in text.

3.   Aemilia Lanyer, *The Poems of Aemilia Lanyer: Salve Deus Rex Judaeorum,* ed. Susanne Woods (New York: Oxford University Press, 1993), 12–16; hereafter cited in text as Woods (1993).

4.   Pallas Athene herself does not escape sexualized interpretation: in "Of Virginite," a chapter in Juan Luis Vives's humanist treatise on female education, *A very frutefull and pleasant boke called the Instruction of a Christen Woman,* trans. Richard Hyrde (1529; hereafter cited in text), Pallas is introduced as an exemplary figure for the wise woman. Her mythical birth from the brain of Jupiter is interpreted by Vives as an authoritative affirmation of the proper conjunction (in a woman) of "virginite and wysedome." Vives goes on to point out that the ancients also "dedicated the noumbre of seven bothe to chastite and wysedome: And sayde that the muses, whom they called the rulers of all sciences, were virgins" (sig. G1v).

5.   The phrase "early modern" has in turn been put in question for its oppositional representation of the Middle Ages as "premodernity, the other that must be rejected for the modern self to be and know itself"; see Lee Patterson, "On the Margin: Postmodernism, Ironic History, and Medieval Studies," *Speculum,* 65 (1990), 99.

6.   Joan Kelly-Gadol, "Did Women Have a Renaissance?" in *Becoming Visible: Women in European History,* ed. Renate Bridenthal and Claudia Koonz (Boston: Houghton Mifflin Co., 1977), 139.

7.  See the annotated entry for Kelly-Gadol (1977) in this volume's Selected Bibliography.

8.  See, for example, Susan Cahn, *Industry of Devotion: the transformation of women's work in England, 1500–1660* (New York: Columbia University Press, 1987); Roberta Hamilton, *The Liberation of Women: A Study of Patriarchy and Capitalism* (London: Allen and Unwin, 1978); C. G. A. Clay, *Economic expansion and social change: England 1500–1700*, vol. I (Cambridge: Cambridge University Press, 1984). All three works hereafter cited in text.

9.  The expectation that a man would support his household was justified with reference to St. Paul. Henry Bullinger, for example, states: "If a man provide not for his owne household, he denieth the faith and is worse then an infidele," in *The Christen State of Matrimonye*, trans. Miles Coverdale (1541), sig. I2; hereafter cited in text. While this expectation was inscribed in the Poor Laws, among the lower classes it was an impossible ideal; wages were often so low that they would support only the worker. Women workers were paid lower wages than men. Vagrancy and destitution were common among both sexes. See Hamilton (1978), 40–41.

10.  See Douglas Bush, *The Renaissance and English Humanism* (Toronto: University of Toronto Press, 1939), 78; and H. Baron, "Secularization of Wisdom and Political Humanism in the Renaissance," *Journal of the History of Ideas* 21 (1960), 131–50.

11.  A classic celebration of human potential is Pico della Mirandola's "Oration on the Dignity of Man" (1486).

12.  See James J. Murphy, ed., *Renaissance Eloquence: studies in the theory and practice of Renaissance Rhetoric* (Berkeley: University of California Press, 1983).

13.  Ruth Kelso, *Doctrine for the Lady of the Renaissance* (1956; reprinted, Urbana: University of Illinois Press, 1978), 36; Ann Rosalind Jones, "Surprising Fame: Renaissance Gender Ideologies and Women's Lyric" in *The Poetics of Gender*, ed. Nancy K. Miller (New York: Columbia University Press, 1986), 74–75. Both studies hereafter cited in text.

14.  Lorna Hutson, "The Housewife and the Humanists," chapter one of *The Usurer's Daughter: Male Friendship and Fictions of Women in Sixteenth-Century England* (London: Routledge, 1994); hereafter cited in text.

15.  Sir Thomas Smith, *De Republica Anglorum. The Maner of Government or policie of the Realme of England* (1583), 12.

16.  A. G. Dickens provides a useful summary of Protestant tenets in his "The Ambivalent English Reformation," in *Background to the English Renaissance*, ed. J. B. Trapp (London: Gray-Mills, 1974), 48. See also his *The English Reformation* (1964; reprinted, London: Collins, 1967).

17.  Martin Luther, for example, could argue against Aquinas in declaring that women were not imperfect men, but in his commentary on Genesis he remarks that "it is evident therefore that woman is a different animal to man . . . being far weaker in intellect." Luther resorts to physiology in arguing that

woman's wide hips and narrow shoulders are a sign that she should stay in the home. Cited in Ian Maclean, *The Renaissance Notion of Woman: A Study in the Fortunes of Scholasticism and Medical Science in European Intellectual Life* (Cambridge: Cambridge University Press, 1980), 9–10; hereafter cited in text.

18.   For a selection of writings on women and marriage, see Joan Klein, ed., *Daughters, Wives, and Widows: Writings by Men about Women and Marriage in England, 1500–1640* (Urbana: University of Illinois Press, 1992).

19.   See Constance Jordan, *Renaissance Feminism: Literary Texts and Political Models* (Ithaca, N. Y.: Cornell University Press, 1990), 214–20. The common conflation of "woman" and "wife" is supported by the legal position of women as T. E. summarizes it in *The Lawes Resolutions of Womens Rights: or The Lawes Provision for Women* (1632), 6: "[Women are] understood either married or to bee married."

20.   William Gouge calls the family both "a little Church, and a little commonwealth" in his *Of Domesticall Duties* (1622), 18. Robert Cleaver in his Epistle Dedicatory to *A Godly Form of Householde Governement* (1598) comments likewise on the value of the report that a man "hath a church in his house" (sig. A4v), and later reminds his reader that the "good and carefull housholder . . . himselfe is as a Pastour over his familie" (139); hereafter cited in text.

21.   Elizabeth L. Eisenstein, *The Printing Revolution in Early Modern Europe* (Cambridge: Cambridge University Press, 1983), 145–48; hereafter cited in text.

22.   But see Wendy Wall, *The Imprint of Gender: Authorship and Publication in the English Renaissance* (Ithaca, N. Y.: Cornell University Press, 1993), 20, for a critique of essentialist positions that "claim that print transforms the social order into a uniform, fixed, and totalized world"; hereafter cited in text.

23.   Margaret Ferguson points to the imbalance in Jacob Burckhardt's assessment of women's position in the Renaissance in her introduction to *Rewriting the Renaissance: The Discourses of Sexual Difference in Early Modern Europe*, ed. Margaret W. Ferguson, Maureen Quilligan, and Nancy J. Vickers (Chicago: University of Chicago Press, 1986), xv; hereafter cited in text.

24.   See Maclean, who discusses changing notions of women in the fields of theology, law, medicine, and moral philosophy.

25.   David Cressy, *Literacy & the Social Order* (Cambridge: Cambridge University Press, 1980), 176. Cressy compares an estimated figure of 70 percent illiteracy among men.

26.   Cf. also Vives's justification of the brevity of his text: "though the preceptes for men be innumerable: women yet maye be enformed with fewe wordes . . . for a woman hath no charge to se to, but her honestie and chastyte. Wherfore whan she is enformed of that, she is sufficiently appoynted" (1529, sig. B2).

27.   Richard Mulcaster, *Positions* (1581), ed. Robert Hebert Quick (London: Longmans, Green and Co., 1888), 133–34; hereafter cited in text.

28.  Richard Brathwait, *The English Gentlewoman* (1631), 183; hereafter cited in text.

29.  Bullinger asserts that "What so ever is to be done without the house, that belongeth to the man. . . . The wyves workynge place is wythyn her howse ther to oversee and to set all thinge in good order, and to beware that nothynge be loste, seldome to go forth, but when urgent causes calle hir forth" (1541, sigs. I2v–I3).

30.  Cited in Kelso 1978, 62.

31.  Antonio de Guevara, *The Diall of Princes*, trans. Thomas North (1557), f. 126v; hereafter cited in text.

32.  Cf. Richard Hyrde's preface to Margaret More Roper's translation of Erasmus, *A Devout treatise upon the Pater noster* (1526), sigs. a4v–b1 (hereafter cited in text as Roper), where he argues that one of the "great commodyteis" of Margaret Roper's learning is the entertainment it provides her husband; and Mulcaster (168), whose concern is for the duties of motherhood. An example of a more liberal opinion is to be found later in the period in Jacques Du Bosque's *The Compleat Woman*, translated by N. N. (1639); hereafter cited in text. Du Bosque (or Du Bosq, Du Boscq), in his chapter "Of Prudence and Discretion," remarks that "it is also a tyranny, and a custome, which is no lesse unjust, then old, to reject them from the publike government; as if their spirits were not as capable of affayres of importance, as well as that of men . . . they have some-times brought good remedies to the most desperate maladyes of States and Provinces" (18). Men, he argues, should take the advice of "judicious women."

33.  Lawrence Stone, *The Family, Sex and Marriage in England, 1500–1800* (London: Weidenfeld and Nicolson, 1977), 203. See also Suzanne Hull, *Chaste, Silent and Obedient: English Books for Women 1475–1646* (San Marino: Huntington Library, 1982), 57; hereafter cited in text.

34.  See Book 3 of Baldassare Castiglione, *The Book of the Courtier* (1528), trans. Sir Thomas Hoby, ed. J. H. Whitfield (London: J. M. Dent and Sons, 1974); hereafter cited in text.

35.  Pierre Erondelle, *The French Garden* (1605, sig. B2); hereafter cited in text.

36.  *A Mirrhor mete for all Mothers, Matrones, and Maidens, intituled the Mirrhor of Modestie* (1579) was Thomas Salter's translation of an Italian treatise by Giovanni Michele Bruto entitled *La Institutione di una Fanciulla Nata Nobilmente* (1555); hereafter cited in text.

37.  Lisa Jardine, *Still Harping on Daughters: Women and Drama in the Age of Shakespeare* (London: Harvester Wheatsheaf, 1983), 57–58; Margaret L. King, "Book-Lined Cells: Women and Humanism in the Early Italian Renaissance," in *Beyond Their Sex: Learrned Women of the European Past*, ed. Patricia A. Labalme (New York: New York University Press, 1980), 79–80. Both studies hereafter cited in text.

38.  Thomas Heywood's *Nine Bookes of Various History Concerning Women* (1624) was reissued as *The Generall Historie of Women* (1657); hereafter cited in text.

39. Edward Hake, *A Touchstone for this time present* (1574, sig. C4); hereafter cited in text.

40. Cf. Vives: "And she that hath lerned in bokes to caste this and suche other thynges, and hath furnyshed and fensed her mynde with holy counsailes, shal never fynde to do any vilany" (1529, sig. D3).

41. See Linda Woodbridge, *Women and the English Renaissance: Literature and the Nature of Womankind, 1540–1620* (Brighton: Harvester Press, 1984), for an extended discussion of the controversy; hereafter cited in text.

42. Ann Rosalind Jones, *The Currency of Eros: Women's Love Lyric in Europe 1540–1620* (Bloomington: Indiana University Press, 1990); hereafter cited in text. Much of the literature concerning male-female relations can be interpreted as working out relations between men, as illustrated in a verse by the ballad writer Humfrey Crouch (cited in Hull 1982, 118): "I scorn as much to stoop to women kinde / For if I should then all men would me hate / Because from manhood I degenerate / And surely I should have the love of no men / If I were such a slave unto a woman." Peter Stallybrass, in his "Patriarchal Territories: The Body Enclosed," discusses the contradictory emphases on gender and on class in the Renaissance deployment of woman's body (in Ferguson 1986, 133).

43. Peter de la Primaudaye, *The French Academie*, trans T. B. (1586), 517; hereafter cited in text. Cf. Brathwait's advice that women, when they do speak, "make choyce of such arguments as may best improve your knowledge in houshold affaires, and other private employments" not "State-matters" or "high poynts of Divinity" (89–90).

44. See, for example, the anonymous *Anatomy of a Woman's Tongue*, 5th ed. (1638), reprinted in *Harleian Miscellany*, vol. 2 (London: T. Osborne, 1744), 167–78 (hereafter cited in text as *Anatomy*); and *The Virgins A.B.C.* (1630?), a ballad that associates quietness and obedience. See also Jardine's chapter on representations of shrews and scolds (1983, 103–40).

45. Edmund Tilney's *A briefe and pleasant discourse of duties in Marriage, called the Flower of Friendshippe* (1568; hereafter cited in text) includes a debate on the extent of obedience in a wife. Lady Isabella questions obedience on the grounds that "women have soules as wel as men, they have wit as wel as men, and more apte for procreation of children than men. What reason is it then, that they should be bound, whome nature hath made free?" (sig. D8) Lady Julia, however, follows Erasmus's assertion that "divine, and humaine lawes, in our religion giveth the man absolute authoritie, over the woman in all places" (sig. D8v).

46. In Richard Tofte's translation of Varchi's *The Blazon of Jealousie* (1615), 34. Cf. Heywood: "Two things there are, that be great corrupters of Modestie, and provokers to Sinne; namely, Wanton and unbridled Discourse, and vaine and fantasticke prodigalitie in Attyre" (1657, 438–39).

47. Maclean (1980, 56) outlines two common strands of thinking about female virtue in Renaissance moral philosophy. One argues that feminine virtues complement masculine virtues (thus a woman's silence complements a man's eloquence); another argues that men and women have identical virtues,

but these differ in expression according to their different roles. Brathwait's "moving Rhetoricke" seems to derive from this latter strand. Cf. Francesco Barbaro's *De re uxoria* (1416): "women should believe that they have achieved the glory of eloquence if they honor themselves with the outstanding ornament of silence" (cited in Jones 1990, 21).

48.   See Jardine (1983), 121–33. Cf. *Anatomy* (1744), Epigram XVIII, where the female speaker claims that "her Tongue, although a Member bad, / Was all the 'fensive Weapon that she had." Peter Stallybrass notes that in English law, a man accused of slandering a woman as a "whore" could defend himself by claiming he meant not "whore of her body" but "whore of her tonge" (in Ferguson 1986, 126).

49.   Kelso 1978, 24, identifies other virtues, such as shamefastness, simplicity, peaceableness, patience, humility, piety, constancy, temperance, and modesty.

50.   Vives repeats this advice in his instruction for wives (1529, sig. h2v) as well as maidens.

51.   See, for example, Vives (1529, sig. N4), and Tilney (1568, sig. C2v). Antonio de Guevara provides reasons for such home-keeping: "the houre that she goeth out of the house, she oughte to thynke, that the handemaydes will straye abroade, the children wyll ronne out to playe . . . and that whyche is worst of all, some wyll steale the goodes oute of the house, and the others wyll speake evyll of the renowne of the wife" (1557, f. 89v).

52.   Cf. Stallybrass's discussion of the articulation of woman as property through surveillance of three areas: the mouth, chastity, and the threshold of the house (in Ferguson 1986, 126).

53.   Often, however, women were discursively represented as a single group, regardless of their class. This is evident, for example, in Robert Crowley's vocational advice in *The voice of the laste trumpet* (1549): women are addressed only after 11 male estates from beggars to magistrates have been dealt with (cited in Hull 1982, 162–63). Ruth Kelso (1978, 1) has also noted this discursive lack of attention to class distinctions relative to doctrine for the gentleman: "the lady, shall we venture to say, turns out to be merely a wife."

54.   See Jones (1990, 24–25).

55.   John Taylor, *The Needles Excellency* (1631); hereafter cited in text.

56.   See Iris Brooke, *English Costume of the Seventeenth Century*, 2d ed. (London: Adam & Charles Black, 1950), 26–27.

57.   Cf. Thomas Powell's advice to the lesser gentry: "Let greater personages glory their skill in musicke, the posture of their bodies, their knowledge in languages, the greatnesse and freedome of their spirits, and their arts in arreigning of mens affections at their flattering faces: This is not the way to breede a private Gentlemans Daughter"; *Tom of all Trades or The Plaine Pathway to Preferment* (1631), ed. Frederick J. Furnivall (London: New Shakspere Society, 1876), 173; hereafter cited in text.

58. On reading as a store of resources with transformative power, see, for example, Hutson (1994, 30–31), and Terence Cave, *The Cornucopian Text: Problems of Writing in the French Renaissance* (Oxford: Clarendon Press, 1979), 172–78; hereafter cited in text.

59. See William Haller and Malleville Haller, "The Puritan Art of Love," *Huntington Library Quarterly* 5 (1942), 252; and Marie Bowlands, "Recusant Women 1560–1640," in *Women in English Society 1500–1800*, ed. Mary Prior (London: Methuen, 1985), 165–66. (Prior hereafter cited in text.) Radical sects in the Civil War took this possibility to its logical conclusion as spiritual equality provided grounds for women to change husbands for the sake of conscience; see Keith Thomas, "Women and the Civil War Sects," *Past and Present*, 13 (1958), 42–62.

60. John Foxe, *Actes and Monuments* (1563). Salter says: "if she love to bee delighted in vertue, let her reade that worthie booke of Martyres, compiled by . . . Foxe" (1579, sig. C4).

61. Mary Ellen Lamb, *Gender and Authorship in the Sidney Circle* (Madison: University of Wisconsin Press, 1990), 8; hereafter cited in text.

62. Medical writings, for example, linked women's weaker intellect and reason with the effects of the uterus and with her "cold moist" humours (Maclean 1980, 42). For a discussion of female "misreading," see Susan Noakes, "On the Superficiality of Women," in *The Comparative Perspective on Literature*, ed. Clayton Koelb and Susan Noakes (Ithaca, N. Y.: Cornell University Press, 1988), 339–55.

63. Hull (1982, 1).

64. The relative value of speech and writing was debated in the context of both Renaissance humanism and Protestantism; see Cave (1979) and Malcolm Evans, *Signifying Nothing* (Brighton: Harvester Press, 1986), 41–67.

65. Martin Billingsley, *The Pens Excellencie or The Secretaries Delighte* (1618), sigs. B4–B4v; hereafter cited in text.

66. Thomas Bentley, *The Monument of Matrones: conteining seven severall Lamps of Virginitie, or distinct treatises; whereof the first five concerne praier and meditation . . .* (1582), sig. B1v; hereafter cited in text.

67. See Wall (1983, 11–17), and J. W. Saunders, "The Stigma of Print: A Note on the Social Bases of Tudor Poetry," *Essays in Criticism*, 1 (1951), 139–64; hereafter cited in text. Margaret Ezell emphasizes the importance of manuscript writings of women in this context; see *The Patriarch's Wife: Literary Evidence and the History of the Family* (Chapel Hill: University of North Carolina Press, 1987), 64–65; hereafter cited in text.

68. Cited in *Vives and the Renascence Education of Women*, ed. Foster Watson (New York: Longmans, Green & Co., 1912), 189.

69. Mary Ellman, *Thinking about Women* (New York: Harcourt, 1968), 29; Christiane Rochefort, from "Are Women Writers Still Monsters?" reprinted in *New French Feminisms*, ed. Elaine Marks and Isabelle de Courtivron (London: Harvester Wheatsheaf, 1981), 184.

70.  Francesco Barbaro, cited in Jones 1990, 21.

71.  Sandra Gilbert and Susan Gubar, *The Madwoman in the Attic* (New Haven: Yale University Press, 1979), 6.

72.  *Ben Jonson*, ed. C. H. Herford, Percy and Evelyn Simpson, vol. 8 (Oxford: Clarendon Press, 1947), 222. Cf. Janet Halley's discussion of the sexual dynamics invoked by Donne and his circle in "Textual Intercourse: Anne Donne, John Donne, and the Sexual Poetics of Textual Exchange," in *Seeking the Woman in Late Medieval and Renaissance Writings: Essays in Feminist Contextual Criticism*, ed. Sheila Fisher and Janet E. Halley (Knoxville: University of Tennessee Press, 1989), 187–206; hereafter cited in text.

73.  See Wall (1983) on the gendered figuration of authorship in the English Renaissance.

74.  Lamb (1990, 12–13) links this popularity with the growing perception of translation as a feminized form of writing.

75.  See, for example, Fisher and Halley (1989, 1–17); and Gary Waller, "Struggling into Discourse: The Emergence of Renaissance Women's Writing," in *Silent but for the Word: Tudor Women as Patrons, Translators, and Writers of Religious Works*, ed. Margaret P. Hannay (Kent, Ohio: Kent State University Press, 1985), 238–91 (hereafter cited in text).

*Chapter Two*

1.  The quotation is taken from *The Diary of Lady Margaret Hoby 1599–1605*, ed. Dorothy M. Meads (London: Routledge, 1930), 98; hereafter cited in text as Meads.

2.  Elizabeth Jocelin, *The Mothers Legacie to her unborne Childe* (London, 1624), sig. B6.

3.  Betty Travitsky, *The Paradise of Women: Writings by Englishwomen of the Renaissance* (1981; reprinted, New York: Columbia University Press, 1989), 69; and Estelle C. Jelinek, ed., *Women's Autobiography: Essays in Criticism* (Bloomington: Indiana University Press, 1980), 19. Both works hereafter cited in text.

4.  Juliet Mitchell, *Psychoanalysis and Feminism* (Harmondsworth: Penguin, 1975), 14. See also Patricia Meyer Spacks, "Women's Stories, Women's Selves," *Hudson Review*, 30 (1977), 33.

5.  Claudio Guillén, "Notes toward the Study of the Renaissance Letter," in *Renaissance Genres*, ed. Barbara Kiefer Lewalski (Cambridge, Mass.: Harvard University Press, 1986), 81. See also Jonathan Goldberg, *Writing Matter: From the Hands of the English Renaissance* (Stanford, Calif.: Stanford University Press, 1990), 149–57. Both works hereafter cited in text.

6.  Maureen Bell, George Parfitt, and Simon Shepherd, eds., *A Biographical Dictionary of English Women Writers, 1580–1720* (Boston: G. K. Hall, 1990), 270–71; hereafter cited in text as Bell.

7.  References are to the following editions: Lord Braybrooke, ed., *The Private Correspondence of Jane Lady Cornwallis, 1613–1644* (London: S. & J.

Bentley, 1842); G. B. Harrison, ed., *The Letters of Queen Elizabeth I* (London: Cassell, 1935); and Thomas Taylor Lewis, ed., *Letters of the Lady Brilliana Harley* (London: Camden Society, 1854); each of these editions hereafter cited in text. See also L. M. Baker, comp., *The Letters of Elizabeth Queen of Bohemia* (London: Bodley Head, 1953); Elizabeth Cooper, *The life and letters of Lady Arabella Stuart, including numerous original and unpublished documents,* 2 vols. (London: Hurst and Blackett, 1866); Ruth Hughey, ed., *The correspondence of Lady Katherine Paston, 1603–1627* (Norfolk: Norfolk Record Society, 1941); and Alison Wall, ed., *Two Elizabethan women: correspondence of Joan and Maria Thynne 1575–1611* (Devizes: Wiltshire Record Society, 1983). For criticism, see especially *New Ways of Looking at Old Texts,* ed. W. Speed Hill (Binghamton: Renaissance English Text Society, 1993); Barbara Kiefer Lewalski's chapters on Lady Arbella Stuart and Elizabeth, Queen of Bohemia, in her *Writing Women in Jacobean England* (Cambridge, Mass.: Harvard University Press, 1993; hereafter cited in text); Alison Wall, "Elizabethan Precept and Feminine Practice: The Thynne Family of Longleat," *History,* 75 (1990), 23–38; and Sara Jayne Steen, "Fashioning an Acceptable Self: Arbella Stuart," *English Literary Renaissance,* 18 (1988), 78–95. Mary Ellen Lamb briefly discusses the letters of the Cooke sisters (in Hannay, 1985, 120–24).

     8.    Elizabeth Tudor (1533–1603) became queen in 1558. Many of her letters prior to her accession have survived, but since they were written before the period covered in this book, I make no reference to them. Harrison publishes letters written as early as 1544, when Elizabeth was a child of 11.

     9.    Jane Meautys (1581–1659) was first married to Sir William Cornwallis in 1608, and then to Nathaniel Bacon in 1614, although she kept her first husband's name until 1626, when Charles I ruled that Knights of Bath were to take precedence over Knights Bachelors (Braybrooke 1842, 137).

     10.    Lucy Harington (1581–1627) was married to Edward Russell, third Earl of Bedford, in 1594; she was a notable patron of literature and the arts. For discussions of her life and activities as courtier and patron, see especially Lewalski 1993, 95–124; and Margaret M. Byard, "The Trade of Courtiership: The Countess of Bedford and the Bedford Memorials; A Family History from 1585 to 1607," *History Today* (1979), 20–28.

     11.    Lewalski comments that this "sober religious persona" is captured in a portrait of the countess, dated 1620, in which she is dressed in black with black jewelry and against a black background, although a "hint of the earlier showy display remains" in coronet, lace trimmings, and hair (1993, 103).

     12.    Brilliana Conway (1600–1643) became the third wife of Sir Robert Harley in 1623. She died while she was defending the Harley estate, Brampton Bryan, from Royalist forces; a letter to her son, dated 2 July 1642, shows her resolve in these circumstances: "at first when I sawe how outrageously this cuntry carried themselfes aganst your father, my anger was so up, and my sorrow, that I had hardly patience to stay; but now, I have well considered, if I goo away I shall leave all that your father has to the pray of our enimys, which they would

be glad of; so that, and pleas God, I purpos to stay as long as it is poscibell, if I live; and this is my resolution, without your father contradict it. I cannot make a better use of my life, next to sarving my God, than doo what good I can for you" (Lewis 1854, 182). For a biography emphasizing Harley's motherhood, see Margaret George, *Women in the First Capitalist Society: Experiences in Seventeenth-Century England* (Urbana: University of Illinois Press, 1988), 193–202.

13.   Mary Cornwallis (d. 1627) was the youngest daughter of Sir Thomas Cornwallis, sister of Sir William.

14.   See, for example, James Olney, "Autobiography and the Cultural Moment: A Thematic, Historical, and Bibliographical Introduction," in *Autobiography: Essays Theoretical and Critical*, ed. James Olney (Princeton, N. J.: Princeton University Press, 1980), 3–27; Dean Ebner, *Autobiography in Seventeenth-Century England: Theology and the Self* (The Hague: Mouton, 1971; hereafter cited in text); and Elizabeth W. Bruss, *Autobiographical Acts: The Changing Situation of a Literary Genre* (Baltimore: Johns Hopkins University Press, 1976). Specific discussions of women's autobiographical writing are to be found in Paul Delany, *British Autobiography in the Seventeenth Century* (London: Routledge, 1969), 158 ff.; Elspeth Graham, Hilary Hinds, Elaine Hobby and Helen Wilcox, eds., *Her Own Life: Autobiographical Writings by Seventeenth-Century English Women* (London: Routledge, 1989; hereafter cited in text as Graham 1989); Mary G. Mason, "The Other Voice: Autobiography of Women Writers," in Olney, 207–35; Sara Heller Mendelson, "Stuart Women's Diaries and Occasional Memoirs," in Prior (1985, 181–210; hereafter cited in text); Cynthia S. Pomerleau, "The Emergence of Women's Autobiography in England," in Jelinek (1980, 21–38); Mary Beth Rose, "Gender, Genre, and History: Seventeenth-Century English Women and the Art of Autobiography," in *Women in the Middle Ages and the Renaissance: Literary and Historical Perspectives*, ed. Mary Beth Rose (Syracuse, N. Y.: Syracuse University Press, 1986), 245–78; Sidonie Smith, *A Poetics of Women's Autobiography: Marginality and the Fictions of Self-Representation* (Bloomington: Indiana University Press, 1987); Domna C. Stanton, ed., *The Female Autograph* (1984; reprinted, Chicago: University of Chicago Press, 1989); and Helen Wilcox, "Private Writing and Public Function: Autobiographical Texts by Renaissance Englishwomen," in *Gloriana's Face: Women, Public and Private, in the English Renaissance*, ed. S. P. Cerasano and Marion Wynne-Davies (London: Harvester Wheatsheaf, 1992).

15.   Linda Anderson, "At the Threshold of the Self: Women and Autobiography," in *Women's Writing: A Challenge to Theory*, ed. Moira Monteith (Brighton: Harvester Press, 1986), 60.

16.   References are to the following editions or manuscripts: V. Sackville-West, ed., *The diary of the Lady Anne Clifford* (London: Heinemann, 1923); Meads (1930); and Grace Mildmay's manuscript journal (1617; hereafter cited in text as Mildmay), now at the Central Library, Northampton. Extracts of Mildmay's journal appear (though with some inaccuracy) in Rachel Wiegall, "An Elizabethan Gentlewoman: The Journal of Lady Mildmay, circa

1570–1617 (unpublished)," *Quarterly Review*, 215 (1911), 119–38 (hereafter cited in text). See also the recent edition of Clifford's diaries and memoirs, *The Diaries of Lady Anne Clifford*, ed. D. J. H. Clifford (Wolfeboro Falls, N. H.: Alan Sutton, 1991).

17.   Margaret Dakins (1571–1633) was brought up in the household of the Earl and Countess of Huntingdon; a wealthy heiress, she was widowed twice before 1596, when she married Sir Thomas Posthumous Hoby (son of Elizabeth Cooke Hoby, later Lady Russell).

18.   Ebner (1971) discusses the dramatic shaping of the Puritan autobiography in a chapter on *Grace Abounding*. Mendelson points out that the model behind many of the early diaries by women was "the Puritan duty of pious self-examination" (in Prior 1985, 186). She cites a guide published in 1646 that includes a list of 38 questions for women to ask themselves each night; the list addresses time of rising, spiritual exercises, household business, dinner, company, and recreation. Lady Hoby's diary appears, initially at least, to be answering similar questions.

19.   "I thought good to set them downe unto my daughter, and her children, as familiar talke and communication with them, I being dead, as yf I were alive" (Mildmay, 4). Grace Sharington (1552–1620) married Anthony Mildmay in 1567, whose father Sir Walter died in 1589, whereupon she became the mistress of Apethorpe Manor, Northamptonshire. Her only child, Mary, married Sir Francis Fane, later Earl of Westmoreland; their heir, Mildmay Fane, is specifically addressed in the journal (Mildmay, 67). The journal is discussed by Retha M. Warnicke in "Lady Mildmay's Journal: A Study in Autobiography and Meditation in Reformation England," *Sixteenth Century Journal*, 20 (1989), 55–68. For biographical information, see also Wiegall (1911), and Herbert A. Mildmay, *A Brief Memoir of the Mildmay Family* (London: privately printed, 1913).

20.   The autobiographical preface covers 89 manuscript pages, while the meditations themselves extend to more than 900 pages; the meditations are edited from a single volume of several that she had written down over the previous 50 years as described in Warnicke (1983, 57). The mother's-advice book is discussed in Beilin (1987, 266–85); and in Travitsky (1981, 50–68).

21.   Warnicke (1983, 59); Mildmay (9). In the same way she encourages her grandson, Mildmay Fane, to preserve the blood of his "honorable Grandmother, the Lady le Dispencer . . . unspotted evermore as she hath done, Chaste and upright in all her vertuous conversation" (Mildmay 1923, 70).

22.   Anne Clifford (1589–1676) was the daughter of the Earl and Countess of Cumberland, who were estranged soon after her birth. Her father, at his death in 1606, willed his estate to his brother, but she and her mother Margaret (Russell) Clifford maintained her legal claim to part of the inheritance by entail dating back to the reign of Edward II in the early 14th century. Anne was married to Richard Sackville, Earl of Dorset, in 1609; after his death she married Philip Herbert, Earl of Pembroke and Montgomery, in 1630, but lived

separately from him after a few years. She gained the estates she had so long struggled for at the death of her uncle and his son in 1643, and moved north to take over her property in 1649, a year before Herbert's death. For the rest of her life she was actively engaged in the administration and development of her property. See George C. Williamson, *Lady Anne Clifford, Countess of Dorset, Pembroke & Montgomery, 1590–1676: Her Life, Letters, and Work* (Kendal: T. Wilson, 1922); and Martin Holmes, *Proud Northern Lady: Lady Anne Clifford, 1590–1676*, (Chichester: Phillimore, 1975). See also the chapter on Clifford in Lewalski (1993, 125–51); Mary Ellen Lamb, "The Agency of the Split Subject: Lady Anne Clifford and the Uses of Reading," *English Literary Renaissance*, 22 (1992), 347–68 (hereafter cited in text); and R. T. Spence, "Lady Anne Clifford, Countess of Dorset, Pembroke, and Montgomery (1590–1676): A Reappraisal," *Northern History*, 15–16 (1979–80), 43–65.

    23.  Lewalski (1993, 368, n. 1) notes that two copies exist, an 18th-century manuscript copy made by the Duchess of Portland, in the Portland Papers at Longleat House, Wiltshire; and a (?) 19th-century copy now at the Center for Kentish Studies, Maidstone, Kent (on which Sackville-West's edition is based).

    24.  Lewalski argues that Anne Clifford justifies her resistance in the diary "in terms of the paradigm provided by Foxe's female martyrs, enacting a secular and self-interested version of their patient endurance and firm adherence to the right . . . she seems to see herself engaged in an almost mythic battle" (1993; 147, 151).

    25.  Lamb argues that "Clifford remained a split subject, caught in the contradictions between obedient wife and aristocratic heir" (1992, 349).

    26.  Letter dated 22 September 1615, cited in Lewalski (1993, 135).

    27.  The household at Knole alone was 10 times the size of the Yorkshire and Nottinghamshire estates of the Hobys and the Mildmays, with their dozen or so servants.

    28.  See Lamb (1992, 360–66) for an interesting discussion of this portrait.

    29.  Virginia Woolf, *A Writer's Diary*, ed. Leonard Woolf (London: Hogarth Press, 1959), 13–14.

*Chapter Three*

    1.  Rachel Speght, *Mortalities Memorandum with a Dreame Prefixed, imaginarie in manner; reall in matter* (1621), 4; hereafter cited in text.

    2.  "The Cooke Sisters: Attitudes toward Learned Women in the Renaissance," in Hannay (1985, 21).

    3.  H. S. Bennett has estimated that translation comprised one-fifth of all texts printed in the second half of the 16th century; *English Books and Readers 1558 to 1603* (Cambridge: Cambridge University Press, 1965), 104 (hereafter cited in text). The huge disparity in the number of published translations pro-

duced by the two sexes gives a clear indication of the gendered nature of writing as a practice. Bennett counts over 1000 items translated in the Elizabethan period alone, but less than a dozen actually written by women can be identified in the same period; a mere seven items are listed as printed between 1558 and 1603 in Patricia Gartenberg and Nena Thames Whittemore, "A Checklist of English Women in Print, 1475–1640," *Bulletin of Bibliography and Magazine Notes*, 34 (1977), 1–13.

    4.   The representation of translation and the translator is discussed by Lori Chamberlain in "Gender and the Metaphorics of Translation," in Lawrence Venuti, ed., *Rethinking Translation: Discourse, Subjectivity, Ideology* (London: Routledge, 1992), 57–71.

    5.   Florio's prefatory remarks to his translation of Montaigne's *Essayes* (1603) are discussed by Lamb in Hannay (1985, 115–17).

    6.   Nothing is known of Margaret Tyler other than the information, given in her dedication to Lord Thomas Howard, that she had in the past been in service to Howard's parents. She offers her translation "as a simple testimony of that good will which I bere to your parents while they lived then being their servant" (sig. A2v). The *Mirrour* is discussed by Tina Krontiris in her *Oppositional Voices: Women as Writers and Translators of Literature in the English Renaissance* (London: Routledge, 1992), 49–62; hereafter cited in text.

    7.   The dedication of Man's work indicates some connection between her own family and that of the Earl of Strafford: "I had the Honour to be admitted into the House of my Lord Your Father, where my Parents did introduce me" (sig. A2v). She may be the daughter of William Man of Lyndsell, Essex; see Maureen Bell (1990, 132). John Barclay's Latin *Argenis and Polyarchus* had been translated into English by Kingesmill Long (1625) and by Sir R. Le Guys and Thomas May (1628).

    8.   Lady Mary Wroth's *Urania* (1621) is discussed in chapter eight. Philip Sidney's *Arcadia* was translated into French by Geneviève Chappelain in 1624–25; see Sir Philip Sidney, *The Countess of Pembroke's Arcadia*, ed. Victor Skretkowicz (Oxford: Clarendon Press, 1987), xliv. I have been unable to trace any reference to the *New Amarantha*.

    9.   Nothing is known of Du Verger (or Du Vegerre, Duvergerre) beyond her publication of *Admirable Events: selected out of foure bookes, written in French by the Right Reverend John Peter Camus . . .* (1639).

    10.   Anne Dowriche was born Anne Edgcombe and "was 'under age' in 1560, the date of her father's will" (Bell 1990, 67). Her husband, Hugh Dowriche, was made rector of Honiton in Devon in 1587. *The French Historie*, as Beilin has stated, is based on Thomas Timme's translation of Jean de Serre, *The Three Partes of Commentaries, containing the whole and perfect discourse of the civill warres of Fraunce* (1574). See Beilin (1987, 101–7, hereafter cited in text); and Elaine Beilin, "Writing Public Poetry: Humanism and the Woman Writer," *Modern Language Quarterly*, 51 (1990), 258–67.

    11.   Iambic couplets with alternate lines of 12 and 14 syllables.

12.  Bale's play was originally written c. 1534, and was revised in several stages over the next 20 years or so, during a period of acute religious controversy; see Peter Happé, ed., *The Complete Plays of John Bale*, 2 vols. (Cambridge: D. S. Brewer, 1985), I, 9–11.

13.  Title page; the verse is from 1 Timothy 3:2.

14.  See, for example, the speech of Francis Collute to his sons as they are about to be butchered (ff. 33–33v), and that of Masson de Rivers (ff. 34v–35v), who is made a figure of Christ in his death.

15.  Little is certainly known of Tyrwhit; she may have been governess or lady-in-waiting to Princess Elizabeth in 1548 (Bell 1990, 199; Beilin 1987, 81). Certainly the appearance of her prayers following those of Elizabeth, Catherine Parr, and Jane Dudley suggests an elevated position.

16.  Frances Manners, daughter of the Earl of Rutland, was married to Henry Nevill, Lord Aburgavenny (or Bergavenny, Abergavenny). See Beilin (1987, 81–86), for a discussion of both Tyrwhit and Aburgavenny.

17.  Indeed, Aburgavenny's prayers are advertised as maternal advice in the heading to her work: "committed at the houre of hir death, to the right Worshipfull Ladie Marie Fane (hir onlie daughter) as a Jewell of health for the soule" (139).

18.  Prowse was born Anne Vaughan c. 1535, had married Henry Locke by 1553, married the preacher Edward Dering c. 1573, and had married her third husband, Richard Prowse, by 1583. She was a close friend and confidante of John Knox, and Patrick Collinson discusses her life as an example of women's participation in the English Reformation in his *Godly People: Essays on English Protestantism and Puritanism* (London: Hambledon Press, 1983), 276–87; hereafter cited in text. Her work as a translator is briefly discussed in Beilin (1987, 61–63).

19.  The full titles are: *Sermons of John Calvin, upon the Songe that Ezechias made after he had bene sicke, and afflicted by the hand of God, conteyned in the 38. Chapiter of Esay*; *Of The markes of the children of God, and of their comforts in afflictions*. There is some debate with regard to the authorship of the verse "Meditation" that follows the Sermons, since it is introduced by the statement that it "was delivered me by my frend with whom I knew I might be so bolde to use and publishe it as pleased me" (sig. A3). It is unclear whether this statement derives from Prowse or from the printer. Collinson suggests that the "Meditation" may perhaps be the work of John Knox and not Anne Locke Prowse (1983, 280).

20.  Celeste M. Schenck, "Feminism and Deconstruction: Re-Constructing the Elegy," *Tulsa Studies in Women's Literature* 4 (1986), 13; hereafter cited in text.

21.  Elias Ashmole, *The Antiquities of Berkshire*, 3 vols. (London: E. Curll, 1719), vol. II, 465–69, 491. Lady Russell's elegies are briefly discussed in Betty Travitsky (1980, 23); and by Lamb in Hannay (1985, 119–20).

22.  Travitsky (1980, 23) notes that the elegy was "transcribed by Paul Hentzner, a sixteenth-century traveler," and printed among his writings in

1757. Very different in its impersonal voice is the epitaph of Margaret Clifford, Countess of Cumberland (?1560–1616), to Richard Candish, inscribed on a wall at Hornsey Church, Middlesex, in 1601; with no sense of the speaker's personal grief and no specification of the relation between speaker and subject, the poem takes its place as a public exercise. Charlotte Kohler reproduces the epitaph from Joseph Ritson's *Bibliographica Poetica* (1802); see her "Elizabethan Woman of Letters, the extent of her literary activities" (Ph.D. dissertation, University of Virginia, 1936), 292; hereafter cited in text. Margaret Russell married George Clifford, Earl of Cumberland, in 1577, and was mother of Anne Clifford.

23. Printed among the poems of John Soowthern (or Southern) in his *Pandora, The Musique of the beautie, of his Mistresse Diana* (1584, sigs. C3v–C4v); hereafter cited in text. Anne de Vere (1556–88) was the daughter of Mildred Cooke and William Cecil, Lord Burghley. Married to Edward de Vere in 1571, she was repudiated by her husband after the birth of her first child, Elizabeth, in 1575. The son of the sonnets was born in 1583 after a reconciliation. Ellen Moody discusses the poems in the context of de Vere's life in "Six Elegiac Poems, Possibly by Anne Cecil de Vere, Countess of Oxford," *English Literary Renaissance*, 19 (1989), 152–70; hereafter cited in text.

24. In fact, de Vere had three more children, all girls, before she died in 1588 (Moody 1989, 159).

25. Edmund Lodge, ed., *Illustrations of British History, Biography, and Manners . . .*, 2d ed., vol. 3 (London: John Chidley, 1838), 241. Anne Dacre Howard (1558–1630) was married to Philip Howard, Earl of Arundel, in 1571. She and her husband professed Catholicism in 1582 and 1584, respectively, and the earl was imprisoned and executed in 1595. See Kohler (1936, 170–71); and Travitsky (1980, 33–34). Lodge (241), who rediscovered the poem, suggested that it was written on the execution of the Earl of Arundel in 1595, but there is nothing but circumstantial evidence (and the desire to locate writing by women in a domestic framework) to substantiate this claim. It is more likely, as Margaret Ezell suggests, that the elegy was written on the occasion of the death of Prince Henry in 1612; see her *Writing Women's Literary History* (Baltimore: Johns Hopkins University Press, 1993), 124; hereafter cited in text. A collection that I have been unable to locate, entitled *Miscentur seria locis, Elegies, Exequies . . .* (1647), apparently includes an elegy by Anne Howard on the death of the prince.

26. See Lewalski (1993, especially 110–15, 120–22) for a discussion of the countess's literary relations with Donne. Lewalski (121–22) reprints the elegy, which also appears in Ann Stanford, ed., *The Women Poets in English* (New York: McGraw-Hill, 1972), 34–35.

27. Ben Jonson wrote "The Court Pucell," a vicious epigram on Bulstrode, sometime before her death in 1609.

28. A similar coterie group may be the origin of a fictional prose contract drawn up by Lady Frances Southwell, daughter of Charles Howard, Earl of Nottingham, and lady-in-waiting to Queen Anne in 1609. Lady Southwell's

"Certaine Edicts from a Parliament in Eutopia" was first printed as an addition to the sixth impression of Sir Thomas Overbury's *Conceited Newes* in 1615, among a collection of satirical pieces by Overbury and his friends. See James E. Savage, ed., *The "Conceited Newes" of Sir Thomas Overbury and His Friends* (Gainesville: Scholars' Facsimiles and Reprints, 1968), 218–22. Savage (xxiii) argues that the "Newes" and "Edicts" that make up this collection "are part of an elaborate courtly game" analogous to Jonson's "vapours" in *Bartholomew Fair*, a game which wittily satirized the court of King James and its conduct (xxix). Southwell's 17 "Edicts" are alternately addressed to the men and women of the court, and show particular concern for the conduct of relationships between the sexes.

29.   See Arthur Clifford, ed., *Tixall Poetry* (Edinburgh: James Ballantyne and Co., 1813); all quotations derive from this edition.

30.   Most of the poetry appears to have been written in Ireland, before her return to London (c. 1631) with her second husband, Sir Henry Sibthorpe, but few poems can be dated with certainty; Southwell may have continued revising her poems until her death in 1636. The manuscript is held in the Folger Shakespeare Library (V.b. 198) and has recently been published by the Renaissance English Text Society, ed. Jean Klénè. Anne Southwell (1574–1636) was the daughter of Sir Thomas Harris of Cornworthy, Devon; a maid of honor to Elizabeth I, she married Sir Thomas Southwell of Norfolk, who settled in Ireland. After his death in 1626, she married Sir Henry Sibthorpe. For a discussion of her library and of one of the letters in the commonplace book, see Jean C. Cavanaugh "The Library of Lady Southwell and Captain Sibthorpe," *Studies in Bibliography*, 20 (1967), 243–54 (hereafter cited in text); and her "Lady Southwell's Defense of Poetry" (1984), reprinted in *Women in the Renaissance: Selections from English Literary Renaissance*, ed. Kirby Farrell, Elizabeth H. Hageman, and Arthur F. Kinney (Amherst: University of Massachusetts Press, 1990), 175–78 (hereafter cited in text as Farrell, 1990).

31.   In this, she echoes her own defense of poetry in a letter to Lady Ridgway: "To heare a Hero & Leander or some such other busye nothing, might bee a meanes to skandalize this art. But can a cloud disgrace the sunne? will you behold Poesye in perfect beautye: Then see the kingly Prophett, that sweete singer of Israell, explicating the glorye of our god . . . O never enough to bee admired, devine Poesye: It is the subject, that commends or condemmes the art" (f. 3v). The letter is reprinted by Cavanaugh in Farrell (1990, 176–77).

32.   A few poems in the manuscript diverge from piety in addressing a lover or husband. One, for example, appropriates the advice of the marriage manuals for the lament of an aging wife who has lost the love of her husband:

Am I a yoakffelowe, or slave

What is my due I looke to have

Or else Ile digg my self a grave

      and Ly at rest. (f. 11)

Another, "Like to a lampe wherein the light is dead" (f. 9v), laments a tempo-
rary separation from the lover in lines that are reworked later in "An Epitaph
upon the Countess of Sommersett" (f. 23).

33.   The title page is dated 2 December 1626, and Cavanaugh (1967,
244) notes that the manuscript book, which includes old entries by the Sibthorpe
family, was presented to her by her second husband after their marriage.

34.   See Leicester Bradner, ed., *The Poems of Queen Elizabeth I* (Providence,
R. I.: Brown University Press, 1964); all quotations derive from this edition,
hereafter cited in text. Several poems and translations written by Elizabeth
before her accession survive, notably poems written during her imprisonment at
Woodstock and her early translation of Marguerite de Navarre's *Le Miroir de
l'âme pécheresse* ("The glasse of the synnefull soule" in Elizabeth's translation),
which she presented in manuscript to Catherine Parr in 1544. During her reign
she translated from several classical texts, including Boethius's popular moral
tract, *The Consolation of Philosophy*, Plutarch's essay on curiosity, and part of
Horace's *Art of Poetry*; see Bradner (1964, 13–68). Again, the choice of material
differentiates the sovereign's work from that of other women. Her adult translation from both Greek and Latin functions primarily as a display of the queen's
humanist learning.

35.   The poem is reprinted from *Nugae Antiquae* (II. 411–16), in
Alexander Dyce, ed., *Specimens of British Poetesses* (London: T. Rodd, 1827),
67–75; hereafter cited in text. After James's accession to the English throne,
Elizabeth (1596–1662) spent several years in the care of the Haringtons prior to
her marriage to Frederick, Elector Palatine, in 1613.

36.   The full title of Primrose's text is *A Chaine of Pearle. Or, A Memoriall
of the peerles Graces, and Heroick Vertues of Queene Elizabeth, of Glorious Memory*.
Little is known of Primrose. She may have been the wife of Gilbert Primrose (c.
1580–1641) who returned to England from France, where he had been the
head of the Reformed Church; he was made chaplain to King Charles by 1628,
after several petitions for help (Bell 1990, 161–62). Greer, however, suggests
she may have been a daughter or daughter-in-law of Gilbert's cousin James, an
Edinburgh printer; see *Kissing the Rod: An Anthology of 17th Century Women's
Verse*, ed. Germaine Greer, Jeslyn Medoff, Melinda Sansone, and Susan Hastings
(London: Virago Press, 1988), 83 (hereafter cited in text as Greer 1988).

*Chapter Four*

1.   The quotation is from Mary Sidney's dedicatory poem "Even now
that Care" (l. 87); see G. F. Waller, ed., *The Triumph of Death and Other
Unpublished and Uncollected Poems by Mary Sidney, Countess of Pembroke
(1561–1621)* (Salzburg: Institut für Englische Sprache ünd Literatur, 1977);
hereafter cited in text as Waller 1977.

2.   Mentions of Mary Sidney's life and work are included, for example,
in biographical studies of Philip Sidney by Mona Wilson, John Buxton, Roger
Howell, James M. Osborn, and Katherine Duncan-Jones.

3.  The countess was involved in the preparation and publication of the first authorized version of Philip Sidney's romance in 1593, fully titled *The Countesse of Pembrokes Arcadia*; this text brings together the three books revised by her brother before his death and the final two books, derived from an earlier version in her possession. Sidney also ensured the publication of Philip Sidney's *The Defence of Poesie* in 1595 and the authorized edition of his works in 1598, which included the complete sonnet sequence of *Astrophil and Stella*. Only recently have Sidney's own works become more widely available. An edition of her complete works, prepared by Margaret P. Hannay and Noel Kinnamon, is forthcoming.

4.  Gary Waller, *Mary Sidney, Countess of Pembroke: A Critical Study of Her Writings and Literary Milieu* (Salzburg: Institut für Anglistik ünd Amerikanistik, 1979); hereafter cited in text.

5.  Ringler identifies only seven references to Philip Sidney as a writer in the 270 poems of the three Oxford and Cambridge memorial volumes, and only 21 further such allusions in all the tributes paid him in the four years after his death. W. A. Ringler, "Sir Philip Sidney: The Myth and the Man," in *Sir Philip Sidney: 1586 and the Creation of a Legend*, ed. Jan Van Dorsten, Dominic Baker-Smith, and Arthur F. Kinney (Leiden: Leiden University Press, 1986), 11; hereafter cited in text as Van Dorsten 1986.

6.  See Fulke Greville, "Building Sidney's Reputation: Texts and Editors of the *Arcadia*," in Van Dorsten 1986, 111–20. In a letter to Sir Francis Walsingham written soon after Philip Sidney's death, Greville is anxious to ward off the publication of the "old Arcadia" since the "correction of that old one . . . [is] fitter to be printed than the first"; cited in John Buxton, *Sir Philip Sidney and the English Renaissance*, 3d ed. (London: Macmillan, 1987), 179.

7.  "'Doo What Men May Sing': Mary Sidney and the Tradition of Admonitory Dedication," in Margaret P. Hannay (1985, 155). Hannay's excellent biography of Mary Sidney discusses her encouragement of the "hagiography that has developed into the Sidney legend" at length; see *Philip's Phoenix: Mary Sidney, Countess of Pembroke* (Oxford: Oxford University Press, 1990), 60 ff. Both hereafter cited in text.

8.  All three poems are reprinted in Waller (1977, 88–95, 176–79); subsequent quotations derive from this edition. The remaining poem, "A Dialogue betweene two shepheards, *Thenot* and *Piers*, in praise of *ASTREA*," was first published in Francis Davison's *A Poeticall Rhapsody* (1602), and is reprinted in Waller (1977, 181–83).

9.  *Astrophel* by Edmund Spenser was published with *Colin Clouts Come Home Again*. See Waller (1977, 176–80).

10.  A presentation copy of the Sidney Psalms was prepared for the planned visit of Queen Elizabeth to Wilton in 1599, a visit which never took place; see Hannay (1985, 276 n. 2). The manuscript that W. A. Ringler identifies as "J" (dated 1599) in *The Poems of Sir Philip Sidney* (Oxford: Clarendon Press, 1962), 550–51 (hereafter cited in text as Ringler 1962), contains both dedicato-

ry poems and may be the presentation copy . Ringler notes that J is a transcript of an earlier manuscript, designated "A," that was prepared by John Davies of Hereford in "a single beautiful Italian hand," and postulates that the A manuscript may have been prepared for presentation but "not presented because the many corrections made in the process of copying marred its appearance" (547).

11.   Mary Sidney's "To the Angell Spirit of the most excellent Sir Philip Sidney," which was printed in Samuel Daniel's *Whole Workes, in Poetrie* (1623), is reprinted in Waller (1977, 190–92); subsequent quotations (identified as "Spirit") derive from Waller's edition.

12.   The debate is summarized in *The Works of Edmund Spenser: The Minor Poems*, vol. I, ed. C. G. Osgood and H. G. Lotspeich (Baltimore: Johns Hopkins Press, 1943), 500–505; hereafter cited in text as Osgood 1943. See also Waller (1979, 89–93), and Hannay (1990, 63–67). The attribution to Spenser has not yet been firmly rejected, although critical opinion appears to be currently in favor of the countess.

13.   Even Waller (1979, 92) supplements his argument in favor of the countess by stating that "some of the 'Lay's' careless or strained lines are hardly up to Spenser's standard of competence."

14.   Osgood's list of parallels with Edmund Spenser's work could usefully be compared to parallels with Mary Sidney's own writing. For example, Osgood compares line 55, "Oh death that hast us of such riches reft," with Spenser's description of Philip Sidney as the "worldes chiefest riches" in *The Ruines of Time* (1591). Yet in Sidney's dedicatory poem to Queen Elizabeth she complains that with Sir Philip's death, "the poorer [is] left, the richer reft awaye" (l. 22). Moreover, in both poems prefaced to the presentation copy of the Psalms, as in the "Lay," the rhyme words "reft" and "left" are used in the same elegiac context. Cf. "The Dolefull Lay" (ll. 50–52, 57–79), and "To thee pure sprite" (ll. 15–16).

15.   Waller (1979, 92) also points to the typographical separation of the "Lay" from the poems that precede and follow it in the collection, and to differences in tone between the "Lay" (which he compares with formal Greek elegy) and Spenser's "Astrophel" (a narrative lyric "suggestive of the Homeric hymns").

16.   Frances Young conjectured in her biography of Mary Sidney that the "Idle passion" and "toy" that Sidney requests Sir Edward Wotton to return to her (in a letter written about 1594) may have been the "Lay"; *Mary Sidney, Countess of Pembroke* (London: David Nutt, 1912), 56–57 (hereafter cited in text). In *The Ruines of Time*, completed in 1590, Spenser alludes to Mary Sidney's elegiac voice in the context of an address to her dead brother: "but who can better sing, / Than thine owne sister, peerles Ladie bright, / Which to thee sings with deep harts sorrowing" (ll. 316–18).

17.   Osgood (1943, 185).

18.   Significantly, the "shepheards lasses" are represented not as mistresses of Astrophel, but as the readers of his riddles and singers of his lays of love.

19.   Osgood draws a parallel between the figure of the fair flower and "Astrophel" (ll. 181 ff.); but compare line 32 ("Hath cropt the stalke which bore so faire a flowre") with Sidney's translation of Petrarch's *Triumph of Death* (l. 115): "So cropt the flower, of all this world most faire" (Waller 1977, 70).

20.   In Hannay (1985, 149–65); see also Hannay (1990, 3–14 and passim) on the Sidney-Dudley alliance.

21.   William Harvey, *Disputations Touching the Generation of Animals*, trans. Gweneth Whitteridge (Oxford: Blackwell Scientific Publications, 1981), 192.

22.   This assertion should no more be taken at face value (though it often has been) than Philip Sidney's "looke in thy heart and write" (*Astrophil and Stella*, sonnet 1, l. 14; Ringler 1962, 165).

23.   "'To the Angell spirit . . .': Mary Sidney's Entry into the 'World of Words,'" in *The Renaissance Englishwoman in Print: Counterbalancing the Canon*, ed. Anne M. Haselkorn and Betty S. Travitsky (Amherst: University of Massachusetts Press, 1990), 271; Haselkorn and Travitsky 1990 hereafter cited in text.

24.   E. Kite (1898), cited in John Briley, "Mary Sidney—A 20th Century Reappraisal," in *Elizabethan and Modern Studies*, ed. J. P. Vander Motten (Gent: Seminarie voor Engelse en Amerikaanse Literatuur, 1985), 54.

25.   *Certain Sermons or Homilies*, ed. John Griffiths (London: Society for Promoting Christian Knowledge, 1914), 537.

26.   The prose tract is reprinted in *The Countess of Pembroke's Translation of Philippe de Mornay's "Discourse of Life and Death,"* ed. Diane Bornstein (Detroit: Michigan Consortium for Medieval and Early Modern Studies, 1983). Mary Sidney's translation of Robert Garnier's play is reprinted as "The Tragedie of Antonie" in *Narrative and Dramatic Sources of Shakespeare*, ed. Geoffrey Bullough, vol. 5 (London: Routledge and Kegan Paul, 1964), 358–406. Waller (1977) reprints the *Triumph of Death*. See Bornstein (1983), Bullough (1964), and Waller (1977); hereafter cited in text. J. C. A. Rathmell has edited the Psalms from the Penshurst Place manuscript (manuscript A). See *The Psalms of Sir Philip Sidney and the Countess of Pembroke* (New York: New York University Press, 1963); hereafter cited in text. Philip Sidney versified the first 43 psalms; Mary Sidney versified Psalms 44 to 150.

27.   The popularity of the *Trionfi* led to Ascham's lament in *The Scholemaster* (1563–68) that Italianate Englishmen had more reverence for the *Triumphs* of Petrarch than for the *Genesis* of Moses; see Robert Coogan, "Petrarch's *Trionfi* and the English Renaissance," *Studies in Philology* 67 (1970), 306. The importance of the Psalms is suggested by the volume of editions published in the Renaissance; the Sternhold and Hopkins Psalter alone went through 280 editions by 1640. See Hallett Smith, "English Metrical Psalms in the Sixteenth Century and Their Literary Significance," *Huntington Library Quarterly*, 9 (1946), 251; hereafter cited in text.

28.   Alexander Maclaren Witherspoon has argued that Mary Sidney, aiming to "impart a more intellectual atmosphere to English tragedy" (75), led

the way for a group of writers who produced a dozen plays using Garnier as a general model. He includes in that number Thomas Kyd's translation of Garnier's *Cornelia*, two plays written in direct imitation of *Antonie* (Daniel's *Tragedie of Cleopatra* and Brandon's *The vertuous Octavia*), and several plays based on the French Senecan model (including Greville's *Mustapha* and *Alaham*, four plays by Alexander, Daniel's *Philotas*, and Elizabeth Cary's *Tragedie of Mariam*). See Alexander Maclaren Witherspoon, *The Influence of Robert Garnier on Elizabethan Drama* (1924; reprinted, Hamden, Conn.: Archon Books, 1968), 84–85. It appears that Sir Fulke Greville also wrote a tragedy on the Antony and Cleopatra story, probably in the same mode, but later burned it to avoid contemporary analogy with the fall of Essex (Bullough 1964, V, 216–17). Of all these plays, Samuel Daniel's *Cleopatra* (1594) is the most directly influenced by Mary Sidney's translation. Daniel announced his debt to Sidney in the verse epistle of his play, where he calls it "the worke the which she did impose" (sig. H5). The play, dedicated to Sidney and imitating her verse translation in style and structure, complements *Antonie* in its focus on Cleopatra's suicide. For a rebuttal of the idea that Mary Sidney "attempted to influence English drama to conform to a more dignified classical standard," see Mary Ellen Lamb, "The Myth of the Countess of Pembroke: The Dramatic Circle," *Yearbook of English Studies*, 11 (1981), 194–202.

29.   Sixteen extant manuscript copies of the Sidney Psalms have been located, and a further eight copies hypothesized in reconstructions of the relationship between manuscripts. See Waller (1979, Appendix, 284–86), and Ringler (1962, 546–52). One of the extant manuscripts, labeled "G" by Ringler, was prepared for publication in the 1640s; see Michael G. Brennan, "Licensing the Sidney Psalms for the Press in the 1640s," *Notes and Queries*, 229 (1984), 304–5. *The Triumph of Death* was clearly in circulation by 1600, since the single extant manuscript is bound with a letter dated 19 December 1600 from Sir John Harington to Lucy Russell, Countess of Bedford, in which he sends her the "truly devine translation" of three of the Sidney Psalms along with other miscellaneous pieces. See Hannay (1990, 107).

30.   The *Discourse* is dated 13 May 1590, while *Antonie* is dated 26 November 1590. On the Stoicism in the two texts, see Lamb (1990, 121–32); and Bornstein (1983, 6–7). All quotations from the *Discourse* are taken from Bornstein's edition.

31.   Tina Krontiris (1992, 70) argues that the play "legitimates Cleopatra's relationship with Antony by appropriating conventional marriage terminology and gender roles." All quotations from *Antonie* are taken from Bullough (1964).

32.   See, for example, the Chorus that concludes Act II, ll. 743–819. In the light of Hannay's argument about the Protestant politics of the Sidney Psalms, the choice of *Antonie* may also be politically significant, particularly since it was translated soon after the death in 1588 of the Earl of Leicester, favorite of Elizabeth and leader (like Antony?) of the cause against Rome.

33.   All quotations from Petrarch's *Triumphus Mortis* are taken from *Rime, Trionfi e Poesie Latine*, ed. F. Neri, G. Martellotti, E. Bianchi, and N. Sapegno (Milan: Ricardo Ricciardi, 1951), 517–30.

34.   All quotations from Sidney's *Triumph of Death* are taken from Waller (1977).

35.   All quotations from Lord Morley's *Triumph* are taken from *Lord Morley's Tryumphes of Fraunces Petrarcke*, ed. D. D. Carnicelli (Cambridge, Mass.: Harvard University Press, 1971).

36.   Philip Sidney, *A Defence of Poetry*, ed. J. A. Van Dorsten (Oxford: Oxford University Press, 1966), 73; hereafter cited in text as *Defence* 1966.

37.   See, for example, the editor's note in *Rime, Trionfi e Poesie Latine*, 529.

38.   See Coogan, 7; and Roland Greene, "Sir Philip Sidney's *Psalms*, the Sixteenth-Century Psalter, and the Nature of Lyric," *Studies in English Literature*, 30 (1990), 19.

39.   See Rivkah Zim, *English Metrical Psalms: Poetry as Praise and Prayer 1535–1601* (Cambridge: Cambridge University Press, 1987), 7–23, for a discussion of contradictory Renaissance views on translation; hereafter cited in text.

40.   *The Sidney Psalms*, ed. R. E. Pritchard (Manchester: Fyfield Books, 1992), 10.

41.   Zim (1987, 1–2) identifies more than 70 English versions of the Psalms (in prose and verse) published in the 16th century.

42.   See Barbara Kiefer Lewalski, *Protestant Poetics and the Seventeenth-Century Religious Lyric* (Princeton: Princeton University Press, 1979), 41–49; hereafter cited in text.

43.   Cited in David Norton, *A History of the Bible as Literature*, vol. 1 (Cambridge: Cambridge University Press, 1993), 188; hereafter cited in text.

44.   Ringler (1962, 500–501) argues that this was a task begun by Philip Sidney about 1585, a date that he supports by citing Thomas Moffet's assertion in his life of Sir Philip that the project was begun after the writing of the *Arcadia* and *Astrophil and Stella*. See Thomas Moffet, *Nobilis,* ed. V. B. Heltzel and H. H. Hudson (San Marino, Calif.: Huntington Library, 1940), 12. Waller suggests that Mary Sidney probably had her brother's manuscript in her possession at his death, and picked up where he left off, with less than a third of his task fulfilled, at Psalm 44 (1979, 155).

45.   See Philip Sidney's *A Defence of Poetry* (25). Philippe de Mornay is cited in Norton (1993, I, 188).

46.   Reprinted in Rathmell (1963, ix–x).

47.   The dedicatory verse is addressed "To the Right Honourable, the Lady Marie, Countesse of Pembrooke."

48.   *The Poems of Joseph Hall,* 271, cited in Richard Todd, "'So Well Attyr'd Abroad': A Background to the Sidney-Pembroke Psalter and Its Implications for the Seventeenth-Century Religious Lyric," in *Texas Studies in Literature and Language*, 29 (1987), 79.

49.   Cited in Rathmell (1963, xxvii).

50.   Given license by contemporary views of the Psalms as a compendi-um of poetic modes and by scholarly opinion that the Hebrew psalms were themselves written in poetry, such virtuosity also had literary precedents. Rathmell (1963) and Waller (1979, 159) have established that Sidney consulted a number of "authoritative" sources in her versification of the psalms, from the contemporary prose versions of Coverdale's Great Bible (1539) and the Calvinist Geneva Bible (1560), to the courtly but immensely popular French Huguenot psalter versified by Marot and Beza. From such texts she could draw ideas for imagery and interpretation, in the same way that she used the Psalm commen-taries of Calvin and of Beza.

51.   For discussion of such formal skill, see, for example, Rathmell (1963, xv–xxii); Waller (1979, 190–211); Lewalski (1979, 241–44); Beilin (1987, 145–49); and Beth Wynne Fisken, "'The Art of Sacred Parody' in Mary Sidney's *Psalmes*," *Texas Studies in Women's Literature*, 8 (1989), 223–39 (here-after cited in text).

52.   *The Poems of Joseph Hall*, 271, cited in Todd (1987, 80).

53.   All psalm quotations derive from Rathmell's edition unless other-wise specified.

54.   All psalm quotations from the Geneva Bible, the Great Bible (1539), and the Bishops Bible (1568) are taken from *The Hexaplar Psalter*, ed. William Aldis Wright (Cambridge: Cambridge University Press, 1911).

55.   John Calvin, *A Commentary of the Psalms of David*, 3 vols. (Oxford: Thomas Tegg, 1840), vol. III, 164; hereafter cited in text.

56.   The Sternhold-Hopkins psalter was not displaced from liturgical use until the late 17th century (Norton 1993, I, 178). Quotations from Sternhold-Hopkins are taken from the version appended to the Geneva Bible, facsimile edition (Geneva: Geneva Publishing Company, 1991); hereafter cited in text as Geneva Bible 1991.

57.   While the argument of the stanza is constructed out of four tercets, each of which translates a verse of the biblical text, rather than the sonnet's three quatrains and final couplet, the first line of each tercet (ll. 4, 7, and 10) is tied back by its rhyme to double as the final line of a hidden quatrain, and the final two lines likewise work as a couplet (*abbaccaddaee*).

58.   G. F. Waller, "The Rewriting of Petrarch: Sidney and the Languages of Sixteenth-Century Poetry," in *Sir Philip Sidney and the Interpretation of Renaissance Culture*, ed. Gary F. Waller and Michael D. Moore (Totowa, N. J.: Barnes and Noble, 1984), 74.

59.   This interpretation develops Calvin's view that the text refers to the spiritual adultery of dividing hope and heart "among a variety of objects" (1840, vol. II, 288).

60.   Cf. *"l'armée pudique / De nos pucelles"* of the Marot-Beza psalter. Théodore de Bèze, *Psaumes mis en Vers Français (1561–1562)*, ed. Pierre Pidoux (Geneva: Librairie Droz, 1984), 107; hereafter cited in text.

61.   Waller also notes a variant of line 36 in a manuscript copy in the British Library which reads "dames" for "doves" (1977, 124).

62.   Cf. Calvin's emphasis on the "greatness of the prey" when "even timorous women also were partakers" (1840, vol. II, 204).

63.   In the bottom right corner of the engraving is a notice that reads: "to be sold by Jo: Sudbury and Geo: Hamble in Popeshed Alley." The engraving may have been prepared as an illustration for a projected publication of the Sidney Psalms.

64.   From Matthew Parker's versified psalter of 1567, cited in Lewalski (1979, 234).

65.   George Ballard, in his *Memoirs of Several Ladies of Great Britain who have been celebrated for their writings or skill in the learned languages, arts and sciences* (Oxford: W. Jackson, 1752), interprets this portrait as a claim of authorship: "it seems to me, to be inconsistent with her modesty, if the performance had not been her own, to have been drawn in that manner" (262); hereafter cited in text.

*Chapter Five*

1.   The quotation is taken from Aemilia Lanyer's dedicatory poem to Anne Clifford, Countess of Dorset, in *Salve Deus Rex Judaeorum* (1611); see Woods (1993, 41). All subsequent quotations are taken from Woods's edition.

2.   Elizabeth Middleton's "The Death, and Passion of our Lord Jesus Christ, As it was Acted by the Bloodye Jewes, And Registred by The Blessed Evangelists" exists in a manuscript volume dated 1637 in the Bodleian Library, Oxford (Bod. Don. e. 17), from which all quotations are taken. The text remains unpublished. Stanzas 23–29 are included in Greer (1988). Alice Sutcliffe's "Of our losse by Adam, and our gayne by Christ" is appended to her *Meditations of Man's Mortalitie. Or, A Way to True Blessednesse* (1634). Greer (1988) reprints seven stanzas (5–7, 21–24) from the poem. Lines 43–301 of Rachel Speght's *Mortalities Memorandum* (1621) are reprinted in Greer (1988). Aemilia Lanyer's *Salve Deus Rex Judeorum* (1611) has reappeared in three editions in the last two decades, the first being that of A. L. Rowse, *The Poems of Shakespeare's Dark Lady* (New York: Clarkson N. Potter, 1978); hereafter cited in text. Woods's old-spelling edition (1993) has recently been complemented by the modern-spelling edition in *Renaissance Women: The Plays of Elizabeth Cary, the Poems of Aemilia Lanyer*, ed. Diane Purkiss (London: William Pickering, 1994); hereafter cited in text.

3.   Middleton's poem appears between a Calvinist prose tract and part of William Austin's "Ecce Homo." See Greer (1988, 94–99), who suggests that Middleton may be related to the Middletons (or Myddeltons) of Denbighshire in Wales.

4.   Greer (1988, 96) suggests that the dedicatee Sara Edmondes may be the sister of Sir John Harington of Exton (and thus aunt to Lucy Russell, Countess of Bedford), who married Sir Thomas Edmondes in 1626 at the age of 60.

5.  Cf. Matthew 26: 7–13, and Mark 14: 3–9.

6.  Cf. the "30 pieces of silver" of Matthew 26:15 (Authorized Version).

7.  Greer (1988, 94) points out that stanzas 145–47 are nearly identical to ll. 49–54, 61–67, and 163–68 of "Saint Peter's Complaint," first published in 1595 after Southwell's execution.

8.  Alice Sutcliffe, daughter of Luke Woodhows (or Wodehouse, Woodhouse) of Kimberly in Norfolk, was married to John Sutcliffe by 1624, who was already an "Esquire of the Body to King James" (see Greer 1998, 90–93).

9.  In the following discussion, I include quotes in pentameter layout rather than in the printed format.

10.  *Meditations of Man's Mortalitie* was first entered in the *Stationers' Register* on 30 January 1633; extant copies of 1634 are described as "The Second Edition, enlarged" on the title page.

11.  Beilin calls the "Dreame" a "countermyth to Eden," "a new myth of woman's intellectual experience" (1987, 111–12). Rachel Speght (1597–?), the daughter of London minister James Speght, takes the conventions of the medieval dream allegory (well-known from such texts as Chaucer's *The Book of the Duchess*) and employs them as a frame for gender politics. For discussions of Speght's writing, see especially Beilin (1987, 110–17; 1990, 267–71); and Lewalski (1993, 153–75).

12.  Speght's contribution to the *querelle des femmes* debate is discussed in Woodbridge (1984, 87–92); and in Diane Purkiss, "Material Girls: The Seventeenth-Century Woman Debate" in *Women, Texts & Histories 1575–1760*, ed. Clare Brant and Diane Purkiss (London: Routledge, 1992), 90–95; hereafter cited in text as Brant 1992. Mary Moundford (or Moundeford) was the wife of physician and author Thomas Moundford.

13.  Purkiss argues that such names "do not clearly illustrate female agency; rather, they illustrate the taking-up of the position of a disorderly woman for the purpose of signifying disorder of some kind, domestic or political" (Brant 1992, 85).

14.  Aemilia Lanyer (1569–1645) was the daughter of Margaret Johnson and the court musician Baptista Bassano, who were both dead by the time she was 18. It seems that she moved in court circles during her youth and was mistress to Henry Hunsdon, Elizabeth's aging Lord Chamberlain. She was married to Alphonso Lanyer in 1592 in order that he might "provide" for her when she became pregnant, but was forced to provide for herself after his death in 1613. In 1617 she set up a school for children of "divers persons of worth and understandinge" (Chancery petition, cited in Woods 1993, xxviii) in an attempt to support herself, and ran it for two years. She is later found making repeated claims against her brothers-in-law for her share of the profits of a patent she had transferred to them after her husband's death. The most reliable biographical information is provided in Woods (xv–xxx); Rowse's researches made an important contribution to our knowledge of Lanyer's life, but are marred by the spurious conclusions he draws from mixed evidence.

15.  See, for example, Wall (1993, 321); Barbara Lewalski, "Of God and Good Women: The Poems of Aemilia Lanyer," in Hannay (1985, 204); and Beilin (1987, 203).

16.  Lorna Hutson, "Why the Lady's Eyes are Nothing Like the Sun," in Brant (1992, 13).

17.  Lynette McGrath, "'Let Us Have Our Libertie Againe': Amelia Lanier's 17th-Century Feminist Voice," *Women's Studies* 20 (1992), 331–48; hereafter cited in text.

18.  Whatever success Lanyer's writing achieves in such proof, she herself has been made a "dark secret to be disclosed" by the historian A. L. Rowse, who published his edition of *Salve Deus* in 1979 as *The Poems of Shakespeare's Dark Lady*. In his introduction, Rowse puts forward a spurious argument grounded on ill-assorted evidence that Lanyer was Shakespeare's dark mistress, and that the "rampant feminism" of her text was an angry retort to the publication of the sonnets in 1609. Lanyer herself becomes an "occasion of discursive virtue among men," with Rowse and Shakespeare the beneficiaries.Other critiques of Lanyer's work include Lynette McGrath, "Metaphoric Subversions: Feasts and Mirrors in Amelia Lanier's *Salve Deus Rex Judeorum*," *Literature, Interpretation, Theory*, 3 (1991), 101–13 (hereafter cited in text); Barbara K. Lewalski, "Re-writing Patriarchy and Patronage: Margaret Clifford, Anne Clifford, and Aemilia Lanyer," *Yearbook of English Studies*, 21 (1991), 87–106; Barbara K. Lewalski's revised version of "Of God and Good Women" in *Writing Women in Jacobean England* (1993; hereafter cited in text); and Aliki Barnstone, "Women and the Garden: Andrew Marvell, Emilia Lanier, and Emily Dickinson," *Women and Literature*, 2 (1982), 147–67.

19.  Beilin argues that Lanyer puts women "at the heart of Christianity" (1987, 179).

20.  Few copies of *Salve Deus* remain; the Huntington Library copy is the only known example of the rare first issue, and eight copies of the second issue survive. Those that exist show some variation in the organization of the prefatory material, with differing combinations of dedicatory addresses. The British Library copy, for example, omits the dedications to Arabella Stuart and to the Countesses of Kent, Pembroke, and Suffolk, as well as the address to the "Vertuous Reader." One copy of the text was presented by Lanyer's husband as a gift to Thomas Jones, Lord Chancellor of Ireland and Bishop of Dublin. For details of the variant copies, see Lewalski (1993, Appendix B).

21.  For more extensive discussion of the figure of the "glasse," see especially Hutson (in Brant, 1992); McGrath (1991); and also Wall (1993, 322).

*Chapter Six*

1.  The quotation is taken from Cary's *Tragedie of Mariam* (1613), ed. A. C. Dunstan, Malone Society Reprints facsimile (Oxford: Oxford University Press, 1914), l. 1244; all subsequent quotations are derived from this edition, hereafter cited in text as *Mariam*.

2.   John Davies, *The Muses Sacrifice,* sig. *₊*2; hereafter cited in text.

3.   Margaret Ferguson, "Running On with Almost Public Voice: The Case of 'E.C.,'" in *Tradition and the Talents of Women*, ed. Florence Howe (Urbana: University of Illinois Press, 1991), 45; hereafter cited in text as Howe 1991. Even Ferguson initially states that Davies "urged [the women] . . . to publish their work" (44).

4.   Donald A. Stauffer first suggested Elizabeth Cary's authorship; see "A Deep and Sad Passion" in *Essays in Dramatic Literature*, ed. Hardin Craig (New York: Russell and Russell, 1935), 312–14, hereafter cited in text. The debate has continued: see Barbara Kiefer Lewalski's summary in Appendix A of her *Writing Women in Jacobean England* (1993, 317–20). A modern-spelling edition of both *Mariam* and the folio *History of the Life, Reign, and Death of Edward II* is now available in Purkiss's *Renaissance Women* (1994).

5.   The memoir of Elizabeth Cary (c. 1655) was first published in the 19th century as *The Lady Falkland: Her Life*, ed. R[ichard] S[impson] (London: Catholic Publishing & Bookselling Company, 1861). See also the account based on this memoir by Lady Georgiana Fullerton, *The Life of Elisabeth Lady Falkland, 1585–1639* (London: Burns and Oates, 1883). Both works hereafter cited in text.

6.   Lewalski, following Beilin (1987), has suggested that the dedicatory poem may have been recalled either because Elizabeth Cary's sister-in-law did not wish to have her name associated with the publication, or because the initials would make public the identity of the author (1993, 191 and n. 57).

7.   Elizabeth Cary's "The mirror of the Worlde translated out of French" translates Ortelius's *Mirroir du Monde* (Amsterdam, 1598); Lewalski notes that the manuscript, signed E. Tanfeelde and held at the vicarage in the village of Burford, Oxfordshire, where the Tanfield family home was located, is "a schoolgirl exercise in careful printing" (1993, 383, n. 4).

8.   Elizabeth Cary, *The reply of the most illustrious cardinall of Perron, to the answeare of the king of Great Britane* (Douay, 1630). The memoir states that Cary "procured it to be printed, dedicating it to her Majesty; but Dr. Abbots, then lord of Canterbury, seized on it coming into England, and burnt it; but some few copies came to her hands" (Simpson 1861, 39).

9.   British Library, Egerton MS 2725, f. 60; reprinted in Lewalski (1993, 383, n. 5).

10.   The letter, dated 8 December 1626, is included in Simpson's appendix (1861), and cited in Fullerton (1883, 69).

11.   It is perhaps the implicit critique of Sir Henry here, rather than anything "too feminine" about it, that makes the biographer's brother erase this passage.

12.   Fullerton (1883, 84 and 89), and the letters from Cary to Secretary Coke and to Charles I are included in Simpson's appendix (1861).

13.   Thomas Lodge, *The Famous and Memorable Workes of Josephus* (1602); hereafter cited in text. The date of the play is circumscribed on the one hand by

Cary's marriage in 1602 and the publication in the same year of Thomas Lodge's translation of Josephus, and on the other by Davies's reference in his dedication of *The Muses Sacrifice* (1612). Cary's sister-in-law would have been properly addressed as "Mistris Elizabeth Carye" after her husband was knighted in 1605; Sir Henry Cary returned from the Continent in 1606 (though he may have been absent frequently after this date to pursue his career in James I's court). It is certainly unlikely that Cary would have written the play after the birth of her first child in 1609. (See Lewalski 1993, 190.)

14.   Maurice Valency discusses English drama based on the story in *The Tragedies of Herod and Mariamne* (New York: Columbia University Press, 1940). For a discussion of Cary's productive use of the genres of closet drama and sonnet in *Mariam*, see Nancy A. Gutierrez, "Valuing *Mariam*: Genre Study and Feminist Analysis," *Tulsa Studies in Women's Literature*, 10 (1991), 233–51; hereafter cited in text.

15.   Gutierrez (1991, 245) points out that the male characters Constabarus and Pheroras also act as foils to Mariam in the context of the state rather than the family.

16.   See, for example, Ferguson (1991, 51–53); Lewalski (1993, 197–98); and Catherine Belsey, *The Subject of Tragedy: Identity and Difference in Renaissance Drama* (London: Methuen, 1985), 173–74; hereafter cited in text.

17.   The Catholic Church had long permitted divorce *a vinculo matrimonii* on the basis of impotence; see Belsey (1985, 140).

18.   Gwynne Aylesworth Kennedy, "Feminine Subjectivity in the Renaissance: The writings of Elizabeth Cary, Lady Falkland, and Lady Mary Wroth" (unpublished Ph.D. dissertation, University of Pennsylvania, 1989), 153–56; hereafter cited in text.

19.   See Belsey's discussion of the debate on divorce (1985, 139–44).

20.   Mercedes Maroto Camino, "'The Stage am I': Epistemology, the Erotics of History, and Early Modern Rapes of Lucrece" (unpublished Ph.D. dissertation, University of Auckland, 1994), 5; see also Marion Wynne-Davies, "'The Swallowing Womb': Consumed and Consuming Women in *Titus Andronicus*," in Valerie Wayne (ed.), *The Matter of Difference: Materialist Feminist Criticism of Shakespeare* (Ithaca, N. Y.: Cornell University Press, 1991), 129–51.

21.   Mariam's refusal may develop a hint from Cary's source here, with reference to the story of Mariam's mother Alexandra (who is a much stronger presence in Josephus than in Cary's play). Alexandra, confined in Herod's absence to the royal palace and put under constant surveillance so she could "doe nothing of her owne authoritie," becomes exasperated: "for being full of feminine pride, she disdained to see her selfe thus wrongfully suspected, desiring rather to suffer anything, then to be deprived of the liberty of free speech: and under colour to be honoured, to live continually in servitude and fear" (15:3, 385).

22.   Cf. Maureen Quilligan's view that "the injunction against speech and against publicness is not a means to secure sexual control. Rather, the terms

of sexual control are there to ensure the verbal blankness—so to speak—of the other, the conformability of the will of the wife to her husband"; from "Staging Gender: William Shakespeare and Elizabeth Cary," in *Sexuality and Gender in Early Modern Europe: Institutions, texts, images*, ed. James Grantham Turner (Cambridge: Cambridge University Press, 1993), 227.

23. The folio and octavo editions of *Edward II* are hereafter cited in the text as *Life* and *History* respectively. The abridged octavo edition has been reprinted in the *Harleian Miscellany*, vol. I (London: T. Osborne, 1744), 64–91.

24. See Lewalski (1993, 201–3 and appendix A); and Isobel Grundy, "Falkland's *History of . . . King Edward II,"* *Bodleian Library Record* 13 (1988), 82–83.

25. The biographer tells us: "She had read very exceeding much; poetry of all kinds, ancient and modern, in several languages, all that ever she could meet; history very universally, especially all ancient Greek and Roman historians; all chroniclers whatsoever of her own country, and the French histories very thoroughly; of most other countries something, though not so universally; of the ecclesiastical history very much, most especially concerning its chief pastors" (Simpson 1861, 113). Viscount Falkland's papers included a manuscript of Cary's translation of Perron's reply, annotated in the margins in her husband's hand.

26. F. J. Levy, *Tudor Historical Thought* (San Marino, Calif.: Huntington Library, 1967), 237 and 244; hereafter cited in text.

27. See V. F. Snow, "Essex and the Aristocratic Opposition to the Early Stuarts," *Journal of Modern History*, 32 (1960), 224–33 (especially 225).

28. Richard Grafton, *A chronicle at large . . . of the affayres of Englande from the creation of the worlde, unto the first yere of queene Elizabeth*, 2 vols (1568); Christopher Marlowe *The troublesome reigne and lamentable death of Edward the second, King of England* (1594). Donald Stauffer (in Craig 1935, 297, 309) and Gwynne Kennedy (1989, 119, n. 25) both consider Grafton to be the primary historiographical source for Cary's *Edward II*. Kennedy (33–108) also compares Cary's history with the verse histories of Michael Drayton ("Peirs Gaveston," 1593, and "Legend of Piers Gaveston," 1619) and Frances Hubert ("The Historie of Edward the Second," 1629), and with the chronicle histories of Robert Fabyan, Raphael Holinshed, John Speed, and John Stow.

29. The only instance to be dramatized of an encounter between Isabel and Mortimer comes near the end of the text, when Mortimer argues that Edward should be murdered. While the Queen withdraws her refusal when Mortimer threatens to abandon her, the terms that both characters use in their speeches maintain the ambiguity of their relationship. Isabel addresses Mortimer as "dear Friend" and "gentle Mortimer" and argues that she does not wish to taint their "innocent" souls (*Life*, 151–52). Mortimer addresses her as "Madam," blames himself for giving his "heart" to "such a female Weakness," and concludes that "since you refuse his judgment, you neither prize his safety, nor his service" (*Life*, 152–53). The language of service makes nothing of a sexual liaison.

*Chapter Seven*

1. The quotation is taken from Isabella Whitney's "Wyll and Testament" (l. 205), a verse legacy reprinted from her miscellany *A sweet Nosgay* (1573) and discussed by Betty Travitsky in "The 'Wyll and Testament' of Isabella Whitney," *English Literary Renaissance*, 10 (1980), 76–94; all quotations from the "Wyll" in the text below are taken from this version.

2. See Bennett (1965, 292–93); J. W. Saunders (1951); and J. W. Saunders, *The Profession of English Letters* (London: Routledge and Kegan Paul, 1964), 39–42, 56–60.

3. E. H. Miller, in *The Professional Writer in Elizabethan England* (Cambridge, Mass.: Harvard University Press, 1959), 14, cites Nashe's declaration that when "the bottome of my purse is turnd downeward . . . I prostitute my pen in hope of gaine."

4. The term "professional" needs some qualification here, since it has several connotations in relation to writing practices of the Renaissance. When J. W. Saunders writes *The Profession of English Letters* (1964) or G. E. Bentley writes *Profession of Dramatist in Shakespeare's Time, 1590–1642* (Princeton, N. J.: Princeton University Press, 1971), they are primarily using the term "profession" to describe a chosen career, a career that is also a way of making a living. I use the term "professional" here primarily in the restricted modern sense, in opposition to "amateur," rather than in the sense of a vocation—writing for money, that is, rather than as a chosen career. In the case of Isabella Whitney, however, there is a certain degree of overlap.

5. Richard Helgerson, *Self-Crowned Laureates: Spenser, Jonson, Milton and the Literary System* (Berkeley: University of California Press, 1983); hereafter cited in text. See also Helgerson's earlier discussion: *The Elizabethan Prodigals* (Berkeley: University of California Press, 1976).

6. Esther Inglis (1571–1624) was born in France and raised in Edinburgh. She spent many years in England with her husband, Bartholomew Kello. Bibliographical information on Inglis's manuscripts is to be found in Dorothy Judd Jackson, *Esther Inglis: Calligrapher 1571–1624* (New York: Spiral Press, 1937); and in A. H. Scott-Elliott and Elspeth Yeo, "Calligraphic Manuscripts of Esther Inglis (1571–1624): A Catalogue," *PBSA* 84 (1990), 11–86 (hereafter cited in text).

7. The majority of Inglis's manuscripts copy selections from Proverbs or the Psalms, moral verse from the French writers Pybrac and de Chereuze, and Georgette de Montenay's emblems.

8. Cited in David Laing, "Notes Relating to Mrs Esther (Langlois or) Inglis," *Proceedings of the Society of Antiquaries of Scotland*, 6 (1865), 304.

9. A Book of Psalms dedicated to Queen Elizabeth in 1599, for example, accompanied a letter from Inglis's husband, Bartholomew Kello, to the queen; Kello draws attention to the skill and variety of his wife's gift, and suggests that it supplements a recommendation from King James: "It may pleas

your Majestie the booke of psalmes wreaten be my wyfe in french and in divers soirtis of Carectaris adornit everie way so far as wes possible to ane simple woman, being presentit to Your Majestie togidder with ane letter of my souverane lords the kings Majestie of Scotland in my recommendatioun." He continues to request the queen's favor in giving order for his "spedie dispatch," since he has been "constraynit to my great hurt heir to stay . . . in respect of your Majesties deliberation past therin" (Scott-Elliott and Yeo 1990, 35). Cf. also Inglis's dedication of a book of Proverbs to the Earl of Essex, 1599, where she speaks of *"la faveur particuliere departie de vostre grace a mon mary"* ("the particular favor shown by your grace to my husband"; 38); and her presentation of a treatise translated by her husband to a member of Prince Henry's household in 1608 (63).

10.   Scott-Elliott and Yeo have identified a treatise by David Hume in Inglis's hand (1990, 49).

11.   See, for example, Esther Inglis's dedications to the Earl of Essex, 1599, and Sir Thomas Hayes, 1607 (Scott-Elliott and Yeo 1990, 38, 60).

12.   Cf. also Inglis's dedication to Prince Charles in 1624, where she speaks of the "two yeeres labours of the small cunning, that my totering right [hand], now being in the age of fiftie three yeeres, might affoord" (Scott-Elliott and Yeo 1991, 81).

13.   Some of Inglis's calligraphic styles even appear to imitate needlework. See, for example, octonarie xxi in the Folger Library's manuscript, *Octonaries upon the vanitie and inconstancie of the world* (1607), reproduced in S. Schoenbaum, *Shakespeare: The Globe & The World* (New York: Oxford University Press, 1979), 80; and quatrain lxvii in *Quatrains du Sieur de Pybrac* (1599), reproduced in Scott-Elliott and Yeo (1990, fig. 18).

14.   Goldberg also suggests that this manuscript by Inglis is dedicated to Prince Henry, who would have been an infant at the time, whereas Scott-Elliott and Yeo (1990, 42) state that this manuscript (Folger Shakespeare Library, V.a.91) has no dedication, and argue that the insertion of the later portrait may indicate that Inglis kept it as "a master copy for the English translation of the *Octonaires.*"

15.   The full titles of these two collections by Isabella Whitney are *The Copy of a letter, lately written in meeter, by a yonge Gentilwoman: to her unconstant Lover. With an Admonition to al yong Gentilwomen, and to all other Mayds in general to beware of mennes flattery* (1567), and *A sweet Nosgay, or pleasant Posye: contayning a hundred and ten Phylosophicall Flowers* (1573). Both collections are reproduced with Hugh Plat's *The Floures of Philosophie* (1572) in a facsimile edition edited by Richard J. Panofsky (Delmar: Scholar Press, 1982), hereafter cited in text. All quotations from these texts, with the exception of Whitney's "Wyll and Testament," are taken from this edition. Whitney has been identified as the sister of Geoffrey Whitney, whose *Choice of Emblemes* appeared in 1586; see R. J. Fehrenbach, "Isabella Whitney, Sir Hugh Plat, Geoffrey Whitney, and 'Sister Eldershae,'" *English Language Notes*, 21 (1983), 7–11.

16. George N. Turbervile, *The Heroycall Epistles of the learned Poet Publius Ovidius Naso* (1567).

17. Sir Hugh Plat, *The Floures of Philosophie* (1572), reprinted in Panofsky (1982).

18. See Guillén in Lewalski (1986, 70–101).

19. Juan de Segura's *Proceso de cartas de amores*, the first purely epistolary novel composed of the fictional letters of two lovers, was published on the Continent in 1548 (Guillén in Lewalski 1986, 74). Panofsky has pointed out that the organization of *A sweet Nosgay* provides a "strong narrative occasion" for Whitney's versification of Plat's moral aphorisms (xii).

20. George Gascoigne revised his text two years later, after it was interpreted as scandalous roman à clef. I disagree here with Krontiris, who suggests that in *A sweet Nosgay* Whitney appears "more restrained, and more conformist" than in *The Copy of a letter* (1992, 40). See also Wendy Wall, who argues that the *Nosgay* "provides an experimental foray into a more internally differentiated complaint form," framed with a "montage of autobiographical, moral, and fictional forms" (1993, 297).

21. See Krontiris (1992, 43); and Jones (1990, 41 and n. 10).

22. See Keith Wrightson, *English Society 1580–1680* (New Brunswick, N. J.: Rutgers University Press, 1982), 51.

23. See the Life of Artaxerxes, in *Plutarch's Lives*, trans. Bernadotte Perrin, vol. XI (London: Heinemann, 1926), 134–35; Whitney mistakenly identifies Artaxerxes with Darius (his father) in this passage.

24. Wall argues that the legacy revises complaint and blazon to "pose a proprietary claim for the writing subject's 'will' over and against the privileged codes of manuscript exchange" (1993, 309).

25. Jones argues persuasively that, in *The Copy of a letter*, "Whitney shifts the voices of Ovid's solitary heroines into the speaking position of a marriage counselor whose opinions are legitimated by decades of advice books" (1990, 43).

26. For an alternative view of this figuration, see Wall (1990, 298–99) on the *Nosgay*'s tropes of contagion.

27. Thomas Tusser, *A hundreth good pointes of Husbandry* (1570), ff. 36v–37; hereafter cited in text. The first edition of Tusser was published in 1557; in 1562 it was augmented to include "a Hundredth good poynts of Huswifery." By 1573, the manual had been expanded further, to become *Five hundreth points of good husbandry united to as many of good huswiferie. . . .*

28. The full title of Mary Fage's work is: *Fames Roule: or the Names of our dread Soveraigne Lord King Charles, his Royall Queen Mary, and his most hopefull posterity: Together with, The names of the Dukes, Marquesses, Earles, Viscounts, Bishops, Barons, Private Counsellors, Knights of the Garter, and Judges. Of his three Kingdomes, England, Scotland, and Ireland: Anagrammatiz'd and expressed by acrosticke lines on their names (1637).* Hereafter cited in text.

29. Games of wit based on names are advertised as an appropriate activity for the courtier by Master Bernard Bibiena in Castiglione's *Book of the*

*Courtier*, 151–52. George Puttenham asserts that the anagram is a "courtly conceit" particularly appropriate for women: "a thing if it be done for pastime and exercise of the wit without superstition commendable inough and a meete study for Ladies, neither bringing them any great gayne nor any great losse unlesse it be of idle time"; in *The Arte of English Poesie*, ed. G. D. Willcock and Alice Walker (Cambridge: Cambridge University Press, 1936), 108.

30.    Francis Lenton, *The Innes of Court Anagrammatist: Or, the Masquers masqued in Anagrammes* (1634), and *Great Britains Beauties, or, The Female Glory Epitomized In Encomiastick Anagramms, and Acrosticks* (1638).

31.    Fage, in her verse to the Archbishop of Saint Andrews (158–59), commends him for "Seeking the true and Orthodoxall sence" in "Gods blest Word." As Terence Cave points out, the humanist scholar Erasmus, following Augustine, recommended "'playing' for a while with poetic allegories as a prelude to the reading of Scripture" (1979, 83, n. 9).

32.    The cult of Neoplatonic love that developed around Charles's French queen, Henrietta Maria, is reflected in the court masques of the 1630s; see, for example, Ben Jonson's *Love's Triumph Through Callipolis* (1630), and William Davenant's *Temple of Love* (1635).

33.    Fage may have sent individual poems to each of her patrons; in the verse addressed to James, Lord Eskeine, she advertises the poem as a New Year's gift: "I send unto you Sir, now this new yeere, / A new yeeres gift the Muses bad me beare" (168).

34.    It is highly unlikely that Fage "was acquainted with the royal family," as Travitsky implies in *The Paradise of Women* (1981, 113). The one verse in *Fames Roule* that suggests familiarity with its addressee proves problematic. In the poem to William, Lord Willoughby, Baron of Parham, Fage says she is "Honouring you, within whose Parham hall / Branch'd forth that Beech, which did to me befall" (92, mispaginated as 102, sig. N2v). Possibly her image of the "Beech" refers to her husband, Robert Fage; yet William, Lord Willoughby, died in 1617, 20 years prior to the publication of *Fames Roule*, and was succeeded by his son Francis—a fact Fage might be expected to know if she or her husband had been associated with the Lord's household.

35.    Cf. verses addressed to Montague, Lord Bartue, heir to the Earl of Lyndsey (104); and to Thomas, Lord Coventry, Keeper of the Privy Seal (114–15).

36.    Robert Fage was the translator of Ramus's *Dialectica* and the author of a pamphlet on infant baptism: *Peter Ramus . . . his Dialectica in two bookes* (1632); *The Lawfulnesse of Infants Baptisme* (1645). He does not appear to have been the "hack writer who produced rather dreary histories" that Margaret Ezell mentions (1987, 96). Interestingly, in his preface to the reader, Robert Fage makes the education of women one of his four reasons for publishing his "more easie" translation of Ramus: "And finally, for the zeale I beare to mine owne country, being willing and desirous, that not onely men, but even women, should exercise themselves in the study of the sacred artes" (sig. A4).

37.  Contrast this with Fage's association of the active public life with masculine virtue in her verse to the Earl of Antrim: "A man was borne not for himselfe alone. . . . Cell-men rob Countries, and themselves each one" (200).

38.  The story was not uncommon in dedications; see Bennett 1965, 35. It appears in Turbervile's dedication of *The Heroycall Epistles* (1567), the translation of Ovid that Whitney may have made use of in writing *The Copy of a letter*: "Artaxerxes his good acceptaunce of a handefull of running water, bred me to this boldnesse to offer your Honor a handful of written Papers" (sig. A3v). There is even an acrostic by William Hunnis that refers to the tale; see his dedicatory verse to the Earl of Leicester, *A Hyve Full of Hunnye* (1578).

39.  See, for example, verses addressed to the Earl of Linlithgow (138) and Viscount Sarsfelde of Kilmallocke (218).


*Chapter Eight*

1.  The quotation is derived from the first and last lines of the "crowne of Sonetts dedicated to Love" embedded in Lady Mary Wroth's sonnet sequence, *Pamphilia to Amphilanthus*; see *The Poems of Lady Mary Wroth*, ed. Josephine A. Roberts (Baton Rouge: Louisiana State University Press, 1983), 127, 134. All quotations from *Pamphilia to Amphilanthus* are taken from this edition, hereafter cited in text as Roberts 1983.

2.  Lady Mary Wroth, born Mary Sidney on 18 October 1586 or 1587, was the eldest child of Robert Sidney (later Earl of Leicester) and Barbara Gamage, and niece of Mary Sidney, Countess of Pembroke, and Sir Philip Sidney. Roberts's account of Wroth's life (1983, 3–40) supplements the biographical study by Margaret Witten-Hannah in her unpublished Ph.D. dissertation, "Lady Mary Wroth's *Urania*: The Work and the Tradition," (Auckland, 1978), 14–65. I am indebted to both accounts for the following biographical details. See also Gary Waller's explorations of Wroth's life in *The Sidney Family Romance: Mary Wroth, William Herbert, and the Early Modern Construction of Gender* (Detroit: Wayne State University Press, 1993); hereafter cited in text.

As a young woman, Wroth had some success in court circles; her favor at court in the early years of James I's reign is indicated by her participation in two masques, both written by Ben Jonson, with Queen Anne and her ladies. She performed the role of Baryte, one of 12 "daughters of Niger," in *The Masque of Blackness* (1605) and *The Masque of Beauty* (1608). Wroth's involvement with the court was at its height in these years, and coincided with her marriage in 1604 to Robert Wroth, a keen huntsman whose estates (Durrance in Enfield and Loughton Hall in Essex) provided hunting grounds for the king. As Roberts points out, Robert Wroth seems not to have shared his wife's literary interests; the only book dedicated to him was a treatise on mad dogs by Thomas Spackman (Roberts 1983, 12). Robert Wroth succeeded to his father's title and estates in 1606; he died in March 1614, only a month after the birth of the couple's child, James. Mary Wroth was left with massive debts. After the death of her son in 1616, she lost her control of the Wroth estates. In this period, she also gave birth to two other children, William and Catherine, the illegitimate off-spring of a liaison with her cousin, William Herbert, Earl of Pembroke (see Waller 1993, and Roberts 1983, 24–26). William may have been born in the spring of 1615, about a year after the birth of James and the death of Wroth's husband. A letter written by Robert Sidney to his wife in 1615 suggests the familial embarassment: "You have don very well in putting Wil away, for it had bin to greate a shame he should have stayde in the hous" (cited in Roberts 1983, 25–26). There is little known of Wroth's life after the publication of the first part of her romance in 1621; petitions to the king for protection from her debtors, records of tax payments and the sale of lands suggest financial difficulties. She continued to live at Loughton Hall at least until 1630, and died c. 1652.

3.   The literary texts by Mary Wroth that are extant today are substan-tial, and include both manuscript and printed material. The first part of *The Countess of Mountgomeries Urania* was published in 1621, with an appended son-net sequence (*Pamphilia to Amphilanthus*); while the romance was taken off the market a few months after publication, numerous copies of the edition have come down to us. The probably unfinished continuation of the romance exists in manuscript in the Newberry Library (Case Ms fY 1565.W 95); an edition of the complete *Urania*, with manuscript continuation, is being prepared by Josephine Roberts. Book I of the *Urania* is included in *An Anthology of Seventeenth-Century Fiction*, ed. Paul Salzman (Oxford: Oxford University Press, 1991), 1–208. A manuscript collection of poems, which includes early versions of many of the poems in the published text, is held by the Folger Library (V.a.104). Roberts (1983) lists variants between the Folger manuscript and the printed version of the sonnet sequence in her edition of Wroth's poems, as does Gary Waller in his early edition of *Pamphilia to Amphilanthus* (Salzburg: Institut für Englische Sprache ünd Literatur, 1977). Two manuscript copies of a pastoral tragicomedy, *Love's Victorie*, in different stages of composition, are also extant. One manuscript of the play is held by the Huntington Library (HM 600); the other is owned by the Viscount de L'Isle and remains in the library of Penshurst Place. The latter (and more complete) manuscript has been edited by Michael G. Brennan in his *Lady Mary Wroth's Love's Victory: The Penshurst Manuscript* (London: The Roxburghe Club, 1988); all references to the play are taken from this edition.

4.   All references to the first part of *Urania* are to the original edition of 1621.

5.   Lisle C. John, *The Elizabethan Sonnet Sequences: Studies in Conventional Conceits* (New York: Columbia University Press, 1938), 65 and n. 94.

6.   See Nancy Miller's "Arachnologies: The Woman, the Text, and the Critic," in Miller 1986, 274–75, 285.

7.   The best-known sonnet sequences—those by Philip Sidney, Edmund Spenser, William Shakespeare, Michael Drayton, and Samuel Daniel—were all written in the 1580s and 1590s. Romance, in translation and in the vernacular,

was likewise most popular in the late 16th century. Romance was frequently regarded in this period as the preserve not only of the male writer but also of the male reader, despite the increasing inclusion of addresses to the gentlewoman reader in both prefatory material and text proper. By the second decade of the 17th century, however, romance was increasingly associated with a female (and often nonaristocratic) readership, and this association tended to lower the status of the genre. Mary Ellen Lamb's discussion of the reception of Sidney's *Arcadia* (1990, 8, 112–14) shows that the reading of romance was interpreted in gender-specific terms: romance as read by men was a genre engaged with serious philosophical, moral, and political issues, whereas romance as read by women was a genre of dangerous, titillating, immoral, erotic tales. Wroth's choice of genres no longer in vogue may have offered her a degree of freedom to manipulate and revise old conventions, as Elaine Beilin suggests (1987, 213).

8.   P. J. Croft points to such echoes in his edition of Robert Sidney's sonnets; see *The Poems of Robert Sidney: Edited from the Poet's Autograph Notebook* (Oxford: Clarendon Press, 1984).

9.   George Chapman, *The Iliads of Homer Prince of Poets* (1611), sig. Hh4v.

10.   Joshua Sylvester, *Lachrimae Lachrimarum or The Spirit of Teares Distilled for the untymely Death of The incomparable Prince Panaretus* (1613), sig. H2.

11.   Graham Parry, "Lady Mary Wroth's *Urania*," *Proceedings of the Leeds Philosophical and Literary Society* 16 (1975), 54–55.

12.   May Paulissen, *The Love Sonnets of Lady Mary Wroth: A Critical Introduction* (Salzburg: Institut für Anglistic ünd Amerikanistik, 1982), 65; hereafter cited in text.

13.   *Ben Jonson* (1947), vol. 8, 182. Lamb (1990, 154–59) points to this sexualization in a detailed reading of Jonson's sonnet, comparing it with Sir Edward Denny's verse attack on Wroth.

14.   Gary Waller has called Mary Wroth "the most important woman writer before Aphra Behn" (1993, 192). For recent criticism, see, for example, the collection of articles in *Reading Mary Wroth: Representing Alternatives in Early Modern England*, ed. Naomi J. Miller and Gary Waller (Knoxville: University of Tennessee Press, 1991); Maureen Quilligan, "The Constant Subject: Instability and Female Authority in Wroth's *Urania* poems," in *Soliciting Interpretation: Literary Theory and Seventeenth-Century English Poetry* (Chicago: University of Chicago Press, 1990), 307–35; Anne Shaver, "A New Woman of Romance," *Modern Language Studies*, 21 (1991), 63–77; Lewalski (1993, 242–307); and Waller (1993, 190–219, 246–81).

15.   Margaret Anne McLaren, "An Unknown Continent: Lady Mary Wroth's Forgotten Pastoral Drama, 'Loves Victorie,'" in Haselkorn and Travitsky (1990, 285; hereafter cited in text); and Miller, "Rewriting Lyric Fictions: The Role of the Lady in Lady Mary Wroth's *Pamphilia to Amphilanthus*," in Haselkorn and Travitsky (1990, 295).

16.  Maureen Quilligan, "Lady Mary Wroth: Female Authority and the Family Romance," in *Unfolded Tales: Essays on Renaissance Romance,*" ed. George M. Logan and Gordon Teskey (Ithaca, N. Y.: Cornell University Press, 1989), 257–80; hereafter cited in text as Logan and Teskey 1989.

17.  See, for example, Mary Wroth's response to Antissia's prying questions (77, mispaginated as 67).

18.  See, for example, Quilligan's discussion of the Argalus/Parthenia story in the *Arcadia* (in Logan and Teskey 1989, 263); and Josephine Roberts on John Barclay's romances (1983, 28).

19.  See Josephine A. Roberts, "An Unpublished Literary Quarrel Concerning the Suppression of Mary Wroth's 'Urania' (1621)," *Notes and Queries*, n.s. 24 (1977), 532–35; and Paul Salzman, "Contemporary References in Mary Wroth's *Urania,*" *Review of English Studies*, 29 (1978), 178–81.

20.  See Roberts (1983, 238). Roberts prints six letters written by Mary Wroth and Edward Denny between December 1621 and March 1622 on the occasion of this literary quarrel.

21.  Mary Wroth, letter to Sir Edward Denny, dated 27 February 1622 (Roberts 1983, 240); and her letter to the Duke of Buckingham, dated 15 December 1621 (Roberts 1983, 236).

22.  But cf. Philip Sidney's representation of the *Arcadia* as a foster child; discussed in Wall (1993, 154–56).

23.  Miller explores both the Ariadne and the Arachne stories as figures of writing in her "Arachnologies" (1986, 270–95).

24.  Letter dated 26 February 1622 (Roberts 1983, 238–39).

25.  C. S. Lewis, *Studies in Medieval and Renaissance Literature* (Cambridge: Cambridge University Press, 1966), 159.

26.  Perhaps the classic statement of this idea is made by Cardinal Bembo in Castiglione's *Book of the Courtier*, 312–22.

27.  See, for example, Roberts (1983, 29–31); Witten-Hannah (1978, 47, 64); and Lamb (1990, 185–88).

28.  Haselkorn and Travitsky (1990, 287). For other discussions of *Love's Victorie,* see Barbara K. Lewalski, "Mary Wroth's *Love's Victory* and Pastoral Tragicomedy," in Miller and Waller (1991, 88–108), and Carolyn Ruth Swift, "Feminine Self-Definition in Lady Mary Wroth's *Love's Victorie* (c. 1621)," *English Literary Renaissance,* 19 (1989), 171–88.

29.  Gayatri Chakravorty Spivak, "Displacement and the Discourse of Woman," in *Displacement, Derrida and After*, ed. Mark Krupnick (Bloomington: Indiana University Press, 1983), 184.

30.  My argument here seems to be in accord with Margaret McLaren's reading of *Love's Victorie,* where she argues that the pastoral tragicomedy "resembles [Wroth's] other works in picturing not an exterior, outward world, but an interior, inward realm that begins and ends with the experience of human rather than divine love and sifts the ever-shifting quicksands of the relationships between men and women" (Haselkorn and Travitsky 1990, 281).

*Chapter Nine*

1.   The quotation is taken from one of the Crown sonnets in Mary Wroth's "Pamphilia to Amphilanthus"; see Roberts (1993, 128).

2.   Virginia Woolf, *A Room of One's Own* (1929; reprinted, London: Panther, 1977), 49; hereafter cited in text.

3.   Margaret J. M. Ezell, "The Myth of Judith Shakespeare: Creating the Canon of Women's Literature," *New Literary History*, 21 (1990), 579–92.

4.   Virginia Woolf, "Donne after Three Centuries," in *Collected Essays*, vol. I (London: Hogarth Press, 1966), 40.

5.   See Travitsky's Introduction in Haselkorn and Travitsky (1990, 11).

6.   The belief that women as well as men held a capacity for reason was utilized by women writers as early as Christine de Pizan, whose 15th century *Book of the City of Ladies*, published in English in 1521, figured Reason as an emblematic mother who offered guidance to her daughter: "Then Lady Reason . . . said, "Get up, daughter! Without waiting any longer, let us go to the Field of Letters. . . . I immediately stood up to obey her commands and . . . I felt stronger and lighter than before. She went ahead, and I followed behind, and after we had arrived at this field I began to excavate and dig, following her marks with the pick of cross-examination." See *The Book of the City of Ladies*, trans. Earl Jeffrey Richards, ed. Marina Warner (New York: Persea Books, 1982), 16.

7.   Thomas Nashe, prefatory dedication to his edition of Sir Philip Sidney's *Astrophil and Stella* (1591), sig. A4. Cf. also Michael Drayton's verses of praise in Eclogue VI of his *The Shepheards Garland* (1593).

8.   Thomas Powell, in Furnivall (1876, 173).

9.   Dedicatory verse by Constantia Mundi, prefaced to *The Worming of a mad Dogge* (1617); reprinted in Shepherd (1985, 127).

10.   Cleaver (1598, 223). This qualification is present not only in Protestant writings; Vives, for example, adds a similar caution: "those thynges that be agaynst the lawes of god, she ought nat to do, though her husbande commaunde her never so moche. For she must a knowlege one for better than her husbande, and have in more price, that is Christe" (sig. c1).

11.   Thomas Churchyard, "A Pleasant Conceite penned in verse" (1593), cited in Frances Young (1912, 174).

12.   Reprinted in Rathmell (1963, ix–x).

13.   Aemilia Lanyer, "The Authors Dreame to the Ladie Marie, the Countesse Dowager of Pembrooke," in Woods (1991, 21–31).

14.   Germaine Greer's comments are cited and discussed in Elaine Showalter's *A Literature of Their Own: British Women Novelists from Brontë to Lessing* (Princeton: Princeton University Press, 1977), 11.

15.   Anonymous, *The Female Worthies: or, Memoirs of the Most Illustrious Ladies, of all Ages and Nations . . .* (London: S. Crowder and J. Payne, 1766); hereafter cited in text.

16.   George W. Bethune, *The British Female Poets: with Biographical and Critical Notices* (Philadelphia: Lindsay and Blakiston, 1848), iii; hereafter cited in text.

17.   G. L. Craik, *Pursuit of Knowledge Under Difficulties. Illustrated by Female Examples* (London: C. Cox, 1847); hereafter cited in text.

18.   Frederic Rowton, *The Female Poets of Great Britain, chronologically arranged* (London: Longman, Brown, Green, and Longmans, 1848), xiv; hereafter cited in text.

19.   Sarah Josepha Hale, *Biography of Distinguished Women; or, Woman's Record, from the Creation to A.D. 1869* (1854), 3d ed. (New York: Harper and Brothers, 1868), viii; hereafter cited in text.

20.   Jane Williams, *The Literary Women of England* (London: Saunders, Otley, and Co., 1861), 2; hereafter cited in text.

21.   Kohler (1936); and Ruth Willard Hughey, "Cultural Interests of Women in England, 1524–1640, Indicated in the Writings of the Women" (Ph. D. dissertation, Cornell University, 1932).

22.   For a survey of research activity, see, for example, the bibliographies of recent studies on 16th- and 17th-century women writers in Farrell, Hageman, and Kinney (1990), and continuation of that material by Georgianna M. Ziegler and Sara Jayne Steen in *English Literary Renaissance*, 24 (1994), 229–73.

# Selected Bibliography

## PRIMARY SOURCES

*Published Works*

Cary, Elizabeth. *Renaissance Women: The Plays of Elizabeth Cary, the Poems of Aemilia Lanyer*. Edited by Diane Purkiss. London: William Pickering, 1994.

―――. *The History of the Life, Reign and Death of Edward II*. 1680a.

―――. *The History of the most unfortunate Prince King Edward II*. 1680b.

―――. *The Tragedie of Mariam*. Edited by A. C. Dunstan. Malone Society Reprints facsimile. Oxford: Oxford University Press, 1914.

―――. *The Tragedy of Mariam, the fair queen of Jewry. With, The Lady Falkland: her life*. Edited by Barry Weller and Margaret W. Ferguson. Berkeley, Calif.: University of California Press, 1994.

Clifford, Anne. *The diary of the Lady Anne Clifford*. Edited by V. Sackville-West. London: Heinemann, 1923.

Cornwallis, Jane. *The Private Correspondence of Jane Lady Cornwallis, 1613–1644*. Edited by Lord Braybrooke. London: S. & J. Bentley, 1842.

Dowriche, Anne. *The French Historie*. 1589.

Du Verger, Suzanne, trans. *Admirable Events*. 1639.

Elizabeth I. *The Letters of Queen Elizabeth I*. Edited by G. B. Harrison. London: Cassell, 1935.

Fage, Mary. *Fames Roule*. 1637.

Harley, Brilliana. *Letters of the Lady Brilliana Harley*. Edited by Thomas Taylor Lewis. London: Camden Society, 1854.

Hoby, Margaret. *Diary of Lady Margaret Hoby 1599–1605*. Edited by Dorothy M. Meads. London: Routledge, 1930.

Lanyer, Aemilia. *The Poems of Aemilia Lanyer: Salve Deus Rex Judaeorum*. Edited by Susanne Woods. New York: Oxford University Press, 1993.

―――. *Salve Deus Rex Judaeorum*. 1611.

Man, Judith, trans. *An Epitome of the History of Faire Argenis and Polyarchus*. 1640.

Primrose, Diana. *A Chaine of Pearle. Or, A Memoriall of the peerles Graces, and Heroick Vertues of Queene Elizabeth, of Glorious Memory*. 1630.

Prowse, Anne, trans. *Of The markes of the children of God, and of their comforts in afflictions*. 1590.

―――,. trans. *The Sermons of John Calvin*. 1560.

Sidney, Mary, trans. *The Countess of Pembroke's Translation of Philippe de Mornay's 'Discourse of Life and Death.'* Edited by Diane Bornstein. Detroit: Michigan Consortium for Medieval and Early Modern Studies, 1983.

————. *The Psalms of Sir Philip Sidney and the Countess of Pembroke*. Edited by J. C. A. Rathmell. New York: New York University Press, 1963.

————. *The Triumph of Death and Other Unpublished and Uncollected Poems by Mary Sidney, Countess of Pembroke (1561–1621)*. Edited by G. F. Waller. Salzburg: Institut für Englische Sprache ünd Literatur, 1977.

————, trans. "The Tragedie of Antonie." In *Narrative and Dramatic Sources of Shakespeare*. Edited by Geoffrey Bullough. Vol. 5. London: Routledge and Kegan Paul, 1964.

Speght, Rachel. *Mortalities Memorandum with a Dreame Prefixed, imaginarie in manner; reall in matter*. 1621.

Sutcliffe, Alice. *Meditations of Man's Mortalitie. Or, A Way to True Blessednesse*. 1634.

Tyler, Margaret, trans. *The Mirrour of Princely deedes and Knighthood*. 1578.

Whitney, Isabella. *The Copy of a letter, lately written in meeter, by a yonge Gentilwoman: to her unconstant Lover. With an Admonition to al yong Gentilwomen, and to all other Mayds in general to beware of mennes flattery*. 1567.

————. *The Copy of a letter, A sweet Nosgay*, and Hugh Plat, *The Floures of Philosophie*. Edited by Richard J. Panofsky. Facsimile edition. Delmar: Scholar Press, 1982.

————. *A sweet Nosgay, or pleasant Posye: contayning a hundred and ten Phylosophicall Flowers*. 1573.

Wroth, Lady Mary. *The Countesse of Mountgomeries Urania*. 1621.

————. *Love's Victory: The Penshurst Manuscript*. Edited by Michael G. Brennan. London: The Roxburghe Club, 1988.

————. *The Poems of Lady Mary Wroth*. Edited by Josephine A. Roberts. Baton Rouge: Louisiana State University Press, 1983.

*Unpublished and Miscellaneous Materials*

Ashmole, Elias. *The Antiquities of Berkshire*, vol. II. London: E. Curll, 1719. (Includes elegies by Elizabeth Cooke.)

Bentley, Thomas, ed. *The Monument of Matrones: conteining seven severall Lamps of Virginitie, or distinct treatises whereof the first five concerne praier and medita- tion. . . . *1582. (Includes poems by Frances Aburgavenny and Frances Tyrwhit.)

Clifford, Arthur, ed. *Tixall Poetry*. Edinburgh: James Ballantyne and Co., 1813. (Includes poems by Gertrude Thimelby and Katherine Aston.)

Lodge, Edmund, ed. *Illustrations of British History, Biography, and Manners. . . .* 2d ed., vol. 3. London: John Chidley, 1838. (Includes poem by Anne Howard, Countess of Arundel.)

Middleton, Elizabeth. "The Death, and Passion of our Lord Jesus Christ, As it was Acted by the Bloodye Jewes, And Registred by The Blessed Evangelists." Manuscript dated 1637. Bodleian Library, Oxford, Bod. Don. e. 17.

Mildmay, Grace. Manuscript journal. Central Library, Northampton.

Soowthern, John. *Pandora, The Musique of the beautie, of his Mistresse Diana*. 1584. (Includes poems by Anne de Vere, Countess of Oxford.)

Southwell, Anne. Manuscript commonplace book. Folger Shakespeare Library, Washington, V.b. 198.

———. *The Southwell-Sibthorpe Commonplace Book: Folger Ms V.b. 198*. Edited by Jean Klénè. Birmingham, N. Y.: Medieval and Renaissance Texts and Studies, 1995.

Wroth, Lady Mary. Manuscript continuation of *The Countesse of Mountgomeries Urania*. Newberry Library, Chicago, Case Ms. f Y 1565.W 95. Forthcoming from Renaissance English Text Society, 1996.

*Anthologies*

Goreau, Angeline. *The Whole Duty of a Woman: Female Writers in Seventeenth Century England*. New York: The Dial Press, 1984. A collection of texts, letters, poems, and essays written by 17th-century British women.

Graham, Elspeth, Hilary Hinds, Elaine Hobby, and Helen Wilcox, eds. *Her Own Life: Autobiographical writings by seventeenth-century Englishwomen*. London: Routledge, 1989. A collection of autobiographical writings in a variety of forms such as diary, meditation, conversion narrative, defense, prophecy, romance, verse, and activist tract. Includes Anne Clifford.

Greer, Germaine, Jeslyn Medoff, Melinda Sansone, and Susan Hastings, eds. *Kissing the Rod: An Anthology of 17th Century Women's Verse*. London: Virago Press, 1988. A selection of the work of 17th-century women poets, providing biographical information, brief commentary, and bibliographical notes. Includes extracts from Elizabeth Stuart, Aemilia Lanyer, Elizabeth Cary, Lady Mary Wroth, Rachel Speght, Diana Primrose, Alice Sutcliffe, and Elizabeth Middleton.

Travitsky, Betty. *The Paradise of Women: Writings by Englishwomen of the Renaissance*. 1981; reprinted, New York: Columbia University Press, 1989. A wide-ranging collection of excerpts from writings by Renaissance English women, divided into two sections. The first is composed of religious poetry and prose, familial writings, letters and diaries, controversy literature, prefaces, and "imaginative literature." The second section, "Writings by Exceptional Figures," includes extracts from the work of Elizabeth Cary.

## SECONDARY SOURCES

*Bibliographies and Reference Works*

Bell, Maureen, George Parfitt, and Simon Shepherd, eds. *A Biographical Dictionary of English Women Writers, 1580–1720*. Boston: G. K. Hall,

1990. Informative biographical entries on British women writing in a wide variety of forms; includes appendices on anonymous and pseudonymous texts, and a series of critical essays that discuss certain modes of writing and the cultural context.

Farrell, Kirby, Elizabeth H. Hageman, and Arthur F. Kinney, eds. *Women in the Renaissance: Selections from English Literary Renaissance.* Amherst: University of Massachusetts Press, 1990. Includes annotated bibliographies by Elizabeth Hageman of studies on Tudor women writers and on 17th-century women writers, and by Josephine A. Roberts on Mary Sidney, covering the period 1945–1990; each bibliography provides an excellent summary of research and publication.

Gartenberg, Patricia, and Nena Thames Whittemore. "A Checklist of English Women in Print, 1475–1640." *Bulletin of Bibliography and Magazine Notes* 34 (1977): 1–13. An early checklist of printed books by women published in Britain. Lists full titles, and usefully provides reference numbers for both the *Short-Title Catalogue of Books Printed in England . . . 1475–1640* and University Microfilm reel copies.

Greco, Norma, and Ronaele Novotny. "Bibliography of Women in the English Renaissance." *University of Michigan Papers in Women's Studies* June (1974): 30–57. An annotated listing of publications dealing with English women in the period 1500–1623, under four headings: women writers, women in relation to male writers, female characters in literature, and women in their cultural and historical contexts.

Steen, Sara Jayne. "Recent Studies in Women Writers of the Seventeenth Century, 1604–1674 (1990–mid-1993)." *English Literary Renaissance* 24 (1994): 243–74. A partly annotated bibliography of 17th-century women writers, continuing bibliographies in Farrell, Hageman, and Kinney (1990), with useful review of research and publications.

Weisner, Merry E. *Women in the Sixteenth Century: A Bibliography.* Sixteenth Century Bibliography 23. St. Louis, Mo.: Center for Reformation Research, 1983. Selective bibliography of sources for study of British and European women in the 16th century, organized by subject matter and geographic region.

Zeigler, Georgianna M. "Recent Studies in Women Writers of Tudor England, 1485–1603 (1990 to mid-1993)." *English Literary Renaissance* 24 (1994): 230–42. A partly annotated bibliography, continuing bibliographies of Tudor women writers in Farrell, Hageman, and Kinney (1990), with a useful review of research and publications.

*Books*

Beilin, Elaine. *Redeeming Eve: Women Writers of the English Renaissance.* Princeton, N. J.: Princeton University Press, 1987. Examines the work of women writing between 1524 and 1623 to argue that a female literary tradition was established in the period, founded on pious writings and built through experimentation with use of writing personae and the modification of existing genres. Includes chapters devoted to Mary Sidney, Aemilia Lanyer, and Lady Mary Wroth as well as sections on Elizabeth Cary, Isabella Whitney, Anne Dowriche, and Rachel Speght.

Belsey, Catherine. *The Subject of Tragedy: Identity and Difference in Renaissance Drama*. London: Methuen, 1985. An analysis of the history of the meanings ascribed to subjectivity and gender, using Renaissance drama as a springboard for discussion.

Brant, Clare, and Diane Purkiss, eds. *Women, Texts & Histories, 1575–1760*. London: Routledge, 1992. A significant collection of feminist essays, which examines the changing representation of women and the construction of speaking positions in discourse by women in the early modern period. Includes essays on Aemilia Lanyer and Lady Mary Wroth.

Ezell, Margaret J. M. *The Patriarch's Wife: Literary Evidence and the History of the Family*. Chapel Hill: University of North Carolina Press, 1987. Argues that women participated in the intellectual and literary life of the 17th century to a much greater extent than had been allowed (though the study tends to focus predominantly on the latter half of the century). Includes a particularly useful chapter on women writers and patterns of manuscript circulation and publication.

————. *Writing Women's Literary History*. Baltimore and London: Johns Hopkins University Press, 1993. By examining critical studies of early modern women's writing produced between 1660 and 1990, Ezell argues that current Anglo-American models of feminist historiography are built on assumptions about authorship and about the generation of literature that have resulted in the marginalization of early women writers.

Ferguson, Margaret W., Maureen Quilligan, and Nancy J. Vickers, eds. *Rewriting the Renaissance: The Discourses of Sexual Difference in Early Modern Europe*. Chicago: University of Chicago Press, 1986. A collection of essays that examine the construction of sexual identity and the interrelationship between the "sex-gender" system and the economic, social, cultural, and political arrangements of early modern Europe. Includes sections on the politics and consequences of patriarchy and (female) exceptions to patriarchal rule.

Fisher, Sheila, and Janet E. Halley, eds. *Seeking the Woman in Late Medieval and Renaissance Writings: Essays in Feminist Contextual Criticism*. Knoxville: University of Tennessee Press, 1989. A collection of essays combining historical criticism and postmodern literary theory to address the problem of the absence of women in the texts of the Middle Ages and the Renaissance.

Goldberg, Jonathan. *Writing Matter: From the Hands of the English Renaissance*. Stanford, Calif.: Stanford University Press, 1990. Applies Jacques Derrida's proposal for a material discourse of writing in *Of Grammatology*, trans. Gayatri Chakravorty Spivak (Baltimore, Md.: Johns Hopkins University Press, 1974), in a fascinating study of the material and ideological practice of handwriting in Renaissance England.

Hannay, Margaret P. *Philip's Phoenix: Mary Sidney, Countess of Pembroke*. Oxford: Oxford University Press, 1990. A reinterpretation of the life of Mary Sidney based on primary sources, presenting her as an eloquent, assertive woman who used her position to transcend gender limitations and fashion an identity as a political spokesperson, literary patron, writer, and administrator.

————, ed. *Silent but for the Word: Tudor Women as Patrons, Translators, and Writers of Religious Works*. Kent, Ohio: Kent State University Press, 1985. A collection of essays arguing that in spite of attempts to restrict educated Tudor women to the margins of religious discourse, piety did allow women to find a voice, and sometimes also to articulate more personal and political concerns. Includes essays on Mary Sidney, Aemilia Lanyer, and Elizabeth Cary.

Haselkorn, Anne M., and Betty S. Travitsky, eds. *The Renaissance Englishwoman in Print: Counterbalancing the Canon*. Amherst: University of Massachusetts Press, 1990. An attempt to challenge the canon through a collection of essays that place marginalized writings by Renaissance women alongside canonized texts on similar topics by their male contemporaries. Includes several essays on Elizabeth Cary, Lady Mary Wroth, and Mary Sidney.

Hull, Suzanne W. *Chaste, Silent and Obedient: English Books for Women, 1475–1640*. San Marino, Calif.: Huntington Library, 1982. Identifies and examines books printed in English between 1475 and 1640 that were intended, at least in part, for a female audience. Provides a summary under four headings—practical guidebooks, recreational literature, devotional books, and books on the controversy—and concludes with a useful annotated bibliography.

Hutson, Lorna. *The Usurer's Daughter: Male Friendship and Fictions of Women in Sixteenth-Century England*. London: Routledge, 1994. A significant and wide-ranging study that explores the complex links among legal, economic, and cultural discourses in the 16th century, arguing that the representation of women was central to the project of humanism with its concern to facilitate homosocial relations and "enable the transmission of knowledge."

Jardine, Lisa. *Still Harping on Daughters: Women and Drama in the Age of Shakespeare*. Sussex: Harvester Press, 1983. In arguing against the reading of Shakespeare's plays as reflections of social realities, suggests new ways of interpreting the literary representation of women in drama by considering their cultural context.

Jordan, Constance. *Renaissance Feminism: Literary Texts and Political Models*. Ithaca, N. Y.: Cornell University Press, 1990. Uncovers and examines the broad scope of Renaissance feminist argument in the context of the *querelle des femmes* or debate about women through analyses of a wide range of European texts.

Jones, Ann Rosalind. *The Currency of Eros: Women's Love Lyric in Europe, 1540–1620.* Bloomington: Indiana University Press, 1990. Provocative study of the love lyrics of eight European and English women poets of the Renaissance from a Marxist-feminist perspective, exploring the ways in which these poets negotiated positions for themselves in relation to gender ideologies and the literary conventions of love poetry. Includes chapters on Isabella Whitney and Mary Wroth.

Kelso, Ruth. *Doctrine for the Lady of the Renaissance.* 1956; reprinted, Urbana: University of Illinois Press, 1978. Studies theoretical treatises by western European writers of the 15th and 16th centuries to provide an account of the Renaissance ideal of the lady, uncovering disparate and contradictory images of the lady as mistress, wife, and courtier.

Krontiris, Tina. *Oppositional Voices: Women as Writers and Translators of Literature in the English Renaissance.* London: Routledge, 1992. Studies the secular writings of a number of Renaissance English women in order to explore female opposition to the dominant ideologies and cultural norms of their time. Discusses the works of Isabella Whitney, Margaret Tyler, Mary Sidney, Elizabeth Cary, Aemilia Lanyer, and Lady Mary Wroth.

Labalme, Patricia A., ed. *Beyond Their Sex: Learned Women of the European Past.* New York: New York University Press, 1980. An interdisciplinary collection of essays on educated European women ranging from the 12th century to the 19th century.

Lamb, Mary Ellen. *Gender and Authorship in the Sidney Circle.* Madison: University of Wisconsin Press, 1990. An important discussion that analyzes the writings of male and female members of the Sidney family as a means of understanding women's writing in the Renaissance and the culture that shaped that writing. The book includes chapters on Mary Sidney and Lady Mary Wroth.

Lewalski, Barbara Kiefer. *Writing Women in Jacobean England.* Cambridge, Mass.: Harvard University Press, 1993. Examines the lives and writing of nine Jacobean women of the social elite within "biographical, historical, literary and theoretical contexts," emphasizing the oppositional nature of women's writing in the period. Includes chapters on Princess Elizabeth, Lucy Russell, Anne Clifford, Rachel Speght, Aemilia Lanyer, Elizabeth Cary, and Lady Mary Wroth.

Maclean, Ian. *The Renaissance Notion of Woman: A Study in the Fortunes of Scholasticism and Medical Science in European Intellectual Life.* Cambridge: Cambridge University Press, 1980. Analyzes the evolving notion of woman through a study of Renaissance discourses of theology, ethics, politics, law, and medicine.

Miller, Naomi J., and Gary Waller, eds. *Reading Mary Wroth: Representing Alternatives in Early Modern England.* Knoxville: University of Tennessee

Press, 1991. A collection of essays on the life and writings of Mary Wroth, utilizing feminist, psychoanalytic, and new historicist perspectives. The collection focuses on Wroth's alternative approach to genre as well as on her representations of gender, subjectivity, and sexual difference.

Prior, Mary, ed. *Women in English Society, 1500–1800*. London: Methuen, 1985. A collection of essays studying the lives of particular groups of women (including wet nurses, widows, and traders) living in the 16th, 17th, and 18th centuries.

Rose, Mary Beth, ed. *Women in the Middle Ages and the Renaissance: Literary and Historical Perspectives*. Syracuse, N. Y.: Syracuse University Press, 1986. A collection of interdisciplinary essays that examines texts written by both men and women to explore the effect of patriarchal sexual ideology on women's lives. Includes an essay on Mary Sidney.

Simpson, Richard, ed. *The Lady Falkland: Her Life*. London: Catholic Publishing & Bookselling Company, 1861. An edition of the memoir of Elizabeth Cary written by one of her daughters; includes an appendix of notes and original documents.

Wall, Wendy. *The Imprint of Gender: Authorship and Publication in the English Renaissance*. Ithaca, N. Y.: Cornell University Press, 1993. Examines the way in which gender ideology and social controversies surrounding print shaped the Renaissance concept of authorship. Includes discussion of English women writers and their creation of new models of authorship in confronting the gendered rhetoric of publication.

Waller, Gary. *Mary Sidney, Countess of Pembroke: A Critical Study of Her Writings and Literary Milieu*. Salzburg: Institut für Anglistik ünd Amerikanistik, 1979. An early attempt to redress the neglect of Mary Sidney's literary career through an analysis of her writings in the context of their production.

———. *The Sidney Family Romance: Mary Wroth, William Herbert, and the Early Modern Construction of Gender*. Detroit: Wayne State University Press, 1993. Utilizes feminist, new historicist, and psychoanalytic theories to study the construction of subjectivity and gender in the early modern period, through an analysis of the letters, the literary works, and the familial and sexual relationship of William Herbert and Mary Wroth.

Warnicke, Retha M. *Women of the English Renaissance and Reformation*. Westport, Conn.: Greenwood Press, 1983. Studies the accomplishments of four generations of women during the 16th century in the contexts of humanism and religious reform.

Wilson, Katharina M. *Women Writers of the Renaissance and Reformation*. Athens and London: University of Georgia Press, 1987. An introduction to the lives and works of 25 European women writers of the Renaissance, the Reformation, and the Counter-Reformation. Includes discussion of Elizabeth I, Mary Sidney, and Mary Wroth.

Woodbridge, Linda. *Women and the English Renaissance: Literature and the Nature of Womankind, 1540–1620*. Brighton, England: Harvester Press, 1984.

Argues that the formal controversy about women developed as a literary game that did not necessarily reflect contemporary attitudes, whereas the controversy about transvestism, or cross-dressing, bore a closer relationship to social realities. Examines the way in which new social perspectives and literary conventions arose out of these controversies.

*Parts of Books*

Cavanaugh, Jean C. "Lady Southwell's Defense of Poetry." In *Women in the Renaissance: Selections from English Literary Renaissance*, edited by Kirby Farrell, Elizabeth H. Hageman, and Arthur F. Kinney, 175–78. Amherst: University of Massachusetts Press, 1990. Introduces and reproduces Lady Anne Southwell's letter in defense of poetry, emphasizing its significance as one of the earliest known essays of literary criticism written in English by a woman.

Ferguson, Margaret. W. "Running On with Almost Public Voice: The Case of 'E.C.'" In *Tradition and the Talents of Women*, edited by Florence Howe 37–67. Urbana: University of Illinois Press, 1991. Argues that the mixed ideological messages about the function and status of wives in Elizabeth Cary's *Mariam* are produced by the conjunction of class, gender, and religious ideologies to which she was exposed.

Jones, Ann Rosalind. "Surprising Fame: Renaissance Gender Ideologies and Women's Lyric." In *The Poetics of Gender*, edited by Nancy K. Miller, 74–95. New York: Columbia University Press, 1986. Explores the problematic nature of literary fame for women in the European Renaissance, arguing that women writers of lyric poetry circumvented, subverted, or broke the "rules of gender decorum."

Kelly-Gadol, Joan. "Did Women Have a Renaissance?" In *Becoming Visible: Women in European History*, edited by Renate Bridenthal and Claudia Koonz, 137–64. Boston: Houghton Mifflin, 1977. A seminal article suggesting that, far from experiencing an expansion of opportunity in the Renaissance, women experienced increased dependency and a "contraction of social and personal options."

Miller, Nancy K. "Arachnologies: The Woman, the Text, and the Critic." In *The Poetics of Gender*, edited by Nancy K. Miller, 270–95. New York: Columbia University Press, 1986. Reads the story of Arachne as a "figuration of woman's relation of production to the dominant culture" in an attempt to theorize a feminist poetics that would not displace women.

Pomerleau, Cynthia S. "The Emergence of Women's Autobiography in England." In *Women's Autobiography: Essays in Criticism,* edited by Estelle C. Jelinek, 21–38. Bloomington: Indiana University Press, 1980. Emphasizes the role played by women in the emergence and development of the autobiography as a genre in the 17th and 18th centuries.

Quilligan, Maureen. "Lady Mary Wroth: Female Authority and the Family Romance." In *Unfolded Tales: Essays on Renaissance Romance*, edited by

George M. Logan and Gordon Teskey, 257–80. Ithaca, N. Y.: Cornell University Press, 1989. A provocative analysis of Mary Wroth's reworking of episodes from Philip Sidney's *Arcadia* and Edmund Spenser's *Faerie Queene* to reverse the gendered implications of the original scenes.

————. "Staging Gender: William Shakespeare and Elizabeth Cary." In *Sexuality and Gender in Early Modern Europe: Institutions, Texts, Images*, edited by James Grantham Turner, 208–32. Cambridge: Cambridge University Press, 1993. Reads Elizabeth Cary's *Mariam* against Shakespeare's *The Taming of the Shrew* and *Othello* to argue that the cultural insistence on the silence of women is not a "means to ensure sexual control" but a means of producing masculine subjectivity.

Wilcox, Helen. "Private Writing and Public Function: Autobiographical Texts by Renaissance Englishwomen." In *Gloriana's Face: Women, Public and Private, in the English Renaissance*, edited by S. P. Cerasano and Marion Wynne-Davies, 47–62. London: Harvester Wheatsheaf, 1992. Argues that the autobiographical texts written by women between 1570 and 1676 demonstrate the inseparability of public and private spheres for their authors; discusses the writing of eight women, including Margaret Hoby, Grace Mildmay, and Anne Clifford.

*Articles*

Beilin, Elaine V. "Writing Public Poetry: Humanism and the Woman Writer." *Modern Language Quarterly* 51 (1990): 249–71. Analyzes the ways in which Isabella Whitney, Anne Dowriche, and Rachel Speght used their humanist educations to claim a position for women writers in the public sphere.

Ezell, Margaret J. M. "The Myth of Judith Shakespeare: Creating the Canon of Women's Literature." *New Literary History* 21 (1990): 579–92. Uses Virginia Woolf's *A Room of One's Own* as a point of departure for exposing 20th-century misconceptions about the silence or isolation of Renaissance and 17th-century women writers.

Fisken, Beth Wynne. "'The Art of Sacred Parody' in Mary Sidney's *Psalmes*." *Texas Studies in Women's Literature* 8 (1989): 223–39. Discusses Mary Sidney's appropriation of the conventions of secular poetry in her translation of the Psalms.

Gutierrez, Nancy A. "Valuing *Mariam*: Genre Study and Feminist Analysis." *Tulsa Studies in Women's Literature* 10 (1991): 233–51. Analyzes Cary's transformation of discourse and refashioning of genre in *Mariam* as acts of cultural negotiation.

Hannay, Margaret P. "'Princes you as men must dy': Genevan Advice to Monarchs in the *Psalmes* of Mary Sidney." *English Literary Renaissance* 19 (1989): 22–41. Argues that Mary Sidney used her translation of the Psalms as a means of making a political statement in support of the Protestant cause.

Lamb, Mary Ellen. "The Agency of the Split Subject: Lady Anne Clifford and the Uses of Reading." *English Literary Renaissance* 22 (1992): 347–68. Analyzes the ways in which Anne Clifford used her ownership of books and her reading as a means of constructing an identity as aristocratic landowner over and above that of obedient wife.

Lewalski, Barbara K. "Re-writing Patriarchy and Patronage: Margaret Clifford, Anne Clifford, and Aemilia Lanyer." *Yearbook of English Studies* 21 (1991): 87–106. Studies the role played by Margaret Clifford as "major influence, model and subject" for the writings of Anne Clifford and Aemilia Lanyer, noting her importance as possibly the first English female patron to have a female literary client. Highlights the ways in which Clifford and Lanyer "rewrite patronage in female terms."

McGrath, Lynette. "'Let Us Have Our Libertie Againe': Amelia Lanier's 17th-Century Feminist Voice." *Women's Studies* 20 (1992): 331–48. Argues that Aemilia Lanyer's *Salve Deus* can be defined as a feminist work because it protests the oppression of women as a group, establishes a supportive community of women, and valorizes the construction of a female identity outside that prescribed by ideology.

———. "Metaphoric Subversions: Feasts and Mirrors in Amelia Lanier's *Salve Deus Rex Judeorum,*" *Literature, Interpretation, Theory* 3 (1991): 101–13. Analyzes Aemilia Lanyer's use of metaphor as a strategy for constructing an alternative female subjectivity, in arguing that *Salve Deus* questions the use of religion as a vindication for the silencing of women.

Moody, Ellen. "Six Elegiac Poems, Possibly by Anne Cecil de Vere, Countess of Oxford." *English Literary Renaissance* 19 (1989): 152–70. Introduces and reproduces Anne de Vere's sonnet sequence, summarizing the evidence for and against her authorship.

Scott-Elliott, A. H., and Elspeth Yeo. "Calligraphic Manuscripts of Esther Inglis (1571–1624): A Catalogue." *Publications of the Bibliographical Society of America* 84 (1990): 11–86. A chronological catalog of information on the calligraphic manuscripts of Esther Inglis. Provides biographical facts and background information on the production of the manuscripts, and lists letters and poems.

Travitsky, Betty. "The 'Wyll and Testament' of Isabella Whitney." *English Literary Renaissance* 10 (1980): 76–94. Introduces and reproduces Isabella Whitney's "Wyll and Testament" to the City of London, providing biographical information on Whitney and a brief review of her other writings.

Warnicke, Retha M. "Lady Mildmay's Journal: A Study in Autobiography and Meditation in Reformation England." *Sixteenth Century Journal* 20 (1989): 55–68. An analysis of Grace Mildmay's journal, highlighting the importance of the autobiographical introduction in providing evidence for the ways in which 16th-century women viewed education, religion, and relationships.

Wiegall, Rachel. "An Elizabethan Gentlewoman: The Journal of Lady Mildmay, circa 1570–1617 (unpublished)." *Quarterly Review* 215 (1911): 119–38. A commentary on the life of Grace Mildmay, containing extracts from her journal and her books of prescriptions and recommendations.

*Unpublished Dissertations and Theses*

Kennedy, Gwynne Aylesworth. "Feminine Subjectivity in the Renaissance: The writings of Elizabeth Cary, Lady Falkland, and Lady Mary Wroth." Unpublished Ph.D. dissertation, University of Pennsylvania, 1989. Discusses the construction of feminine subjectivity in the writing of Elizabeth Cary and Mary Wroth; argues that Cary's *Mariam* and *Edward II* explore subjection and the dissent of wronged wives, while Wroth's *Urania* is an "anatomy of the traffic in women" which constructs a constant feminine subject.

Kohler, Charlotte. "The Elizabethan Woman of Letters: The Extent of Her Literary Activities." Unpublished Ph.D. dissertation, University of Virginia, 1936. A ground-breaking early survey of Renaissance women's writing, which includes discussion of their translations, letters, and practical guidebooks, as well as conventional literary genres.

Witten-Hannah, Margaret. "Lady Mary Wroth's *Urania*: The Work and the Tradition." Unpublished Ph.D. dissertation, University of Auckland, 1978. Argues that *Urania* reflects Wroth's experience of the court in its "documentary" quality and its masquelike scenes, and shows her alienation from that society.

# Index

# The Author

Dr. Kim Walker earned her Ph.D. from the University of Edinburgh, Scotland. Currently, she is a Senior Lecturer in the Department of English, Victoria University of Wellington, New Zealand. She has previously published on the Caroline dramatist James Shirley, and on the Irish novelist Maria Edgeworth.